Regional Planning and Sustainable Development

REGIONAL PLANNING AND SUSTAINABLE DEVELOPMENT

Edited by
Amitabh Shukla

KANISHKA PUBLISHERS, DISTRIBUTORS
NEW DELHI 110002

KANISHKA PUBLISHERS, DISTRIBUTORS
4697/5-21A, Ansari Road, Daryaganj
New Delhi -110 002
Phones : 2327 0497, 2328 8285
Fax : 011-2328 8285
E-mail : kanishka_publishing@yahoo.co.in

First Published-2000
Second Edition-2012

ISBN: 978-81-7391-318-8

PRINTED IN INDIA

Published by Madan Sachdeva for Kanishka Publishers, Distributors, 4697/5-21A, Ansari Road, Daryaganj, New Delhi-110 002, Typeset by Sunshine Graphics, Delhi, and Printed at Rajdhani Printers, Delhi.

Preface

'Development' depends upon a scientific planning-system. While, optimum utilisation of natural and physical resources is an essential pre-requisite, generation of fiscal resources and their proper-use assist for an effective implementation of developmental programmes.

Most of the economies of world both developed and underdeveloped are witnessing regional, intra-regional and sectoral imbalances, which are the hurdles for getting higher growth rate. Specially, in a federal set-up effective policies and their implementation is a difficult task due to differences in availability of natural resources, climate, etc., while, even growth of different regions can assist in achieving the targets of national planning.

India's planning system is imbued with several difficulties in which regional imbalances are prime elements creeping in economy ever since the First Five Year Plan came in existence. The planners and researchers are facing terrific task of overcoming it in planning system and several attempts have been made to tackle the problem of regional disparities. In this context 'regional planning' has been considered as an effective system for tackling such problems.

For this purpose measurements of disparities between regions, within regions and between sectors are essential for making plans. Further, adverse effects which are results of developmental process are other burning problems of most of the economies. Environmental degradation and ecological imbalance have created challenges before the planners. Experiences of developed nations shows that pattern of development has adversely effected the environment. Hence, concept of 'sustainability' has received wider attention for policy planners and researchers. The term 'Sustainable Development' is now universally accepted and achieving both 'Sustainability' and 'Development' has become a prime and important task. In this paradoxical situation which is attainment of higher level of development and protection of eco-system, i.e., protection of natural resources through careful and scientific planning is essential.

How regional planning can assist in achieving both the objectives, i.e., development and sustainability?

The answer can be explained in the following manner:

(*i*) regional planning would assist in utilising the locally available natural and physical resources and technology;

(*ii*) it would assist in making plans which would fulfil the local demands;

(*iii*) it would be helpful in reducing the imbalances and disparity across and within the regions;

(*iv*) it would assist in tackling the problems of poverty, unemployment and urbanisation when productive employment would be available at local level;

(*v*) when every region will grow then it would be easier to achieve the targets of higher growth rate of different sectors and higher growth rate of economy too;

(*vi*) regional planning would assist in overcoming the shortcomings or centralised planning and it would assist in making link between sectors and regions;

(*vii*) optimum utilisation of natural resources, fulfilment of local needs through regional planning would be environmentally balanced and it would assist to achieve sustainable development.

An attempt has been made in this book to focus on relationship between 'regional planning' and 'sustainable development' In the present context of Indian economy when we have initiated globalisation process backwardness of some regions and existence of disparities between regions will create hurdles in making our relation with the rest of the world.

This book has presented different aspects of the theme in the following way:

Part I: Need, Significance and Methodological Issues of Balanced and Sustainable Development;

Part II: Regional Disparities in India: Measurements and Factors;

Part III: Poverty, Urbanisation, Environment and Structural Adjustment: Impact Upon Balanced and Sustainable Development;

Part IV: Agricultural Planning and Sustainable Development.

In Part I: 'Need, Significance and Methodological Issues of Balanced and Sustainable Development' theoretical issues and importance of regional planning have been explained and analysed by the authors.

S. Murty in her paper analysed the concept, causes, consequences of regional disparities, she has evaluated the present trend of inter-state disparities and has suggested measures too. In the paper entitled 'Need and significance of Balanced Sectoral development for aggregate sustainable development' N.M. Lall and others have analysed the term 'sustainable development'. According to them it has wider concerns which take into account quality of life of human being also. By analysing theories of development and experiences of developed countries in the path of development the authors argue that balanced sectoral development would assist in achieving sustainability. Regional planning has a very strong base of theories, methodologies and models and one has to understand them for better use of such concept. R.V. Nadkarni has presented pre-requisites, methods and limitations of composite indices which is one of the important tool for measuring regional-disparities. While B.P.K. Sinha has specially explained and analysed the methodological concepts and practical problems while measuring and constructing the indices of human resources development.

In the paper entitled 'Leading theoretical issues of regional economics', O.S. Shrivastava has given very deep insight into the fundamentals of regional economics/planning. He evaluated same basic theories, presented concept and use of some important methods of regional analysis and explained the concept and range of regional economics.

T.K. Das and Lopamudra Mishra in research paper entitled 'Political Economy of Regional Imbalances' calculated per capita NSDP and NSDP of 26 states for measuring regional imbalances in level of economic development of two points of time. By calculating per capita income of four sectors they have prepared indices of development and measured ranking of states. They also established the relationship between investment and income and role of infrastructural facility in economic development of states. They found widening disparities due to failure of regional policies.

Role of state intervention and industrialisation influences regional variation. Hence, priority should be given for sectoral development. This is the conclusion of P.G. Marvanias study entitled "Global Development Experiences: Lessons for Policy Planning in India." Ashutosh Sinha has found increasing inter-state disparities in terms of rates of growth. He concludes that during the liberalisation era the objective of balanced regional development has been ignored. Thus, policies have to be formulated for reduction of regional inequalities on the country. Social sector became important aspect of economic development and it gets place in human development index too. Ms. Neena has measured 'Inter-state Disparities in India's Social Sector' and its relationship with economic development. She concludes that though inadequacy of these facilities are responsible but other factors play a crucial role such as quality of services and governance.

In a federal set-up like in India Central governments play important role in making horizonal and vertical equity or disparities. In India the role of Finance Commission with regard to centre-state financial relation is very crucial. Transfer of resources through Finance Commission is a matter of criticism while discussing existence of inter-state disparities on India. Hence, its a burning theme for researchers. Amitabh Shukla and S.K. Khare in their paper entitled 'Impact of Finance

Commission Transfers on Inter-State Economic Disparities' have analysed the impact of Finance Commissions transfer on economic condition of the states. They found that F.C.s. transfers as percentage of total expenditure of states shows that low income states have benefitted and got higher ranks. States expenditure financed by F.C.s. transfers reflects that variation has been increased between two points of time. The findings of this study reveal that F.C.s. plays import role in making inter-state equity or disparities.

In spite of faster growth of secondary and tertiary sectors in the Indian economy, economic development is essentially influenced by agricultural development which constitutes higher productivity of crops. In the paper entitled 'A Study of Regional Disparities in Rates of Growth of Productivity and Instability on Indian Agriculture' K. Pochanna examines inter-state variation in the performance of yield growth rate and its relation with instability. He finds that inter-state variations in yield growth rate and its positive relation with instability factor, therefore responsible obstacles for low productivity persist in states— have to be removed.

Padmaja Mishra in her paper entitled "An Extra Dimension to regional inequality tries to point out the regional variation with regard to distribution of population by income classes. She draws conclusion that central government have to be aware of regional distribution of income and must take care while allocating resources to the states.

Present pattern of planning in India could not succeed to remove poverty on the one hand but has created other problems— sources of unemployment, migration, environmental, etc., on the other. Since last decade the process of economic reforms has been initiated in which structural adjustment has transformed the economy in a new direction though, it created combined effects on the economy. This situation reveals that a wider and balanced approach is essential. For tackling such unfinished tasks and achieving balanced and sustainable development. Part II is devoted on the lines as described above.

'The poverty alleviation is *sine qua non* of Sustainable Development' and increasing and unmanageable population creates danger for environmental management. Thus, sound population policy is a pre-requisite for attaining sustainable development. This relationship is established by Shankar Chatterjee in his paper 'Poverty Alleviation for Sustainable Development'. He also shows the increasing ratio of population living below poverty-line in the states of India and in the nation as a whole.

Urbanisation is another outcome of increasing population and it creates multiplier adverse effects which are obstacles for balanced development and it stresses upon the need of regional planning. This is the finding of the paper entitled 'Urbanization and Spatial Planning in India: Policy Issues' written by C.R. Pathak. He has analysed the level, trend, structure and distribution of urbanization in India, evaluated the problem of urban development and role of national urbanization policy. He advocated the multi level planning system to tackle urbanization problem in India.

There is a very close and unavoidable link between environment and development even than the faster growth of population and present trend of over exploitation of natural resources resulted in adverse effects on eco-system. Hence only environment friendly approach of development can attain the objective of balanced and Sustainable Development. This has been revealed by Shridhar Pandey in his research paper entitled Ecological Balance: Prerequisite for Balanced Development'.

A.C. Minocha in his paper entitled 'Bio-Diversity, Sustainable Development and Intellectual Properly Rights', has established the Inter-dependency of sustainable development and protection of bio-diversity. He analysed the contradictions between intellectual properly rights and protection and use of traditional crops and commodities. In the Indian context he has warned to safeguard patent rights of traditional agricultural commodities and documentation of traditional Indian knowledge and practices. How and to what extent structural adjustment programme in India has influenced the pattern of development is a matter of investigation. G.B. Nath in his research paper titled 'Structural Adjustment in India and Its Impact on Balanced Regional Development' by analysing disparities in economic growth and agrarian disparities argues that planned economy itself has encouraged the process of economic concentration and switching over to open economy would accentuate the existing regional disparities due to its inherent contradictions.

Agriculture which uses balanced and natural resources has utmost importance in the context of sustainable development. Hence, scientific agricultural planning is essential in this regard, Part III—'Agricultural Planning and Sustainable Development' analyses some important dimension of this theme. M.V. Nadkarni in his paper titled 'Sustainable Development: Concept and Issues with Special Reference to Agriculture' argues that the present trend of maximisation of agricultural production has adversely affected the environment. According to him efforts have to be made to safeguard the environment by minimising the exploitation of natural resources.

In a vast country like India where wide disparities exist with regard to climatic conditions, rainfall, soil types and crops agricultural planning has to be made by taking due care of such symptoms. A major step has been taken by making Agro-climatic zones and sub-zones taking due care of similarity in terms of climate, soil condition, cropping pattern, etc. R. Maria Saleth and V.V. Jugale and Y.V. Jugale have analysed the conceptual and empirical issues of agro-climatic regional planning. They argue that it will assist in utilising the natural and human resources and would be much friendly towards sustainable agriculture.

AMITABH SHUKLA

Contents

List of Contributors

A.C. Minocha — Professor (Rtd.), Department of Regional Planning and Economic Growth, Barkatullah University, Bhopal (M.P.)

Amitabh Shukla — Faculty Member, Department of P.G. Studies and Research in Economics, Rani Durgawati University, Jabalpur (M.P.)

Anjani Kumar Jha — Robinson Centre for Research, Gwalior (M.P.)

Ashutosh Sinha — Faculty Member, Department of Economics and Rural Development, Dr. R.M.L. Awadh University, Faizabad (U.P.)

C.R. Pathak — Professor (Rtd.), Department of Architecture and Regional Planning, I.I.T. Kharagpur (West Bengal)

G.B. Nath	—	Reader and Head, Department of Economics, L.N. College, Jharsuguda (Orissa)
K. Pochanna	—	Reader, Department of Economics, Osmania University, Hyderabad (A.P.)
Lopamudra Mishra	—	Research Assistant, Department of Analytical and Applied Economics, Utkal University, Bhubaneswar (Orissa)
M.V. Nadkarni	—	Professor, Institute for Social Economic Change, Bangalore (Karnataka)
Neena	—	Lecturer, Punjab School of Economics, Guru Nanak Dev University, Amritsar (Punjab)
N.M. Lall	—	Visiting Professor, School of Studies in Economics, Jiwaji University, Gwalior (M.P.)
O.S. Shrivastava	—	Professor (Rtd.), Department of Regional Planning and Economic Growth, Barkatullah University, Bhopal (M.P.)
Padmaja Mishra	—	Reader, Department of Analytical and Applied Economics, Bhubaneswar University, Bhubaneswar (Orissa)
P.G. Marvania	—	Associate Professor, Department of Economics, Saurashtra University, Rajkot (Gujarat)
R. Maria Saleth	—	Professor, Institute of Economic Growth, University Enclave, Delhi
R.V. Dadibhavi	—	Reader and Head, Department of Economics, Karnatak University, Belgaum Campus, Belgaum, (Karnataka).

Shankar Chatterjee	—	Assistant Director (CME), National Institute of Rural Development, Rajendra Nagar, Hyderabad (A.P.)
Sheelwati Agrawal	—	Reader, School of Studies in Economics, Jiwaji University, Gwalior (M.P.)
Shridhar Pandey	—	Professor (Rtd.), Veer Kuer Singh University, Arrah (Bihar)
S. Murty	—	Professor, School of Studies in Economics, Vikram University, Ujjain (M.P.)
Tushar Kanti Das	—	Research Officer, (RBI) Department of Analytical and Applied Economics, Utkal University, Bhubaneswar (Orissa)
V.V. Jugale	—	Professor, NABARD Chair, VAMNICOM, Pune (M.S.)
Y.V. Jugale	—	Lecturer in Economics, Willingdon College, Sangli (M.S.)

Part I

NEED, SIGNIFICANCE AND METHODOLOGICAL ISSUES OF BALANCED AND SUSTAINABLE DEVELOPMENT

1

Regional Disparities: Need and Measures for Balanced Development

—(Mrs.) S. Murty

Meaning of the Term Region

Study of regional disparities involves the determination and definition of the term 'region'. Generally speaking, a region is a geographical area, territory or place. It may be a nation, a state, a district, a taluk, a block or a village, but the word region does not always apply to a particular place or area. It may have to be viewed as an economic, political, social, administrative, climatic or geographical entity according to the need or purpose of any study. Region in the Indian context broadly means a state within the union of India which is formed on linguistic basis, but for the purpose of planning, it may imply an economically backward or forward area within a state.

Meaning of Regional Disparities

Regional disparities mean uneven growth of primary, secondary, tertiary and/or social sectors in a country, state, district or place as the case may be. Every country whether developed or under-developed, agricultural or industrial, big or small, has economically advanced and backward regions. This advancement or backwardness may be prevalent in the sectors of agricultural, industry, trade, commerce, banking, insurance, transport, communication, infrastructural development, social overheads, education, health services, housing facilities etc.

Meaning of Even or Balanced Development

Balanced regional development implies an even growth of different regions to the extent of their development capabilities and needs. It does not mean that every region should be exactly equally developed, neither does it mean equal level of industrialization nor a uniform economic pattern for each state, not even self sufficiency in each region or state. It simply means the fullest development of the potentialities of an area according to its capacity so that the benefits of overall economic growth are shared by the inhabitants of all regions.

Rather it means widespread diffusion of industry in backward areas so far as it is economically feasible. The ultimate aim is to raise the living standards of the people in backward areas to those of the advanced areas and this may be through the development of agriculture or industry, trade or commerce, education or health facilities.

Development of the Concept of Balanced Regional Development

The idea of balanced regional development originated with Stalin who wanted to develop each region of Soviet Russia so that in the event of attack by the enemy, the economic power of the country may not cripple. In England, the idea of dispersal of industries and development of backward areas got strength after the German bombardment during the Second World War. Earlier the Barlow Commission in 1937, and Political and Economic Planning Group in 1939 had stressed the need for dispersal of industries in backward areas. In America, the backward area of Tennesse Valley received the first attention. Thus advanced countries have been conscious of balanced regional development. But the problem of regional disparities in economic development is more prevalent and acute in underdeveloped countries. India being in this category is striving hard for the removal of economic disparities since the inception of Five Year Plans. Today all underdeveloped countries are conscious about balanced regional development.

Causes of Regional Disparities

It is necessary to correlate the regional pattern of economic development with various physical and socio-economic variables in order to identify the variables which have the highest influence on the growth pattern. Though the broad answer to the question 'Why disparity' will not apply to all regions with equal force, still there are sufficient common aspects in it is allow some generalisation. When 'it comes to the ultimate level of case studies of particular regions, these general answers will have to be interpreted in the light of the particular circumstances of that region. The main causes are:

1. Geographical; 2. Historical; 3. Political; 4. State policy; 5. Administrative; 6. Social; and 7. Economic.

1. *Geographical Causes*

When the area of a place is fairly large, the distribution of national resources, power resources, agricultural resources, topography, climate and rainfall are not even throughout. Other things being equal, fair geographical condition leaves a region in a better condition.

2. *Historical Causes*

The level of development in a community also depends on what it has done in the past by way of providing for future. The form of organisation of economic life in the past is an important reason with which is connected the issue of incentive, to workers and entrepreneurs. A feudal system concedes very slight incentive for hard work. An industrial system where workers feel exploited, suffers from restlessness and a planned and restrictive system may arouse little initiative for private investment and cause hindrance to development. The example of some East European countries is before us. A system with freedom to work and invest may progress faster.

3. *Political Causes*

An elaborate but disturbed political set up will not offer as good a living as a less elaborate but sound political structure will. Better a pair of stout shoes than a Maruti car with two wheels missing. Political instability is a great obstacle to development. Again if a government is stable but weak, corrupt or unable to resist selfish and anti-social pressures, it will fail to pursue good policies for development. The political status of all regions is not the same. With so many political parties in the country, it is not always necessary that the M.P. or M.L.A. elected from a particular constituency will belong to the ruling party and if he does not, he cannot get favours done for his constituency with the result that a particular region suffers step-motherly treatment in comparison to the regions who have representative of ruling parties on the treasury benches. This increase the gap of unevenness in the economic development.

4. *State Policy Causes*

In recent times, almost all richer countries are approaching, the concept of welfare state. In these countries, state policies have been initiated which are directed towards greater regional equality. The market forces which result is backwash effects have been offset while those resulting is spread effects have been supported. In poor countries, there have been less of such policies. On the contrary in many poor countries, the natural drift towards inequalities has been supported and magnified by built in feudal and other inegalitarian institutions and power structure which help the rich in exploiting the poor.

5. *Administrative Causes*

Sometimes, the factor of administrative efficiency or inefficiency adds to the gulf of disparities of the regions. Today the state has many functions to perform for which it needs honest, educated, trained, adequately remunerated and efficient administrators because efficient administration results in regional development and *vice versa*.

6. *Social Causes*

Many social factors cause impediments to development. The people in less developed regions do not possess the institutions and attitudes which are conducive to economic development. They believe in more primitive variants of religion, traditional beliefs and social values which are a constant drag on economic development. This social backwardness catches these regions in a whirlpool of economic backwardness. On the other hands the people of developed regions possess such institutions and attitudes which are conducive to development. They believe in more flexible norms of religion, traditions, social beliefs and attitudes. Their is material prosperity and economic progress. These attitudes continuously sustain further expansion in a cumulative manner.

7. *Economic Causes*

Economic causes like differences in the factors of production, cumulative process of various factors, vicious circle of poverty, free play of market forces and their backwash and spread effects and market imperfections start and increase the disparities in economic development.

The first economic cause is qualitative and quantitative difference in the factors of production such as land, labour, capital, organisation and enterprises. Other things being equal, more favourable these factors, better will be the development.

The second economic cause is *cumulative process* of various factors by which a developed economy goes on developing and underdeveloped economy goes on deteriorating unless the state interferes in the form of schemes for inter-regional equalisation.

The first cumulative process is started by the *vicious circle* of poverty. There are two types of vicious circle in a backward economy. The first vicious circle is formed by the underdeveloped resources and backwardness of the people which are the cause and effect of each other. The second vicious circle consists of backwardness of people, low standard of living, low efficiency, low productivity, low income, low consumption, low savings, low investment, less employment and backwardness of people again. According to Nurkse, these factors act and react upon each other in such a way so as to keep a region in a perpetual state of poverty and start a downward cumulative process. On the other hand, there is a circle of prosperity in developed areas. Forward people, high standard of living, better efficiency, higher productivity, more production, more income, more consumption, more savings, more investment, more employment, and again more progressive people start an upward cumulative process, and the result is that the gap between the two types of regions goes on increasing.

Free play of market forces and their *spread and backward effects* are other economic causes of regional disparities. Due to free play of market forces, economic factors like labour, capital, and enterprise, and economic activities like industry, trade, commerce, banking and insurance which in a developing economy tend to give bigger returns, tend to cluster in more developed areas which provide certain internal and external economies. This all happens at the cost of other underdeveloped localities where relative stagnation becomes the pattern due to backwash effects. These poor localities get some advantage from the development of developed localities by way of spread effects, but the spread effects are weaker in comparison to the strong backwash effects, and the result is that there is a cumulative trend upwards in the lucky regions, and downwards in the unlucky regions.

Another economic cause of disparities is due to *market imperfections* such as factor immobility, price rigidity, ignorance of market conditions, lack of specialization, lack of division of labour etc. These act as friction to the development of backward areas. On the contrary, the perfectness of these factors make the already developed areas more developed.

Thus there are so many causes which result in regional disparities in economic development.

Need for Balanced Development

According to Rogestein Roden, for smooth development, a country needs a big push because it has to develop all sectors and all regions simultaneously because of 3 types of individualities.

1. Indivisibility of investment—Accordingly investment will have to be done in all sectors and regions simultaneously for the development of infrastructure—it is the basic need.
2. Indivisibility of demand—Many industries and regions should be developed simultaneously so, that they may create demand for each others products.

3. Indivisibility of savings because lump sum savings are needed for lump sum investment.

As the slow or rapid growth of any part of human body results in an abnormal formation, in the same way, unbalanced growth of regions cause many economic, social, and political problems in a country. Thus arises the need for the study of regional disparities and planning for balanced development. It is said that poverty anywhere is a danger to prosperity everywhere and prosperity anywhere should be shared everywhere. All governments intend to remove or minimise regional disparities because of various reasons. They are:

(*a*) To develop the economy smoothly;
(*b*) To develop the economy rapidly;
(*c*) To utilise and conserve resources;
(*d*) To promote employment opportunities;
(*e*) To reduce extra burden of population on agricultural and capital formation through disguised unemployment;
(*f*) To encourage decentralisation and to overcome social evils of localisation, urbanisation and pollution;
(*g*) To avoid internal conflicts and political instability; and
(*h*) To defend the country from external wars.

(a) To Develop the Economy Smoothly

If all the regions are equally developed, they can be mutually helpful to each other. Otherwise the low level of income in backward areas will cause lack of adequate demand for the products of developed areas and will retard their development. Moreover, balanced regional development also avoids transport and supply bottlenecks, and minimise inflationary pressure within the economy.

(b) To Develop the Economy Rapidly

If the speed of all walkers in a group is alike, the group proceeds further fast. In the same way, the progress of the entire economy depends on the development of all regions, simultaneously, keeping in view their factor endowments.

(c) To Utilise and Conserve Resources

Balanced development of each region helps to exploit and

utilise its natural and human resources to the maximum extent possible. Moreover, when a region develops its resources these resources in turn develop that region and thus their wastage due to non-utilisation of their destructive and exploitative use by others is stopped.

(d) To Promote Employment Opportunities

With the development of infrastructure, and dispersal of industries in backward regions, there is scope for larger employment opportunities in all areas, thereby increasing per capita output and domestic product. Besides this, many other negative effects of unemployment can be overcome.

(e) To Reduce Extra Burden of Population on Agriculture

India is primarily an agricultural country whose 75 per cent population resides in rural areas which are generally backward areas. Thus 75 per cent of population thrives on agriculture in the absence of other means of livelihood and cause extra burden on agriculture, resulting in low productivity and disguised unemployment. Louis is of the opinion that unlimited supply of labour from less productive sector to more productive sector at subsistence wages or a little more than subsistence wages will on the one hand increase the per capita productivity in the first sector and will increase employment, production, and capital information in the other sector leading the country gradually to better stages of economic development. Louis's theory of unlimited supply of labour forces from agricultural sector to industrial sector may work here.

(f) To Encourage Decentralisation

Regional disparities encourage centralisation. The developed areas have the capacity to attract new entrepreneurship, new industries, and new institutions whereas the backward areas have a tendency to distract them. As a result, the problem of centralisation emerges and grows. Centralisation of economic affairs is not a problem in itself, but it gives rise to many other defects, such as localisation, urbanisation, fear of war, internal conflicts etc. Localisation and urbanisation in turn generate many other problems such as overcrowding, congestion, noise, pollution, housing problem and many other evils. The cost of living in these areas is high and breeds poverty and increases discontentment.

(g) To Avoid Internal Conflicts and Political Instability

The developed regions overshadow the underdeveloped regions which go in the background and remain neglected in spite of the fact that they continue to be the constituent parts of the economic development of the state. This leads to the development of a sense of inferiority complex in the minds of the people of these regions. They become either mild and docile or wild and hostile and striking. This leads to internal disputes and resentment. Such complexes are never good for the general well-being of a nation, and need serious thought. Restlessness in backward regions leading to internal disputes not only cause bad feelings in these regions but throughout the country and create a lot of problems for the governments—both state and central.

Regional disparities in income and wealth are the greatest danger to national solidarity. States may want to secede if they are vary rich. They may also demand to secede if they are very poor and feel neglected. Political and economic negligence led Bangladesh as an independent sovereign country.

(h) To Defend the Country from External Attack

Balanced regional development is an essential factor for a proper security of the country in war time from aerial attacks on industrialized areas, because development of a few areas and concentration of industries in them will bring the entire economy to a standstill in the event of their destruction by the enemy.

Estimate of Regional Disparities in India

In India, economists and government agencies have done studies of regional disparities from time to time.

1. The Economic and Scientific Research Foundation of India proved that over the decade 1960-61 to 1970-71 agricultural income from crop production registered a very high growth rate of 142.6 per cent. In case of already developed states, it was very high with Punjab 224 per cent, Haryana 223 per cent, Gujarat 203 per cent, and Rajasthan 200 per cent, while it was lower than the national average in Mysore, Orissa, Jammu and Kashmir, Kerala and other states.

2. In 1982, *The Economic Times* made a study of prosperity in different states and found that nine states had about 50 per cent population below the poverty line. These states were Orissa, Tripura, M.P., Bihar, West Bengal, Tamil Nadu, Assam, U.P., and Karnataka.
3. Prof. Radhakrishnan, in his lecture *The centre and the periphery* in 1980 grouped inter-state disparities into six categories, and found that 72 per cent of the total poor population resided in seven major states, *viz.*, MadhyaPradesh, Uttar Pradesh, Bihar, Maharashtra, West Bengal, Andhra Pradesh, and Tamil Nadu. Most of the least developed states lie in the heartland while most of the outlying area seems to be less deprived. So Prof. Radhakrishnan calls it the centre periphery problem rather than North-South problem in the United Nations terminology.
4. In 1968, the government of India appointed a working group known as Pande Committee for identification of backward areas. The Committee recommended five indicators for measuring development. Subsequently, the Planning Commission in consultation with the National Development Council recommended six indicators. Both Pande Commission and Planning Commission had suggested that for incentives to industrial development, the districts should have a minimum level of infrastructural facilities.
5. Chakravarty Committee on Backward Areas has more methodically examined the problem of identification and classification of backward areas with the help of fourteen indicators. The Chakravarty Committee made use of three methods for aggregating the fourteen indicators which it initially chose. The ranking method classified 164 districts as backward; the index method classified 206 districts as backward; and the principal component method classified 181 districts as backward. 155 districts were classified as backward by all the three methods and were named as hard core of backward areas in the country.
6. The National Committee on Development of Backward Areas recommended problem area approach and viewed six types of fundamental backwardness, *viz.*, Chronically drought prone areas; Chronically flood affected areas;

Desert areas; Hill areas; Coastal areas affected by salinity; and Tribal areas.

7. *Facts for You* in 1982, analysed the regional disparities in states on the basis of per capita income at current prices in comparison to all India average being equal to 100. For the year 1980-81, the state above the national average were Punjab, Maharashtra, Haryana, Gujarat, and West Bengal, their indices being respectively 173, 149, 137, 123 and 103. The states below the national average were respectively Himachal Pradesh (98.5), Jammu & Kashmir (95.2), Karnataka (91), Kerala (90.5), Tamil Nadu (89.1), Andhra Pradesh (85.6), Assam (81.5), Rajasthan (81.3), Uttar Pradesh (79.4), Madhya Pradesh (71.8), Orissa (71.7), Manipur (69.8), and Bihar (59.4).
8. Prof R.T. Tiwari in 1984 prepared a composite index based on nineteen indicators from agriculture, industry, irrigation, power, roads, education and health. The states above the national average were Punjab (157), Kerala (139), Tamil Nadu (137), Maharashtra (123), Gujarat (119), Haryana (116), Karnataka (115), and West Bengal (109). The states below the national average were Andhra Pradesh (98), Himachal Pradesh (98), Uttar Pradesh (87), Orissa (84), Rajasthan (81), Bihar (78), and Madhya Pradesh (76). Thus, Madhya Pradesh the largest state of India in terms of land, came out even half the performance level of Punjab.

Thus different committee and persons have adopted different methods of measuring disparities in India, and different districts and states have emerged as more or less developed. But, generally the states which are identified to be more developed and above the national average are: Punjab, Haryana, Maharashtra, Gujarat, West Bengal, and Himachal Pradesh. The states identified as less developed and generally below the state average are Madhya Pradesh, Uttar Pradesh, Bihar, Orissa, Manipur, and Assam.

Policies for Balanced Development in Indian Plans

1. In the First Plan it was mentioned that due consideration will be given to regional balanced and sustained growth,

but the disparities must have increased in the First Plan as there was wide gap in per capita expenditure of different states, *i.e.* Karnataka Rs. 49 and Madhya Pradesh Rs. 19.

2. The Second Plan emphasized that disparities in the levels of development between different regions should be progressively reduced and the pattern of investment should be so devised as to lead to balanced regional development. In pursuance of this policy, some basic facilities like water, power, irrigation and transport were provided in backward areas; small scale and village industries were located in backward regions, and industrial estates were located near small towns. But the plan failed to reduce regional disparities.
3. The Third Plan devoted a separate chapter to balanced regional development. The Plan report pointed out, "Balanced development of different parts of the country, extension of benefits of economic progress to the less developed regions and widespread diffusion of industry and among the major aims of planned development". Despite its efforts and measures, the Plan could not reduce regional disparities.
4. The Fourth Plan was more realistic in its approach towards the problem of regional disparities. The Plan devised a triple formula for removing regional imbalances. First, weightage in allocation of central assistance; second, location of central projects in backward areas; and third, adjustment in procedures and policies of financial institutions so as to provide concessions to small and medium industries in backward areas.
5. The Fourth Plan approach to the development of backward areas was carried forward in the Fifth Plan.
6. The Sixth Plan emphasized the need for continuing existing policies for removing regional disparities. Besides, it recommended more measures for skill, technology, resources and investment development in backward areas.
7. The Seventh and Eighth Plan, besides carrying forward the already prevalent programmes, started special area development programme such as Hill Area Development Programme, Desert Development Programme, etc. In Eighth Plan special tax holidays were given for development of industries in backward regions.

Policy Measures for Even Development

1. First of all, the study regional disparities should be done by using some uniform criteria, and backward regions which are below the national or state average should be demarcated.
2. Techno-economic and social survey of each region should be done to evaluate its development potentials, economic feasibilities and social attitudes.
3. After the techno-economic survey of the region, the development programme of the region should be made, based on regional potential and needs, and not on political considerations.
4. There should be an integrated programme for development of villages and small scale industries in backward areas. In the initial stages consumer goods and processing industries can be started, followed by manufacturing industries.
5. Next step is the establishment of industrial estates or industrial development area where basic facilities like land, water, power, transport, communications, banking and insurance etc. should be provided. Initially all facilities should be provided by the state.
6. Loans, concessions, and subsidies should be given to entrepreneurs willing to start projects in backward areas.
7. Industrial development is not enough. Agricultural development is more important in the rural oriented economy of India. Hence agriculture in backward regions should be improved by providing improved seeds, fertilisers, pesticides, irrigation and credit facilities to farmers etc.
8. The next step is to develop 'Growing Points' as recommended by Working Group on Incentives for Industrial Development in Backward Areas. Growing points may take the form of market towns for the farmers of backward regions wherefrom they can get their inputs and sell their output. Thus a centre of higher order may become the nucleus of development for surrounding areas. The whole region may be called a Growth Settlement. There may be a growth pole in each region and many

settlements will revolve around this growth pole for services of higher order. This growth pole will be a bigger settlement in itself.

9. Enough funds should be made available by the centre to the states for development of backward areas, after studying their needs and importance.
10. Dandekar Committee on Removing Imbalances in Maharashtra has suggested the establishment of a Statutory Watch Dog Authority to supervise and report on the activities of regional imbalances. The package of incentives should take into account the factor of distance and should compensate if sufficiently.

    Policy of industrial location should be modified in the light of techno-economic changes that are taking place in power supply, transport, communication, industrial organisation etc. With these developments, all the facilities can be provided in far off places, and industrial location need not be near big cities.

Conclusion

Balanced regional development should be planned after finding out the imbalances, striking out the potential of backward regions, and making schemes for their development. Disparities should be removed by lifting up the bottom rather than by putting down the top.

References

1. Balkrishna, R., *Regional Planning in India.*
2. Dayoh, G.H.J., *Studies in Regional Planning.*
3. Datta, A.K., *Some Lessons of Regional Planning in India.*
4. Harvey, D.P., *Regional Resources and Economic Growth.*
5. Harrisons, I.Z., *Economic Factors in Economic Growth.*
6. Mishra, A., *Levels of Regional Development in India.*
7. Prakash, Rao, *Regional Planning.*
8. Roback, S.H., *Regional and Economic Development in India.*
9. Sharma, T.K., *Location of Industries in India.*
10. Tinbergen, J., *Regional Planning.*
11. Agarwal & Singh, *The Economics of Development.*

2

Need and Significance of Balanced Sectoral Development for Aggregate Sustainable Development

—N.M. Lall, Sheelwati Agrawal
& Anjani Kumar Jha

"Thus, the quest for sustainability can be made into a potent force for efficiency, productivity, innovation and growth—if we don't squander it on knee-jerk responses, such as out-lawing what we don't like and instituting inefficient commands and controls. The road to sustainable development passes through an undistorted, competitive and well-functioning market."

—Theodore Panayotou[1]

The need and significance of balanced sectoral development for aggregate-sustainable development is crystal clear from the views expressed by Theodore Panayotou at the Round Table Discussion with Lester Brown on the subject "Is Economic Growth Sustainable?" at World Bank Annual Conference on Development Economics in 1991. Theodore Panayotou rightly argues that the sustainability has a great potential for efficiency, productivity, innovation and growth if the economies follow the path of balanced sectoral growth. Any deviation from the path of balanced sectoral growth will lead to keen-jerk responses, such as out-lawing what we do not like and thereby instituting inefficient commands and controls. Thus, the road to aggregate sustainable development based on balanced sectoral growth will pass through an undistorted, competitive and well-functioning market.

Walt W. Rostow was the first economic historian to open the discussion on "The Take-off into Sustained Growth". Rostow found it convenient to divide the economic history of any country into three stages: a "long period" of a century or more during which the preconditions for take-off are established; two or three decades into which the take-off itself is compressed; and "the long fluctuating story of sustained economic progress" when growth becomes normal and relatively automatic?[2]

Even rich and stagnant countries have troubles who do not follow the path of balanced sectoral growth for aggregative-sustainable development. The maintenance of full employment poses difficult policy questions even in highly developed countries which cease to grow. When an "open society", in which opportunities for individual advancement accompany the unbalanced sectoral growth of the economy as a whole, is transformed into a closed one where individual advancement is possible only at the expense of others., social and political problems are intensified as well. If per capita incomes are low but rising, if sustained growth seems assured, and if the gains in welfare are widely diffused so as to insurrect balanced sectoral growth of the economy, there is irrelatively little cause for concern. Such a society may well be less troubled than one that is rich but stagnant and follows unbalanced sectoral growth. Clearly, however, the economic problem is most serious in countries that are both stagnant and impoverished marching ahead on the path of unbalanced sectoral growth. Above all, therefore, the problem of economic development is launching a take-off into sustained growth in poor and stagnant countries with unbalanced sectoral growth. Thus, by "sustained growth" is meant a discernible rise in national, sectoral and per capita real income, widely diffused throughout the population spread over all the sectors of the economy poised for sectoral balanced growth, that continues for two or more generations.[3]

In presenting his version of balanced sectoral growth, Ragnar Nurkse, in his book *Problems of Capital Formation in Underdeveloped Countries,* advocates "a frontal attack . . . a wave of capital investments in a number of different industries"[4] to achieve the desideratum of balanced sectoral growth *i.e.* equal incremental growth in all the sectors of the economy. The case for balanced sectoral growth rests on the need for a "balanced diet." The doctrine may be expressed by paraphrasing a metaphor coined in a different context: "hundred flowers may grow where a single flower would wither away for lack of nourishment."[5] This presents a case for the prime need of balanced sectoral development for aggregate sustainable development.

While the aggregate sustainable development is a fashionable buzz word in environmental conservation circles in much of the world's international development. It received its most popular exposition in the highly influential Brundtland Report in 1987 which was prepared by the World Commission on Environment and Development.[6] The aggregate sustainable development is the acknowledged subject of much recent development thinking *i.e.* World Commission on Environment and Development. The sustained development is the acknowledged subject of much recent development thinking *i.e.* World Commission on Environment and Development, 1987; Repetto, 1986; Redcliff, 1987; Turner, 1988 and Stockholm Group, 1988. There is no doubt that little headway appears to have been made in terms of rigorous definition of the concept. Therefore, not surprisingly, efforts to 'operationalize' sustainable development and to show how it can be integrated into practical discussion and decision-making have been few and generally unpersuasive.[7]

The current use of the term 'development' rather than 'economic growth', naturally implies acceptance of the limitations of the use of measures such as "Gross National Product" or "Gross Domestic Product" to measure the well-being of the nations. To speak the truth, development embraces wider concerns of the quality of life—educational attainment, nutritional status, access to basic freedoms and spiritual welfare. The stress on the word 'sustainability' suggests that what is needed is a policy effort at making these developmental achievements last well into the future. By implications, some at least of past development efforts have achieved only short-lived gains. A simple definition of sustainable development can be elaborated as a set of minimum conditions for development to be sustainable, the conditions being based on the requirement that the 'natural capital stock' should not decrease over time but the constant or increased.[8]

To probe deeper into the matter, one must be clear since development is a value word, implying change that is 'desirable', there is no consensus as to its meaning. What constitutes development depends on what social goals are being advocated by the development agency, government analyst or advisor. It would be more precise to take development to be a vector of desirable social objectives. It is a list of attributes which society seeks to achieve or maximise. The elements of this vector may include:[9]

* increase in real income per capita;
* improvement in health and nutritional status;
* educational achievement;
* access to resources;
* a fairer distribution of income; and,
* increase in basic freedoms.

Any correlation between these elements or an agreed system of weights to be applied to them, might permit development to be represented by a single pre-indicator, but this is not the issue to be pursued here.

Aggregate sustainable development is a situation in which the development vector does not decrease over time. The term implies the adoption of an infinite time horizon but the aim should be to achieve ever lasting development—whereas practical decision-making requires some finite time horizon. It should also tell us if the rate of change of development *(D)* with respect to time *(t)*, must be positive for each and every time period (for strong sustainability) or whether only the trend of development—

D/dr

must be positive (for weak sustainability). To do this, future benefits and costs are discounted to a similar benefit or cost in the present. The present value maximization is consistent with the extinction of resources. How far these extinctions of resources result in the development objectives themselves becoming unsustainable is open to question. But there should lend some support to the idea that present value maximization is not a sufficient criterion for sustainable development. The sustainable development is the rate of change of development over time as generally positive over some selected time horizon.[10] Thus, the aggregate sustainable development categorically always needs the rate of change of development over time as perfectly positive over the selected time horizons.

To sum up the whole discussion over the balanced sectoral growth and aggregate sectoral development, it can be indubitably stated that there is an imperative need and significance of balanced sectoral development for aggregate sustainable development since the former paves the way for the later and the later can not be dreamt of without achieving the former.

Notes

1. Panayotou, Theodore, *Is Economic Growth Sustainable?* (Round Table Discussion with Brown, Lester)—Proceedings of the World Bank Annual Conference on Development Economics (1991) Washington, p. 358.
2. Rostow, W.W., "The Take-Off Into Self-Sustained Growth", *The Economic Journal*, (March, 1956), pp. 29-30.
3. Higgins, Benjamin, *Economic Development—Problems, Principles and Policies* (1961), pp. 20-21.
4. Nurkse, Ragnar, *Problems of Capital Formation in Underdeveloped Countries* (1953), p. 5
5. Benjamin, Higgins, *op. cit.*, p. 400.
6. Peace, David *et al.*, *Sustainable Development* (1993), p. IX.
7. *Ibid.*, pp. IX-1.
8. *Ibid.*, pp. IX–X–1
9. *Ibid.*, pp. IX–1–2.
10. *Ibid.*, p. 2.

3

Composite Indices for Regional Analysis: Some Methodological Issues

—R.V. Dadibhavi

The purpose of the paper is to study the problems in constructing the composite indices for regional analysis and to suggest remedial measures. The analysis is made with reference to inter-state disparities in infrastructure (Economic) development in India based on the secondary sources of data for seventeen major states covering the period 1970-71 to 1984-85.

The crucial stage in the multivariate analysis is that of contracting a large number of variables into a smaller number of indices so that the geographical (Micro) units, (in the present case the states) can be easily compared with each other. Among the several approaches suggested, the most important are the construction of (*i*) a composite index for each region/state, and (*ii*) an index of composite distance between every pair (Mahalanobis, 1936). However, in the present paper, we have opted to follow the former approach owing to its great relevance.

Paper presented at the International Conference of RSA, Kharagapur I.I.T. during December, 17-19, 1992.

The task of constructing the composite index has two major aspects: elimination of the bias of scale and determination of weightages to different variables.

Elimination of the scale bias: The variables selected for constructing composite indices are measured in different units, and hence in general, not directly additive. It, therefore, becomes, necessary to convert them to some standard 'Units' so that the initial scale chosen for measuring the variables does not bias the results (Anderson, 1958). Any conversion (linear or non-linear) may disturb the relative position of the observations, their relation with the origin and other variables. Selection of scale, therefore, is not a value free decision.

Ranking Method, Standardisation, Division by Standard Deviation, Normalisation, Division by Mean and Division by an 'Ideal' value are some of the methods of scale conversion currently used in regional studies (Kundu, 1980). We propose to employ the method of division by mean as it helps to get rid of the bias of scale without effecting the dispersion or the relative position of observations in the series.

Assigning Weights

Once the bias of the unit of measurement is removed from the observations, the crucial problem that remains is assigning appropriate weightage to the chosen variables. If one has sufficient insight into the nature and magnitude of the interrelations among the selected variables, he might chose to determine the weightage through his judgement. This often incorporates, certain amount of subjectivity and 'arbitrariness' into the analysis, though in the hands of experienced researchers it may produce fruitful results. Regional patterns obtained through such methods, however, stand exposed to *ad hoc* influences of vested interests, one can, perhaps, minimise the dangers of *ad hoc* influences (Political) or group pressures by subjecting the analysis to some standard mathematical technique. We have employed the "Method of Principal Component Analysis" to assign the weights for different variables in the present work.

The method of Principal Component Analysis, a special case of the more general method of Factor Analysis (Harman,

1970) has been widely applied in constructing composite development index since 1970. The method is relatively a straightforward method of transferring a given set of variables or indicators into a new set of composite variables or principal components that are orthogonal (uncorrelated) to each other. It is designed primarily to synthesise a large number of variables into a smaller number of general components which retain the maximum amount of descriptive ability. An empirical method for the reduction of a large body of data with a view to extracting the maximum of the variance was first proposed by Pearson (Pearson, 1901) and later on fully developed as the method of principal components or component analysis by Herold Hotelling (Hotelling, 1933).

Now the problem is to obtain estimates of as (loading). For this purpose we employed the method suggested by Koutsoyiannis (Koutsoyiannis, 1977 and Dadibhavi, 1982).

The problem does not end here if we are interested to construct composite indices of development for different regions on year-wise basis over a period of time. In fact the indices worked out for different years on the basis of single weightage are comparable. Variable weightage system makes the indices non-comparable. In case of single weightage system, the weights may be based

(*i*) on either the beginning year or the terminal year data,
(*ii*) on the average of all the years data,
(*iii*) on the average of beginning and the terminal year data.

The first method does not capture the changes that have taken place in each of the indicators over time. The second method is not useful when the data are not available on year-wise data *i.e.* census data. The third method tries to overcome the above defects. It is proposed to use the third method in our work.

The significant role of infrastructure in the process of economic development has been well recognised both by the economists and planners. Infrastructural development through public investment in irrigation, rural electrification, roads and so on, is expected to distribute the gains from economic growth widely by providing opportunities to the less developed regions.

Water, power, transport and communication are considered as important economic infrastructure requirements of development. In the present paper an attempt has been made to construct the composite indices of economic infrastructure for seventeen major states of India covering the period 1970-71 to 1984-85 using both the methods of weightage system. It also tries to show whether the results based on single weightage system are too much divergent from that of the results based on year to year weightage system.

To indicate the availability of transport, communication, power and irrigation systems in the states, the following indicators are selected. They are:

X_1 = Road length per 100 km^2 area,
X_2 = Road length per lakh population.
X_3 = Surface road length (as per cent of total road length),
X_4 = Number of registered vehicles per lakh population,
X_5 = Railway length in Kms per 1000 km^2.
X_6 = Number of post offices per lakh of population,
X_7 = Percentage of villages electrified,
X_8 = Per capita energy consumption
X_9 = Per capita industrial use of power (in kwh)
X_{10} = Net irrigated area as per cent of NSA

The weights based on the average of 1971-81 data and weight based on year-wise data are given in Table 3.1. From the table it can be observed that the variations in the weights of all the variables for the period 1970-71 to 1984-85 are found to be negligible (see the last row of the table). Since the yearwise changes in the development of infrastructural facilities are marginal, the above results are not surprising. Further, the states ranked on the basis of indices constructed on the single weightage system and year-wise weightage system are given in Tables 3.2 and 3.3, respectively. There is perfect correlation between the ranks of the states based on the single weightage system and the ranks of the states based on yearwise weightage system.

Maharashtra and Madhya Pradesh were the highest and lowest developed states, respectively, in terms of economic infrastructure development in 1970-71. Whereas in the terminal period of study, Punjab and Assam, turned out to be the highest

Table 3.1
Weights of Economic Infrastructural Variables (First Principal Component)

Years	X_1	X_2	X_3	X_4	X_5	X_6	X_7	X_8	X_9	X_{10}	*Per cent explained variation*
1970-71 and 1980-81 (Average)	.7790	0.1065	0.4511	.7454	.4939	.3500	.7306	.8912	.7893	.5220	35.00
1970-71	.4125	.0885	.2391	.4282	.5137	.2918	.6109	.8377	.6698	.3895	24.42
1971-72	.4921	.2217	.3728	.5041	.5161	.2950	.5821	.8066	.6234	.3963	25.72
1972-73	.4811	.1964	.3768	.4831	.5586	.3209	.5536	.8214	.7114	.4355	27.37
1973-74	.4859	.3075	.4352	.3537	.4287	.1629	.6745	.7395	.3959	.4460	22.12
1974-75	.4571	.1774	.4233	.5790	.5430	.3935	.7602	.8005	.6600	.4469	30.58
1975-76	.4073	.2251	.4673	.7630	.5219	.4131	.7143	.7700	.6006	.4392	31.16
1976-77	.3676	.1883	.5127	.8265	.5331	.4599	.8097	.8394	.7198	.5363	37.78
1977-78	.3730	.1440	.5180	.8291	.5267	.4166	.7838	.8089	.6590	.5263	35.45
1978-79	.3385	.1147	.5836	.7651	.4816	.0133	.8336	.8452	.6917	.5486	34.74
1979-80	.3554	.1168	.5682	.8359	.4658	.4008	.7732	.8709	.7522	.5650	37.73
1980-81	.3610	.1640	.5710	.8372	.4640	.3862	.8039	.8842	.7639	.5248	38.35
1981-82	.3449	.1540	.5890	.7166	.4491	.3491	.8308	.8864	.7484	.2568	34.28
1982-83	.3484	.2329	.6037	.8306	.4359	.3975	.7958	.7718	.7608	.5674	37.07
1983-84	.2969	.2579	.5664	.8433	.4035	.4160	.7745	.9017	.7429	.5437	37.82
1984-85	.3008	.2573	.5565	.8670	.4011	.3755	.7535	.7676	.7212	.5054	34.52
Mean (1970-85)	.3875	.1879	.4922	.6974	.4828	.3394	.7369	.8234	.6814	.4751	—
C.V. % (1970-85)	16.8	32.31	21.24	25.35	10.6	34.09	12.29	5.9	13.7	17.9	

Note: Weights are based on respective correlation matrix.

Source: Dadibhavi, R.V., "Regional Variations in Infrastructure Development in India", Report submitted to CSSR, New Delhi, K.U.B.C. Mimeo.

Table 3.2
Rank of Seventeen Indian States in Terms of Composite Index of Economic Infrastructure Based on Single Weightage System

States	*1970-71*	*1971-72*	*1972-73*	*1973-74*	*1974-75*	*1975-76*	*1976-77*	*1977-78*	*1978-79*	*1979-80*	*1980-81*	*1981-82*	*1982-83*	*1983-84*	*1984-85*
Andhra Pradesh	10	9	10	11	10	10	9	10	9	9	9	9	8	8	8
Assam	16	16	15	17	17	17	17	17	17	17	17	17	17	17	17
Bihar	13	12	13	15	13	14	11	13	14	14	16	16	16	16	16
Gujarat	6	6	6	5	5	4	5	4	4	3	3	3	3	3	2
Haryana	5	5	3	1	6	5	2	2	2	2	2	2	2	2	3
Himachal	12	15	16	10	16	11	15	15	15	15	14	13	11	13	12
J & K	15	14	14	14	12	12	12	11	12	13	12	11	12	15	14
Karnataka	8	8	7	8	7	7	7	7	7	7	7	7	5	7	6
Kerala	4	4	4	3	4	6	6	6	6	6	6	6	6	6	5
Madhya Pradesh	17	17	17	16	15	16	16	16	16	16	15	15	13	11	11
Maharashtra	1	2	5	7	3	3	4	5	5	5	5	4	7	4	4
Orissa	9	10	9	6	14	13	13	12	13	12	11	12	15	14	15
Punjab	2	1	1	2	1	1	1	1	1	1	1	1	1	1	1
Rajasthan	14	13	12	13	11	15	14	14	11	11	13	14	14	12	13
Tamil Nadu	3	3	2	4	2	2	3	3	3	4	4	5	4	5	7
Uttar Pradesh	11	11	11	12	9	9	10	9	10	10	10	10	10	10	10
West Bengal	7	7	8	9	8	8	8	8	8	8	8	8	9	9	9

Source: Dadibhavi, R.V., "Regional Variations in Infrastructure Development in India", Report submitted to ICSSR, New Delhi, KUBC Mimeo, p. 47.

Table 3.3
Rank of Seventeen Indian States in Terms of Composite Index of Economic Infrastructure Based on Year to Year Weights

States	*1970-71*	*1971-72*	*1972-73*	*1973-74*	*1974-75*	*1975-76*	*1976-77*	*1977-78*	*1978-79*	*1979-80*	*1980-81*	*1981-82*	*1982-83*	*1983-84*	*1984-85*
Andhra Pradesh	10	9	11	11	10	9	9	11	9	9	9	8	8	8	8
Assam	14	14	14	15	17	17	17	17	17	17	17	17	17	17	17
Bihar	12	12	12	14	11	15	13	13	13	15	16	16	16	16	16
Gujarat	6	6	7	5	6	6	5	4	4	3	4	3	3	3	2
Haryana	5	5	4	1	4	5	2	2	2	2	2	2	2	2	3
Himachal	13	13	15	10	15	11	12	15	16	14	12	11	11	9	10
J & K	16	16	16	16	14	12	11	10	11	12	11	10	12	13	13
Karnataka	8	8	8	7	7	7	7	7	7	7	7	7	5	6	5
Kerala	4	2	3	2	2	3	6	6	6	6	6	6	6	7	6
Madhya Pradesh	17	17	17	17	16	16	16	16	15	16	15	15	13	14	12
Maharashtra	2	4	5	6	5	4	4	5	5	5	5	4	7	4	4
Orissa	9	10	9	8	13	14	15	14	14	13	13	13	15	15	15
Punjab	1	1	1	3	1	1	1	1	1	1	1	1	1	1	1
Rajasthan	15	15	13	13	12	13	14	12	12	11	14	14	14	12	14
Tamil Nadu	3	3	2	4	3	2	3	3	3	4	3	5	4	5	7
Uttar Pradesh	11	11	10	12	9	10	10	9	10	10	10	12	10	10	11
West Bengal	7	7	6	9	8	8	8	8	8	8	8	9	9	11	9

Source: Dadibhavi, R.V., *op. cit.*, p. 58.

and lowest developed states, respectively. Except Madhya Pradesh, the states like Assam, Jammu and Kashmir, Rajasthan and Bihar all along occupied the lower ranks between 13 to 17 during this long period of analysis. Madhya Pradesh improved its rank from 17 in 1970-71 to 11 in 1984-85, whereas Orissa lost its position from 9 in 1970-71 to 15 in 1984-85. In top ranking stages, there is a continuous deterioration in the ranks held by Maharashtra and Tamil Nadu as against the continuous improvement in the ranks held by Gujarat and Haryana. It is also important to note that ranks have fluctuated substantially over the years in the case of Hill states *i.e.*, Himachal Pradesh and Jammu & Kashmir. The middle level ranks are occupied by Andhra Pradesh, Karnataka, Uttar Pradesh and West Bengal. Their position have not changed much. Further the results reveal that the ranks have not undergone any substantial changes between 1970-71 and 1984-85.

To study the trend in regional disparities in the economic infrastructure facilities, we worked out the coefficients of variation of infrastructure indices for all the years. Coefficient of variation increased from 35.79 per cent in 1970-71 to 40.51 per cent in 1979-80 and thereafter it fluctuated around 36 per cent. In other words the development of overhead facilities has gone contrary to the planned objectives of reducing regional disparities in India. Perhaps, this phenomenon, to some extent, may explain the economic disparity in the country. Concerted efforts are needed to reduce this magnitude of disparity.

On the basis of the value of composite indices of economic infrastructure the states may be categorised into four groups *viz.*, Group I—Advanced, Group II—Semi-Advanced, Group III—Partially Advanced, and Group IV—Underdeveloped states. On the basis of 1984-85 infrastructure indices, the states are classified as follows:

Group I—Advanced
Gujarat, Punjab.

Group II—Semi-Advanced
Haryana, Karnataka, Kerala, Maharashtra, Tamil Nadu.

Group III—Partially Advanced
Andhra Pradesh, Assam, Uttar Pradesh, West Bengal.

Group IV—Underdeveloped
Bihar, Himachal Pradesh, Jammu & Kashmir, Madhya Pradesh, Orissa, Rajasthan.

Thus, the states like Bihar, Himachal Pradesh, Jammu & Kashmir, Madhya Pradesh, Orissa and Rajasthan are the most backward states in India in terms of economic infrastructure.

Plan Outlays, State Expenditure and Development of Infrastructure

Of the total public sector outlay of about Rs. 3,54,655.5 crores during the seven Five Year Plans, as much as about 2,72,446.6 crores or 77 per cent of the total outlay was devoted to infrastructure. In other words our planning is concerned with infrastructure which is of crucial importance for the development of the Indian Economy as a whole.

The total plan expenditure in a state consists of expenditures made by the centre called 'Central Plan Expenditure" and expenditure incurred by the states termed 'State Plan Expenditure'. The figures on sector-wise central plan expenditure on different sectors for all the plans are not available, separately, and hence, we considered the total state-wise public sector plan outlays here. To study the impact of public sector plan outlays on disparities in infrastructure development, we have worked out per capita outlay on economic infrastructure *i.e.* irrigation and flood control, energy, transport, communication, information and broadcasting etc. from Fourth Five Year Plan (1969-74) to Seventh Five Year Plan (1980-85) and are given in Table 3.4.

The data reveals that there are wide variations in total state plan outlays on infrastructure and there appears to be no reduction in these variations. It can be observed from the coefficients of variation of state per capita total plan outlays on various infrastructure facilities (see the last row of Table 3.4). There are also indications that the state per capita plan outlays have been low in states with low composite index of infrastructure and high in states with high composite index of infrastructure, and thus the per capita state plan outlays are found to be 'regressive in nature'. For instance, Bihar, Madhya Pradesh and Orissa with low ranks in terms of infrastructure indices have also the low ranks in terms of per capita state plan outlays on infrastructure. Among the states with high indices of infrastructure, the states like Punjab, Haryana and Gujarat have relatively high per capita state plan outlays on infrastructure

Table 3.4
State-wise Per Capita Public Sector Plan Outlays and Public Expenditure on Economic Infrastructure

States	*Public Sector Plan Outlays (Rs.)*			*Public Expenditure (Rs.)*	
	IV FYP (1969-74)	*VI FYP (1980-85)*	*VII FYP (1985-90)*	*1971-72*	*1981-82*
Andhra Pradesh	57	358	496	8	36
Assam	63	319	440	4	17
Bihar	59	318	421	7	13
Gujarat	94	694	935	8	48
Haryana	129	941	1268	19	103
Himachal Pradesh	—	681	1088	17	23
Jammu & Kashmir	130	695	839	30	96
Karnataka	122	347	437	7	28
Kerala	57	290	354	3	16
Madhya Pradesh	48	520	874	7	18
Maharashtra	60	621	835	5	31
Orissa	48	370	590	8	12
Punjab	125	717	1201	15	69
Rajasthan	78	361	473	12	27
Tamil Nadu	45	305	509	8	28
Uttar Pradesh	64	364	551	7	16
West Bengal	27	323	315	3	15
All India	75	483	683	10	35
C.V. %	44.76	41.3	44.6	70.2	80.5

Source: Dadibhavi, R.V., *op. cit.*, pp. 151 and 155.

too. This aspect is further studied by working out the correlation coefficients between the composite indices of infrastructure at the beginning of each plan period and per capita state plan outlays on infrastructure during the plan concerned. Coefficients of correlations between the per capita state plan outlays and composite indices of economic infrastructure were found to be +.16, +.49 (significant at 5 per cent level) +.51 (significant at 5 per cent level) for the Fourth, Sixth and Seventh Five Year Plan period, respectively. This is an indication that the states with low infrastructure have low plan outlays and high outlays with high level of infrastructure leading to further divergence in regional disparities.

Further the expenditure incurred by a state on economic infrastructure *viz*., water and power development, transport and communication are scaled down to per capita terms. The state per capita expenditure on economic infrastructure for 1971-72 and 1981-82 are presented in Table 3.4. The variations in the expenditures on economic infrastructure are very high and are on the increase, the value of C.V. increase from 70 per cent in 1971-72 to 80 per cent in 1981-82. During the period of analysis, the top ranking states in terms of infrastructure facilities spent higher per capita amount than the lower rank states in terms of infrastructure facilities except those in the special categories *i.e.* Hill Area States. The coefficients of correlation between the index of infrastructure and state per capita expenditure on infrastructure were found to be –.10 and + .50 (significant at 1 per cent level) for 1971-72 and 1981-82, respectively. Thus, to reduce the regional disparities in infrastructure facilities among the states, public expenditure on per capita basis on economic infrastructure facilities in the backward states must be stepped up from the present level.

Conclusion

The paper attempts to study the specific problem *viz*.,

(*i*) How to eliminate scale bias?
(*ii*) How to assign weights?
(*iii*) How to make composite indices comparable?

involved in constructing the composite indices for regional analysis. The elimination of scale bias may be made through the division by mean. Weights can be assigned by the 'Method of Principal Component Analysis'. It is suggested to use the single weightage system based on the average value of beginning and the terminal year data to make the composite indices comparable over the years.

The problems under reference are studied by constructing the composite indices of economic infrastructure for seventeen major states of India for the period 1970-71 to 1984-85. The study shows that the stages like Bihar, Himachal Pradesh, Jammu

& Kashmir, Madhya Pradesh, Orissa and Rajasthan are most backward states in terms of infrastructure development. It also points out that the state per capita plan outlays and public expenditure on economic infrastructure were found to be "regressive" in nature in India since Fourth Five Year Plan. Thus, to reduce the regional disparities in infrastructure development there is a need to enhance the state plan outlays and public expenditure on infrastructure such as irrigation, energy, transport and communication in the backward states like Bihar, Himachal Pradesh, Jammu & Kashmir, Madhya Pradesh, Orissa and Rajasthan.

References

1. Anderson, T.W. (1958), *An Introduction to Multivariable Statistical Analysis*, John Wiley and Sons, New York.
2. Dadibhavi, R.V. (1982), "Analysis of Inter-taluka Disparity and Backwardness in Karnataka, 1975-76", *Indian Journal of Regional Science*, Vol. XIX (2).
3. ——, (1989), *Regional Variations in Infrastructure Development in India*, Department of Studies in Economics, K.U.B.C. Belgaum, Mimeo, chapter 2.
4. Harman, H.H. (1968), *Modern Factor Analysis*, The University of Chicago Press, Chicago.
5. Hotelling, H. (1933), "Analysis of Complex of Statistical Variables in to Principal Components," *Journal of Educational Psychology*, Vol. 24.
6. Koutsoyiannis, A. (1977), *Theory of Economics*, The Macmillan Press Ltd.
7. Kundu, A. (1980), *Measurement of Urban Process—A Study in Regionalisation*", Popular Prakashan, Bombay.
8. Mahalanobis, P.C. (1936), "On the Generalised Distance in Statistics", *Proceedings of the National Institute of Science of India*, 2.

4

Methodological Concepts of Measuring Human Resources Development

—B.R.K. Sinha

The study of methodological concepts becomes a matter of great interest when the question of what, how, when and where to measure something arises. Here the question of how to measure human resources development in space and time needs a detailed description of the methods and concepts.

Burman, B.K.R. (1983, pp. 114-15) has mentioned, the methods giving details of the research plan with a special emphasis on the logic and reasonableness of the methodology and has described systematically the approach whether experimental and/or correlational, survey or case study. Methodology must relate directly to the stated objectives, procedures to be followed and instruments or tools to be employed, kinds of data to be obtained and the specific manner in which these data will be collected and analysed to show the pattern of the concerned objectives in space and time. According to Kearl Bryant (1976, p. XXI) methodology includes not simply the technology of collecting and dealing with the data but also all aspects of problem formulation, terms and nature of the subject being studied and other procedures and investigating steps. Concepts are defined as the ways of perceiving phenomena. These are in reality, definition in short hand of a class or a group of facts. In another words concepts are the ideas underlying a class or a group of things.

In this way methodology becomes a scientific approach of the way of defining, identifying, classifying, characterizing the nature and characteristics of specific objectives-oriented variables or data to be collected through surveys and interpreted after its synthesis and analysis, employing systematic procedures or steps and tools for deriving certain conclusions and implementation of these to satisfy the needs of the people of a society in space and time.

Therefore, methodological concepts of measuring human resource development should be considered as one of the important and essential ingredients of human resource system because it gives proper guidelines in achieving the described objective. Thus methodological concepts become instrumental in measuring human resources development in the field of human resource system in geography.

Till now none of the scientists including geographers have carried out any work exclusively on the above theme or format and no final yardstick has yet been developed. Therefore, the present paper highlights the basic elements of methodology in measuring the structure and levels of human resources development.

HUMAN RESOURCES

Before discussing the methodological concepts of measuring human resources development, the definition of human resources becomes essential. Human resources are the sum total of knowledge, skills, talents, energies and other qualitative characteristics actually or potentially available in all people of a region. These qualitative characteristics are the result of the process of education, training, health, nutrition, and of other cleaning or health ameliorating factors. Human resources, in other words, is the functional ability or working capacity or capability of a person which is the result of both the mental and physical health of a person. Thus, human resources in brief, is the composite form of all mental and physical attributes of a person. Some of the characteristics of human resources may be of ascribed form but most of the qualitative characteristics are of achieved form. Both ascribed and achieved characteristics give the totality of human resources which exist at a particular reference of time, as human resources change from one place to another and from one time to another. The existing level of human resources is called as stock of human resources. But the most difficult task is how to measure human resources development of a region at a particular reference of time.

METHODOLOGICAL CONCEPTS

Methodological concepts of measuring human resources development can be explained under three broad headings.

Concepts Related to the Selection of the Variables or Indicators

This is a very important part of the methodological concepts which explains about the selection of indicators or variables to be used in measuring human resources development. As stated above, human resource is the composite form of physical and mental health of the people and the measurement of it becomes the measurement of human resources development.

Different scholars have adopted different criteria or indicators and have measured human resources development differently.

Harbison, F.H. (1973, pp. 12-13) admitted, "there is no reliable statistical indicator of levels of human resources development and utilization, and the construction of such a measure would be very difficult". According to him, no one has yet devised a comprehensive indicator of human resources development. If one has to be constructed, it should probably include a minimum measures of educational achievement, school participation ratios, and number and proportion of persons in labour force with strategic skills, measure of health by data on life expectancy, infant mortality, diseases, food and nutrition etc.

Ghosh, B.N. (1985, pp. 145-47), Shrivastava, S. (1983, p. 332), Harbison, F.H. and Myers, C. (1964, pp. 23-33) considered human resources in the form of qualitative values (the product of physical and mental faculty) actually or potentially available in all people and used educational achievement, human capital formation and health in measuring the levels of H.R.D.

According to Raza, Moonis (1990, p. 96), one has to select quantitative indicators of quality in order to make qualitative assessment, *e.g.* a doctor can use quantitative indicators of health for a tuberculosis patient: body weight, body temperature, blood pressure, counts of red blood and white blood corpuscles.

Ghosh, B.N. (1987, p. 224) has employed life expectancy at birth, infant mortality per thousand people, number of doctors per lakh people, average daily calorie supply, causes of death, homicide and serious assault per lakh people as indicators of health of the people.

Smith, D.M. (1977, p. 47) stated infant mortality as an indicator of the levels of health of the people.

Basu, S. (1992, pp. 212-26) has considered assessment of nutritional status as one of the most important health indicators of a population group. He further considered anthropometric and somatic measurement such as body weight, height, head circumference and various clinical signs of hair, eyes, lips, gums, teeth, skin, gland as the indicators of health of the people.

Trewastha, G.T.; Robinson, A.H. and Hammond, E.H. (1967, p. 546) have regarded average length of life, increase in human stature, number of doctors and hospital beds per unit of population as indicators of measuring health status of the people.

Pacione, M. (1988, pp. 211-12) has tried to measure health of the people employing infant mortality rate, life expectancy, weight of new born baby, safe water supply, adult literacy, per capita income, public expenditure on health and other health care facilities and services.

Harbison, F.H. (1973, pp. 135-36) has considered life expectancy as a crude indicator of measuring health and suggested data on critical diseases, access to health facilities, infant mortality as better index of health measurement of the people.

Mukherjee, B.M. (1986, p. 102) in his concept of health has mentioned capacity to do annual work for at least 4-5 hours a day, clear eye sight and memory, to be able to take active part in household activities and physical mobility as signs of good health.

It is clear from the above that most of the scholars have used different quantitative indicators such as life expectancy at birth, infant mortality, mortality and its causes, number of diseases, height and weight according to age and sex, number of medical institutions, hospital beds, number of doctors (including persons per unit of population), medical and educational facilities, per capita income, and medical cost on health and education, per day calorie intake and number of daily meals and breakfast etc. in measuring human resources development and some others have used qualitative indicators such as nutrition, vitamin, types of food taken, quality of drinking water, quality of air, housing condition, types of diseases, blood pressure, working atmosphere, clinical sign, sign of blood, homoglobin, stature and shape of body, appetite and digestive capacity, problem in eyesight, ENT problem, mental problem, capacity to do mental and physical work for a standard working time under sun and rain, normal head load carrying capacity, state of sleeping, feeling of weakness and tiredness, laziness, habit of drinking and smoking, achievements of education, skills, training, school participation ratio etc. in measuring the mental and physical capacity or human resources development of the persons.

Since some of the above mentioned quantitative and qualitative indicators are applicable for the common people at regional, state and national levels and some others are applicable for individual persons at local level, the author considers only those quantitative and qualitative parameters that are directly or indirectly related to mental and physical capacities or efficiencies of the persons and in turn indicate the human resources development.

There are a number and types of diseases, condition of appetite, digestive capacity, memory capacity, mental tension, blood pressure, eye problems, ENT problems, whirling condition, any physical or mental problems while working continuously for standard working hours (6-8), problems arising while working under sun, rain and in cold, problem in carrying normal head load, state of sleeping, feeling of weakness and tiredness, feeling of laziness, whether enthusiastic to work, whether two time meals and breakfasts are taken, number of visit to government and private Hospital or Clinic, per head total medical cost in the last one year, types of drinking water, number of days of pulses, green and other vegetables taken by individuals in a week, how many days in a month an individual takes milk, ghee or butter, egg, fish, meat and fruits, whether the concerned person is habituated to taking tobacco, alcoholic materials, whether the required medicines are purchased timely or not, and whether the food is adequately available or not at household level, whether the house is ventilated or unventilated, whether breath is sweet or not, educational achievements including training and skills, and income levels etc.

Concepts Related to the Field Surveys and Data Collection

This is another part of the methodological concepts which includes the preparation of questionnaire(s), selection of the geographical spatial units and the procedures of data collection.

Preparation of Questionnaire: After having decided the relevant quantitative and qualitative indicators required in measuring human resources development, the preparation of well framed questionnaire(s) for human resource survey becomes necessary, as it contains detailed columns of different variables. Questionnaire is also considered as an important methodological tool used by an interviewer in collecting the detailed information of each and every individual of a household. In this way, questionnaire helps the interviewer in obtaining a desired item of information accurately and completely. Thus, after preparing the questionnaire for the inventory of human resources, the information on desired quantitative and qualitative indicators as mentioned above should be collected at household level from the study area.

Selection of the Spatial Units in the Study Area: Selection of the geographical units for data collection is a very important part of the methodological concepts. Since the desired data on human resource indicators are generally not adequately available at national level, regional level and local level, the selection of sample geographical units particularly at local level (*e.g.* villages) becomes necessary for intensive study of human resources development. It requires sampling procedures. There are several types of samplings such as random, systematic, stratified, cluster, purposive etc. But from the point of view of the collection of such data the stratified random sampling technique should be preferred. While preparing strata of population the 'natural break up' technique as suggested by Dickinson, G.C. (1970) should preferably be employed and proportionately the number of villages from each strata should be selected to constitute at least 10 per cent of the total geographical units (villages).

Data Collection: Since, there is a dearth of desired data for measuring human resources development from published sources such as census, national sample survey etc., the collection of primary data on various types of quantitative and qualitative attributes for measuring the composite form of human health or human resources becomes essentially important. While conducting household survey for data collection from the sample geographical units (villages), researchers should cover preferably 10 per cent of the total number of households of the villages. All persons belonging to 10 per cent of the households should be covered, interviewing at least one respondent from each household.

Synthesis, Analysis and Presentation of the Facts

This is the last but important step of a research methodology. It includes processing of data and preparation of master data sheet, tabulation, cartographic stage and representation of the facts with conclusions and suggestions.

Data Processing: After the collection of primary data through questionnaires from certain households from the sample geographical units, the work of checking, storing, summarizing, calculating and transmitting the data manually or mechanically into a more logical and useful form should be done.

Master Sheet: Data processing also includes the preparation of master data sheet which contains all information deemed necessary to be incorporated in the table. In fact master data sheet is a data storage device that consolidates all questionnaires information into a much smaller and easily manageable document. In a master data sheet, there should be as many columns as variables/indicators and as many rows as persons covered under the investigation. In this way master data sheet becomes a convenient and a portable document for easy reference.

Ranks and Weightage: While preparing master data sheet, researcher must be careful in putting certain codes and weightages against certain indicators. Many quantitative and qualitative attributes have positive or negative nature. In such a case, equal weightage for positive or negative attributes should be given either on the basis of its rank order or without it as and when required. But some other variables have only positive nature, *e.g.* educational standard and income categories. In such a case, ranks of educational achievement and income categories in ascending or descending order should be arranged and accordingly the weightage should be given.

Composite Value: After putting weightage against each positive or negative attributes of the person the total (positive + negative) composite score of all variables and also the total positive or negative score values of each and every person recorded in each row of the data sheet should be separately found out and serially listed.

Finally, for each and every person, the percentage of total positive or negative composite score values of each individual person should be calculated, considering the total composite score values (total positive scores + total negative scores) of the same person as 100%.

Levels of Human Resources Development: In this way we get and see that the percentage of both the positive or negative composite score values of one person differs from that of another one. Thus, on the basis of variation of percentages of both the positive or negative score values of the persons under investigation, some convenient levels such as very high, medium, low and very low can be prepared to show both the positive and negative dimensions of human resources development in the area under study. However, depending upon the percentage variation of composite scores of the persons, some other levels or grades of human resources development can also be made.

Tabulation: After finding out the levels of human resources development, we can prepare as many tables as required to show the cross relationship of human resources development with the biological, social, economic and cultural status of the persons.

Cartographic Stage and Representation: Depending upon the nature of the tables we can prepare some suitable or relevant maps/diagrams/graphs for easier representation of the results and facts.

Thus, it can be said that the above mentioned variables/ indicators, techniques and procedures can give a reliable composite index for measuring human resources development in a particular region at particular reference of time.

References

1. Basu, S. (1992), "Nutritional Status, Physical Growth Trends and Health Problems Among the Tribal Population of Bastar District (M.P.)" in Tripathi P.D. and Tripathi R.S. (1992), *Dimensions of Scheduled Tribes Development in India*, Uppal Publishing House, New Delhi.
2. Burman, B.K.R. (1983), *Tools and Techniques of Social Science Research: A Rapid Appraisal of Their Scope and Limitations*, Council for Social Development, New Delhi.
3. Dickinson, G.C. (1970), *Statistical Mapping and the Presentation of Statistics*, Edward Arnold Ltd., London.
4. Ghosh, B.N. (1985), *Fundamentals of Population Geography*, Sterling Publishers Pvt. Ltd., New Delhi.
5. Ghosh, B.N. (1987), *Population Theories and Demographic Analysis*, Meenakshi Prakashan, New Delhi.
6. Harbison, F.H. (1973), *Human Resources as the Wealth of Nation*, Oxford University Press, London.
7. Kearl, Bryant (1976), *Field Data Collection in the Social Sciences: Experiences in Africa and Middle East*, Agricultural Development Council, New York.
8. Mukherjee, B.M. (1986), "Ageing Members and Their Health in Changing Techno-Economic Condition", in Choudhury, B. (1986), *Tribal Health: Socio-Cultural Dimensions*, Inter-Indian Publications, New Delhi.
9. Pacione, M. (1988), *The Geography of the Third World: Progress and Prospects*, Routledge, London.
10. Raza, Moonis (1990), *Education, Development and Society*, Vikas Publishing House Pvt. Ltd., New Delhi.
11. Smith, D.M. (1977), *Human Geography: A Welfare Approach*, Edward Arnold Ltd., London.
12. Trewartha, G.T., Robinson, A.H. and Hammond, E.H. (1967), *Elements of Geography, Physical and Cultural*, McGraw Hill Book Company, New York.

5

Leading Theoretical Issues of Regional Economics

—*O.S. Shrivastava*

This paper is written to provide theoretical framework of regional economics. The paper is divided into the following parts:

I. Genesis of Regional Economics and Regional Science.
II. Economics of Location, Central Place Theory and "Economic Space".
III. Location Quotient: Coefficient of Specialisation: Mix and Share Analysis and Other Measures.
IV. Flows of Persons, Commodities and Capital Between Regions: Models.
V. Regional Input-Output Analysis.
VI. Regional Economic Fluctuations: Regional Economic Base Theory and Regional Multiplier.
VII. Dynamic Growth Theory, as Applied to Regions.
VIII. Growth Poles, Growth Centres, Growth Points and Growth Foci.

Based on author's book on *Regional Economics* published by Anmol Publications, 4378/4B, Ansari Road, Daryaganj, New Delhi.

IX. Cumulative Causation Theory and Theses about Divergence and Convergence.
X. Epilogue.

Before we discuss anything about regional planning or regional differentiations in India, a brief note on the fundamentals of regional economics is necessary. Economic research without the under-pinning of the theory becomes sub-standard journalism. A paper will be a paper—succinct but brief and when something is to be in brief many essentials too are likely to be left out. The present piece is to be viewed in that light.

Regional economics is not a parochial science nor a region is a 'nation within a nation'. Regional planning is a tail to a body. It serves and not supersedes national planning.

All planning whether of the regions or for the benefit of the clientele groups (targeted groups) should be through the planning of the real sectors. A welfare state cannot be established in a pauper state. Narrow regionalism has no place. The hybrid science that is regional science is a subject of specialisation and the volume is one which attempts something up-to-date.

I. REGIONAL ECONOMICS AND REGIONAL SCIENCE

Regional science is multi-disciplinary but regional economics is of the genre of international economics. Then a few hybrids appeared—the agglomeration economics, the growth-point economics, the polarisation economics, the industrial location/complex economics intermixed with a little bit of welfare economics, public finance, manpower economics, input-output consistency etc. Regional economics emphasises how sectoral (or sub-sectoral and/or functional) activities can increase the regional income and employment. It is problem-solving economics for a region. Regional economics is heavily tilted in favour of depressed regions but talks very little about depressed persons. Regional planning, which would require transgression of administrative boundaries in most cases, addresses itself to people's problems in different economic/geographical regions.

Definitions succeed the subject and not precede it: Regional economics and regional planning were gaining a lot of importance and in fact some of the "regional scientists" were assuming aggressive postures towards "non-regionalists" till the collapse of centralised planning which made them realise that they cannot win over the market paradigm. However, economies can be made market-friendly but markets cannot be made friendly to the poor. As Professor Pigou once remarked that *all* economists are 'welfare' economists since no economist writes for not furthering economic welfare, the regional economists and regional planners too can be taken as ones who are worried about regional inequalities. Their tasks are as onerous *as trying to please God without offending the Devil.* A regional economist or regional planner is concerned about under-development as well as about over-development. Regional economics will primarily take into account the homogeneity, nodality and programming or planning.

Homogeneous regions are easy to develop but *nodality emphasises the heterogeneous nature of the areas and hence the inter-dependence.* This follows that monetary flows unless they are unilateral (as government grants) will be opposite of the goods and service flows. If the latter go out, money comes and *vice versa.* What follows is that if there are "exports' from a region (exporting industries as "basic" industries for the region) then only the employment can be increased and incomes can be propagated.

Economics of nodal regions is the study of the upstream and downstream linkages between the centres of higher and lower economic order and thus inter-regional framework is hierarchical; some regions dominating the disadvantaged ones. The hierarchy will be:

(*a*) if the thickest flows are to a smaller centre from the node, then the node is 'independent" and

(*b*) if the flows are towards a larger centre, then the node is subordinate.

Some nodes of economic activities emerge in space and these nodal regions are composed of heterogeneous units, but closely connected with each other functionally. Towards the centres of agglomeration of economic activities (the dominant centres) money, men and materials gravitate. There can be found a nucleus or nuclei where most of the business and industrial activities (with high density or intensity) take place. Each node will have a concentric zone of influence around it and all types of flows will be very thick near the region; but, they will thin out with the distance. Two concentric circles of two nodal points may have some over-lapping area and within that area, the two nodal points (centres) will have an 'indifferent clientele.' The outer limits of a nodal centres set the limits of the critical radius. There are two-way flows from the nodes to the periphery and from the periphery to the nodes, though the nature and extent of the flows will differ. The heaviest flows tend to polarise towards and from the dominant node or nodes, usually large cities. Flows vary directly with the size or attraction of the node and inversely with the distance from it. These flows form the basis of the study of the *gravity models* which provide important operational technique for polarisation analysis.

Programming aims to bring planning in conformity with geo-physical or agro-climatic conditions. However, it is to be noted that *a region is not a nation within a nation and regional planning will have to serve the objectives of the national planning.*

II. LOCATION: CENTRAL PLACE AND "ECONOMIC SPACE"

Economic behaviour *is* related to space or various types of regions (macro-major, macro, state, meso, micro and micro-minor regions, including some backward and even 'vestigial' [poor resource regions with poor people]. The rational choice and the allocative efficiency that economics seeks, are sought with reference to the region. The resource base and the land values and connectivity become important in regional economic activities. Space development strategy can be a drag or a boon, depending entirely whether it is collusive and parochial or co-operative and complementary. Growth process is facilitated if resources and factors are efficient and sufficient and the region has 'means' to acquire combine them as inputs for higher real outputs of strong-order goods. Narrow use of the resources leads to specialisation in a region and if diversified uses are discovered, multifarious economic activities can be sustained in a region. Resources are limiting factors in limited cases only. Regional development is seldom promoted without government intervention in the form of infrastructure support, tax remissions and subsidies. In the long-run it is best promoted through technical efficiency of the production function and market-friendly production-exchange relations.

Economics of "location" of functions, activities and more importantly of manufacturing units belongs to that class of work of which each generation produces very few. There are three *umbrella* approaches: the 'least cost approach', 'the market area approach' and the 'profit maximisation approach'. The last comes from the 'general economics of the firm'. The first two emphasise the supply side and the demand sides of "*mini-max*" model. The recent approach is behavioural approach which emphasises that location is the result of the interaction with the techno-economic environment *i.e.*, behaviour of the government and the behaviour of the rival firms. *The essence of the location theory is also this*: If there are locational diseconomies they can be overcome with transport economies and if there are transport diseconomies, these can be overcome with locational economies.

Weber's location theory was very profound yet it was such an elementary wisdom that it is taught even in school economics. All types of costs (relating to raw materials, labour, power, transport etc.) are to be kept low. He wrote about industries based on ubiquitous raw materials, which should be located near the market and the specific raw materials which make the location tied. The higher the location weight to be transported the less possibility of distant location. (His location triangle became famous where he demonstrated that if iron ore and coal are situated at distance the steel industry should be nearer coal). It was demonstrated that the radius (area of advantage) within which the agglomeration force of a production of output is effective, is directly proportional to the value of the agglomeration function. Advantage is proportional to lower friction of distance.

> This economics emphasises that *agglomeration would lead to divergence in regional incomes and dispersal of industries will lead to convergence of incomes.* The causative factors of agglomeration at first cross the minimum threshold, then provide economies but as upper thresholds are crossed

they generate diseconomies greater than economies and dispersal becomes necessary.

Agglomerations are first pulled; then they pull and ultimately repulse. Natural agglomerations (jute factories or tea factories) are due to territorial specialisations. Agglomerations first bring economies of scale and then of scope. Growth rate of the industry in the urban area *minus* growth rate of the nation *weighted* by relative growth of population in the urban area is the measurement of the agglomeration economies for a particular industry. Of course the internal economies are more important for the growth of any industry. Economies of agglomeration in a region are assumed to be a function of the size distribution and the spatial distribution of its urban population centres. Thus, (*a*) the larger the number of cities, (*b*) the greater the relative size of the leading cities, and (*c*) the smaller is average inter-urban distance, the greater are the economies of regional agglomeration. A good urban centre, the chances to earn fabulous incomes, low pollutions and high security are preferred while irksomeness of mobility and distances act as frictions.

Nothing enamoured the geographers more than the central place theory in regional economics. Neat hexagonal designs were drawn and all settlements were seen as fitting their abstract model. Very precise 'k' values were attached. There is no doubt that there is a hierarchy of settlements and functions and that there is interaction between various places to avail or supply functions/facilities. It is also true that the entire space will be covered by the producers and retailers of goods and services; they will either reach out to people or people will have to move to central places to avail functions and facilities. Each higher order settlement serves a number of lower order settlements for different functions. Lower order functions are there in higher order settlements also but higher order functions are not there in lower order settlements. Christaller formulated the theory that there is crystallisation of the 'mass' around the core and then gravitational pulls develop in favour of the central places. More and more functions are added to the central place and new functions get stuck to the mass. The place is 'central' in relative terms only.

Many historical nodal points become indelible location "constants". They have the advantage of the momentum of an early start as a port or administration city. More the location "constants" less the chances of them fitting into hexagonal patterns. Central place theories are proved less realistic by them. Regeneration and degeneration take place around these locational constants or old nodal points. These locational constants are the reason why all centres do not crowd together into one giant centre. Development of a virgin region can give rise to a new node/'locational constant' and then they become immobile. Old centres can be improved but not dismantled. Their growth will cease if they become too congested and then new locational constants will emerge.

The Centre Place Theory or the theory of "empty sectors alternating with the 'full' sectors as in a cogwheel (Losch economic space) which claimed that they gave a 'general equilibrium theory of location' was unrealistic in dynamic setting. Actually locational equilibrium could result in the clustering and/or the dispersion of plants rather the regular dispersion of the CPT/ES. In fact *space can be trivialised also (Richardson* "The problems of CPT raise some interesting issues for the *amusement* of the high priests of regional economic theory, but the practical value is limited. Readers primarily interested in the policy relevance of regional economics *may skip this topic* (Richardson *R.U.E.*, p. 75). Locations 'constants' are preferred (who would start a bangles industry away from Firozabad?) but after some time the 'locational preferences' develop for other centres.

Hotelling principle of location highlights locational interdependence. H. Hotelling argued that producers prefer such locations where they can keep one eye on their competitors. Clustering is thus explained and it can be summarised thus:

Clustering/ "hotelling"	*Dispersion*
1. When the demand is inelastic	1. When the demand is elastic and reduction in costs becomes necessary.
2. When resources are tied	2. When resources are ubiquitous.
3. Low transport costs	3. High transport costs increase costs over the distance.
4. Density of population is high	4. Density of population is low.

Games and location were also found to be related. Isard wrote that the sellers and sellers play game for best location and markets; buyers and buyers play game to get things in sellers market cheap and for sure; and the most important game is between buyers and sellers who operate within their zones of bargaining. Since the games are not constant-sum games, location decisions remain uncertain. There should be such locations that we get mutual improvement sets through *incremax* procedures. From the "zone of *incremax*", the total profits will fall if location is outside a zone of maximum advantage. Intermixing of the Weberian and game theory features would secure better locations and development of the regions.

The *punctiform markets of Weber are not considered relevant for all cases.* Costs reducing factors (chances of achieving economies of scale and scope), revenue increasing factors, including government concessions, and pure personal/accidental/historical reasons count.

Losch's ideal economic space emphasized that there is continuum of settlements rather than hierarchy. According to Losch the population and agricultural activities are distributed like polka dots over the space and hence their location is 'area', and location of industrial activity is punctiform. Population gets so distributed that it has proximity to food as well as industrial production. There are crop gradients of agricultural production according to geo-climatic and economic conditions. The agricultural production is sold to a punctiform city. Punctiform industry is distributed for selling to a really spaced customers. Industrial production is agglomerated but at several places. Economies of scale help in agglomeration; economies of transport in deagglomeration. Cost is not the only thing; demand also counts. Losch introduced the concept of *isotim* or a contour line of equaldelivered price.

III. LOCATION QUOTIENT: COEFFICIENT OF SPECIALISATION: COEFFICIENT OF LOCATION: MIX AND SHARE ANALYSIS ETC.

Regional economists calculate location quotient to find out the over-or-under representation of a region of certain variables. The *LQ* is used for measuring the relative specialisation of a region in selected industries. Employment is conventionally used as unit of measure. Total employment in the country becomes the reference variable in comparison to which employment in a selected industry is studied. *LQ* is also referred as *self-sufficiency ratio*. If employment is taken as the variable to be used then:

$LQ =$

$$\frac{E_r}{TE_r} \div \frac{E_n}{TE_n}$$

E_r employment in Industry in region;
TE_r total employment in the region.
E_n employment in industry in the nation;
TE_n total employment in the nation.

LQ of more than 1 suggests high concentration or regional superiority; if it is less than one it should be under-representation. In case we are studying *LQ* with reference to industries and their exports, a high *LQ* suggests industry to be export industry, a low and less than 1 *LQ* suggests that the industry may not provide sufficient output and it will be import industry. If the *LQ* is just one it would suggest a local service industry.

If *employment in Madhya Pradesh in industry* is 150 (all figures in thousands), and *in India* 10000 (thousands: example only) while the *total employment in Madhya Pradesh* is 260 (T) while *total employment in India is 24000* (T), then

$$\frac{150}{260} \div \frac{10000}{24000} = \frac{18}{13} = 1.38$$

Or it can be said that the *LQ* is high. We can also use it to find out the (say) concentration of scheduled caste population in a sub-region. Thus:

$$\frac{LQ_i}{P_i} \div \frac{P_i}{P} \text{ or } \frac{P_{ij}}{P_i} \times \frac{P_j}{P}$$

P_{ij} = number of persons in the *j*th category (SC) in area *i*
P_i = total population in all the categories of area *i*
P_j = Sum of persons of category *j* in all the *n* areas *i.e.*, population of region under castegory *j*.
P = Sum, of P_i in all the area *i.e.*, total population of region in each catetgory.

If several indicators can taken, say 10, then the summation of all the 10 LQs. will give the idea of the regional differentiations about as many indicators.

LQ can help highlight regional relative efficiencies or otherwise. It can also focus on the potential import substitute or products with export-expansion potential. It can give us an idea about which industrial activities require concentration or dispersal and about which industries, further detailed study is necessary. The study is very useful in the context of linkages analysis, economic base analysis, input-output analysis, mix and share analysis. *LQ* can be computed with regard to any reference variable. Besides, not much effort is necessary to calculate the same.

Yet *LQ* is only a round and ready indicator. Much will depend on the selected variables of specialisation and reference variables as also on the choice of the area. If the regions differ in socio-cultural aspects then only common variables should be taken.

Coefficient of Specialisation can be derived from the LQs. It can show the degree of concentration of industry in a particular region. Deviations from the national pattern can be calculated. The *numerator* represents the ratio of employment in industry in the *region* to employment in primary/manufacturing/ construction/service sector in the region. *The denominator* represents ratio of employment in a particular industry *for the nation* in the same sectors as in the numerators. *The numerator is subtracted from the denominator to arrive at coefficient of specialisation. It will give values between 0 and 1 without any regard to positive or negative sign.* If the region has an industrial mix identical with the nation, the coefficient would be 0. If all the employment in the region is nearly concentrated in one industry, the value of the coefficient would tend to be 1.

To understand the regional disparities, the progress accomplished and the quantification of the tasks to be performed to reduce the regional disparities following measures can also be calculated:

The *coefficient of redistribution* (whether of population or of industrial units or schools/hospitals or anything) for the two time periods can be calculated. Summing up of all positive *or* negative deviations, we get a figure which, when divided by

100, can be designated as the coefficient of redistribution. If it is zero, it means there is no redistribution; if it is one, then it means complete redistribution.

Item	*Which measures*
1. Coefficient of geographical association	The share of employment in manufacturing, industry-wise.
2. Index of dissimilarity in occupation.	Occupational pattern of different states or regions.
3. Index of segregation of occupation.	One special occupation *versus* all occupations in an area; of one to the total.
4. Coefficient of redistribution between two time periods.	Share of *some special population* (as people below the poverty line) can also be calculated for the share of gainfully employed persons to dependants.
5. Coefficient of population concentration.	Statewise population related to area may be of SC/ST.
6. Coefficient of differentiation.	For the same purpose as 5 above *e.g.*, for population of different age-groups or religious groups, educated groups or occupational groups.

Coefficient of Specialisation: While the coefficient of localisation measures the concentration of one industry in a region, the coefficient of specialisation measures the degree of overall specialisation in the regional economy, considering all the industrial groups. The opposite of specialisation is diversification and hence we can construct the index of diversification also from the coefficient of specialisation. Some industries are known by the regions; some regions are known by the industries. If there is over-concentration of industries in a region, we call it *burst type of economy.*

Mix and Share Analysis: During the course of development, there is one important structural change: the primary sector activities contribute lesser and lesser to the GDP in percentage terms even if the physical and monetary contributions are going up. The same is true of employment. There are 'sun-rise' and 'sun-set' activities of which changing importance is studied in the "mix and share" analysis. Leads and lags of one region *vis-a-vis* other regions should be studied. There are *several ways* to compute that: one such can be as under with $R = N + M + S$

N is the national growth,
M is the industry mix.
S is regional share.
R is the total change in regional employment.

N depends upon growth rate in the GDP, external effect and the efforts of the people/nation for higher employment (five year plans). M is the distribution of regional employment among higher and lower growth industries, relative to the industry mix prevailing nationally. Change in the mix bring changes in the regional employment and distribution. S is the change in regional share of total national employment in each industry.

From N we can compare the deviations between growth rate of employment in the region and the nation. M effect will be positive, if a region specialises in the same industry in which the nation is growing at a fast rate. It will be negative if it specialises in that industry which is growing slowly or which is declining in the nation.

S effect is calculated through the regional *versus* national totals in each industry.

The following table shows the hypothetical changes in the regional and national employment in a certain time period.

('000)

Activity	*Employment* T_o	T_i	*Employment* $T_o - T_i$ *Absolute*	*Change in percentages*
Agriculture	150	120	–30	–20
Manufacturing	50	80	30	60
Services	50	95	45	90
Government	10	20	10	100
Total	260	315	55	21

Employment in the country increased by 50 per cent but by 21 per cent in the region, not a happy situation. *Mix and share analysis does **not** give us earth-shattering findings.* This M & S analysis is largely descriptive in nature. MS analysis cannot explain all those reasons which enter into different rates of growth nor more than necessary inferences should be drawn. For example, if an industrial activity is experiencing a slow growth and the region even more so, there will be a double drag on employment. But the workers may be migrating elsewhere in high growth and high productivity industries. The sources and quality of data used, the choice of base and terminal years and the level of industry aggregation all seriously influence the results. M & S analysis by its very nature takes one variable—like employment or value-added. It cannot take all variables at the same time into account and to that extent its inferences will have limited value. It need not become a past time in the hands of those who have calculators.

IV. FLOWS OF PERSONS, COMMODITIES AND CAPITAL

While 'development adjusts environment to suit people', 'migration helps in the adjustment of people to adjust them to development process or to the lack of it in certain regions'. Regional economics records the four streams of migration: U-U, R-R, R-U and U-R (where R is for rural and U for urban). Females move in all cases after marriage and most of them migrate RR migration is mostly of this type. The outstanding stream is of R-to-U due to push and pull (gravity mode) factors while U-R migration always is a thin stream of back migrants. U-U migration is towards centres of higher order functions or simple transfer cases. Regional economics records some important models of migration. Ravenstein makes the rate of migration between two points being inversely related to the distance between two points of migration which may be in certain stages and the pull factors are partly deterministic and partly probabilistic. Raimon and Fabricant (separately) developed their migration models as being related to the "income differentials" (demand factor) plus a "barrier function" (distance, kinship ties and residential difficulties). Blanco considered labour migration as being the function of "unemployment differential." Zip and Stewart regarded the "gravitational pulls" far more important than push factors which become important only in serious distress cases. *Lee*'s model contained "plus" (pull), "minus" (push) and "Zero-sum neutral" factors. These neutral factors were eliminated from serious discussion of migration. Lewis' model developed a suggestive model which recommended that migration be promoted till surplus manpower is fully utilised for real capital formation in the capitalist sector. Todaro's model explains migration in terms of incomes expected at the new places rather than the actual incomes earned later on. It also depends upon the expected level of differences between real incomes and between rural and urban job opportunities. Migration to urban areas is based upon the expectations of permanent incomes in the long-run, migrants bear temporary difficulties in the hope of improving their future—at least in comparison to what it would have been in villages. This is the essence of his "thought process thesis about migration".

Bogue, Blau and Duncan Developed Model of "Migrant Selectivity": They wrote about "where the people go". If the degree of urbanisation is low and urban size hierarchy is less developed, migration will not conform to the 'stage migration model' *i.e.*, migrants will not be trapped in the towns in between. "Negative selectivity" *i.e.*, return migration to villages is simply not there for the skilled and educated persons. Single persons can move to far off places; so can the skilled ones. The lower the rate of outmigration from rural and small town areas to large cities, the greater the selectivity. The longer a rapid rate of urbanisation is maintained, the more probability of a decline in selectivity of migrants from rural areas. Most of the migrants are those whose kinship group are already in the big cities.

Gravity model of migration, *though a rehash of words*, became typically associated with regional economic theory. Distance dispels; "mass" (the size of the economic advantage at the new place of migration) attracts. Gravitational force between two masses is a function of the product of the masses themselves and inversely proportional to the distance between them. Backward regions have a low mass. Higher the facilities/incomes/employment opportunities, higher the mass of the new places in the eyes of those who are coming from the areas of low mass.

Isard, who wrote a monumental book on regional economics, developed the "income potential model" which in sum said nothing extra except that if the potential gains are higher than the diseconomies of covering distance, people will migrate. Income "density" is present income, "potential incomes" is what is perceived by the migrant and the "mass" is the social physics which tells about the total changed package of socio-economic facilities. Word "friction" is used for the surrogate of all troubles of moving over distances.

Commodity Flows

"Imports" and "exports" of goods and services over from/to other regions decide how much money will flow in. These are in turn a function more of the technical efficiency (real outputs) than of marketing efficiency. Marketing, storing, transportation etc. will come later. *No one knows about inter-district flows* as no data is kept. The records of railways and road transporters will not suffice because goods are carrierd as head loads, cart loads and in private vehicles. Not even inter-state flows are well quantified. The up-stream (backward) and down-stream (forward) linkages are also not easily quantified. Thus what part becomes *entrepot* trade for the region is also seldom quantified. These studies are easily theorised but can only be *guesstimated.*

Savings and Capital Flows: Markov's Chain Model

While the neo-classical theory emphasised that capital will be distributed over the space in such a way that the marginal productivity/profitability is equal in all uses, the regional economics highlights the importance of equalising the socio-economic MPK. There is adoption of the theory of balancing the investments in infrastructure *versus* services *versus* directly productive investment. Regional planner would be happy if the capital flows are promoted as well as directed, where necessary.

There is an *absorbing region* in Markov's model where the investment demand are more than the savings of the region. These savings come from the *transient region* where savings are high but the use is low. Bombay (Mumbai) region absorbs savings of other regions, for example]. Of course a transient region can become an absorbing region.

Markov has his own terminology. Savings invested in fixed and sunk assets is absorbed and locked. Such savings are "lost" and they "disappear". Savings which are invested in portfolios of various types are "non-absorbed" and "transferable". In case of the sunk assets, the savings-investment process is irreversible. The investment climate (opportunities, profits, interest, tax concessions) will help in all savings getting absorbed in different regions. Usually the savings will be transferred from the 'transient regions' to the absorbing regions. When all the savings are utilised, the process is exhausted and an equilibrium is reached—which itself will be transient as fresh savings will emerge in net additional terms. If there is decline in savings, then less savings will flow to transient and absorbing regions. Thus increment in the capital stock is equal to the long-term savings of different regions.

In Markov's illustrative model, *only one region is absorbing; other regions are transient*! The investment in the absorbing region is *sequential* in character and is also influenced by agglomeration economies.

Regional economists/planners have over-publicised their theories. Markov's chain model and gravity model of labour migration are such examples. Markov's model is neither a comprehensive theory of agglomeration, nor of external economies, nor of the generation of savings, nor of the transfer of savings nor of capital formation or investment. How much long or short a chain of investment can be in different regions at different times or over a period of time? This chain can get elongated or can snap short. These factors are not analysed by Markov. The interaction of the market mechanism and the controlled mechanism cannot be predicted or estimated. Thus investment need not be sequential and no chain can be traced.

V. REGIONAL INPUT-OUTPUT ANALYSIS

Regional input-output (I-O) analysis involves double disaggregation: National aggregates are broken by industry and by region and inter-regional production and trade are incorporated. Intermediate outputs (steel ingots) shall become inputs in some other sector while outputs of fountain pens/ ballpoint pens shall always become goods of final consumption. The I-O table has rows which give the distribution of the output of the sector while the columns represent the production structure of a sector.

The I-O table gives an idea where the outputs can be used as also about wherefrom the inputs shall come. The match-mismatch positions can be judged. It is possible to calculate a table of co-efficiency which would show the effects of a given increase of output of one industry on the purchases of all others. Columns show outputs and the rows show inputs. We get "inputs of knowledge". The table is, however, prepared with the help of linear production function. The table is prepared industry/ trade-wise and if the data is available, hundreds of such activities can be included. *For various intermediate outputs, subsequent production activities are needed; and for final production activities, inputs are needed. There will have to be physical consistencies* If iron and steel unit is to be established, physical consistency exercises would require planning/estimates about coal, cement, ore mining etc. for backward linkages and subsequent use of the end product for the forward linkages. These are to be worked out and planned to come out as envisaged.

Input-output analysis does not throw light on the migration, mobilities and locational shifts. Since input coefficients vary with change in technology, the value of I-O model for even forecasting is limited. It cannot be treated as a theory of regional development. In the dynamic set up, the inter-regional flows of output and inputs cannot be incorporated because the technical coeficients differ in different sectors/regions in different ways. *The erstwhile USSR could not save its economy from collapsing despite the most comprehensive national/regional input-output tables.* Dynamism was introduced in the I-O tables with appropriate incorporation of possible changes but to no avail. *I-O tables*

The econometric exercises not incorporated in this theoretical piece.

have conceptual elegance but "informed estimates" and "expert projections" are more reliable. These tables are good as "snapshot static picture" and inappropriate for long-run investigations. Frequently an I-O tables becomes irrelevant by the time it is completed as the data itself changes. Consistency framework is coveted but is seldom realised. The market smoothens the edges. It functions blindly but not arbitrarily. The straitjacket of I-O table is not a law of economics.

VI. REGIONAL ECONOMIC FLUCTUATIONS: REGIONAL ECONOMIC BASE THEORY AND REGIONAL MULTIPLIER

Regional incomes and rate of growth differ. Regional economics gives profound importance to those industries which "export" goods to other regions. They are 'basic' industries. National business cycle can be weighted average of the regional business cycles. Agglomerations and the industrial development on the principle of "comparative advantage" increase inequalities while planning for balanced growth brings dispersal of economic activities. If one industrial region depends upon another region for raw materials, the fluctuations in industrial output will become a function of the agricultural outputs of the other region. Most backward regions remain insulated against regional cycles because their linkages with other regions are tenuous in nature.

> *On the up-turns, expanding regions usually lead and the contracting regions lag.*
> *On the down turns, the contracting regions lead and the expanding regions lag.*

The regional multiplier theory is based on the "export base" theory which states that the growth of a region depends upon the growth of its "exports" industries. This theory suggests that it is expansion in demand, external to the region, which is crucial in determining growth within the region. *Regional multiplier is thus total employment divided by the employment in the basic industries.* The total employment is the employment in the basic + non-basic industries. It can be calculated for the relationship at a point of time and also over a period of time if *incremental values of the two are taken.* Thus the total employment is equal to the base multiplier, multiplied by the base employment. The basic difference between the 'economic base theory' and 'regional multiplier theory' is that the multiplier, calculated in money terms (as compared with employment in the economic base theory), is much more akin to the short-run Keynesian income type multiplier of macro-economics. It incorporates the effects of 'imports' and 'taxation' also, which are leakages, along with 'savings' which is a leakage of closed economy multiplier). Regional multiplier can be written as:

$$K = \frac{1}{S + M + T}$$

Where K is multiplier, S is the marginal propensity to save, M is marginal propensity to import in a region and T is marginal rate of taxation.

If the basic and non-basic both activities are taken into account then the export base multiplier will be as under for the two sectors:

$$dY_t = \left(\frac{1}{1 - \frac{Y_n}{Y_t}} \right) dY_b$$

Y_t is total income Y_b is basic income Y_n is non-basic income, K is multiplier and d denotes change.

All exogenous and endogamous factors of fluctuations cannot be taken into account in the export base theory. Subsidies, credit flows, investments and grants etc. are not incorporated in these theories. One cannot approve "exporting" industries from territorial specialisation in some agricultural crop only. Besides, as the 'frontiers' of the region are open and no administrative machinery records the inter-regional flows, the value of multiplier cannot be calculated. The concepts remain of theoretical importance.

The question of unutilised capacity or of versal "auto-corrective" effects of regional multiplier are not discussed. An exporting region after getting the income is bound to increase its propensity to "import". Inter-regional "exports-imports" do not have the same significance as international exports-imports for income and employment multiplier, when the labour market of the regions is not closed. We cannot recommend that the "leakages" to other regions be plugged. It is not the case of "export-led" growth model for the region. Higher production for "domestic consumption" is even more important.

VII. DYNAMIC GROWTH THEORY, AS APPLIED TO THE REGIONS

Regional economists have variously considered "classical model", "neo-classical model", "Keynesian model" and "Harrod-Domar models" as being relevant for regional theories. It is obvious that Keynesians considered 'export base theory' and 'regional multiplier' quite important. Classicism (Bible of the liberal bourgeoisie) presented a stadial view of the development of the society occurring through the exercise of self-interest based on the principle of comparative advantage. What is good for the producer is good for the society, believe the supply sider neo-classical economists. It is the *real output* which is important. If population increases, then

(*a*) either the wages have to be low, or
(*b*) population has to be controlled, or
(*c*) real productivity has to increase.

Economic growth is, thus, the marginal product of capital times the proportionate increase in capital, plus the marginal products of labour times the proportionate increase in labour, plus the proportionate increase in output owing to technological change. If technical change is nil, and the proportionate marginal products of labour and land (or capital) add to the increased income, we are back at the Cobb-Douglas production function.

Harrod-Domar type models emphasise that for higher regional growth, there should be higher savings, lower regional capital-output ratio, net capital import and net accretion in whatever resources/labour that can come in. *Over-production is a condition when all the producers in sum produce* too little. If something remains unsold, it means many persons do not have necessary purchasing power. To ensure that *something else must be produced. This is how regions/countries can grow at the increasing rate.*

VIII. GROWTH POLES, GROWTH CENTRES, GROWTH POINTS AND GROWTH FOCI

Growth Poles: F. Perroux first propounded the concept. He defined growth pole as "a centre in abstract economic space from which centrifugal forces emanate and to which centripetal forces are attracted. Each centre being a centre of attraction and revulsion has its own field, which is the field of other centres". Growth pole *is not a place but a set of industries* and such industries are those which have the largest linkage effects on the hinterland. *The concept is "functional" in nature.* These are the industries which innovate and lead. The growth poles are key industries of key sectors. A growth 'pole' has gravitational pulls. *Perroux's growth pole is "economic space" rather than geographical space (as of Boudeville), which Perroux regarded as 'banal'.*

Pottier's growth pole is "development axis" where the net work of transport and other "external economies" converge. Hirschman and Myrdal too wrote about the growth poles. They too regarded growth pole as the leading industries with spread effects far exceeding the backwash effects. If backwash effects exceed the spread effects, growth becomes immiserising. Growth pole first relieves the pains and then becomes pole of development. There is high income elasticity of demand for the product of the pole industries so that demand is not a constraint and whatever is produced, is sold also. There is bunching or clustering effect of growth.

> Growth pole strategy is strategy of "unbalanced growth" and naturally those who advocate balanced growth are not appreciative of the concept being turned into a policy proposition. Some economists argue in favour of "planned poles" instead of "market/natural poles". Those who favour balanced growth do not want the hypothesis of growth pole to be mystified. *Growth pole concept and the 'balanced' growth are as contradictory as the concept of "boiling-ice cream" but growth poles have helped the growth of many areas.*

Growth Centres: A growth centre can be without 'growth pole' but may have many industrial units. The industrial estates near many big city centres are examples of growth centres. They are much more decentralised that the growth poles. Any geographical agglomeration of activities is *not* automatically developmental unless growth is "spoı.sored" by the government. Growth centres serve as guide-posts of development for the hinterland/rural areas. They become important centres of production, trade and taking away all types of "inputs" of development.

Growth Points : Regional economics emphasises that a growth points has its 'zone of influence', while a central place has a 'complementary region'. A growth point sustains the regions, while the central place is sustained by its region. The polarisation flows will be more intense and more varied in character around a growth point than around a central place wither the flows consist mainly of commuting for shopping, leisure and other services. Growth points are *nodal points* of growth. They can be 'natural' or 'planned'. Growth point concept represents a link between the naturally evolved structure of nodal regions and physical and regional planning.

Growth Foci : It is conceived not as a centre only but the entire set of conditions of development *at levels lower than growth points.* It has to provide facilities and functions of development as also the 'extension culture and social atmosphere'. The five-tier upper hierarchy can provide facilities of diffusion of technology, information and in fact the culture of materialism. Villages have their own service centres and central village. Primary activities are supported from growth foci but of the lower order. Growth centre provides middle order facilities and a growth pole/bigger growth centre can provide higher order things (tractor, for example).

IX. CUMULATIVE CAUSATION THEORY AND THESES ABOUT DIVERGENCE AND CONVERGENCE

Prof. Gunnar Myrdal formulated the theory of cumulative causation for regions/countries. He believed that for backward regions/countries the backwash effects had been cumulative while the spread effects were just a few and disjointed or discontinuous. There was clustering of development efforts in certain pockets only. While the forward regions/countries experienced the saga of "nothing succeeds like success", in case of the backward regions it was a case of "nothing fails like a failure". The terms of trade for commodities of backward regions/countries go adverse.

The backwash effects exceed the spread effects and the rebounded effects and circular causation effects are the net result of the backwash effects and the spread effects. Poverty is further perpetuated by poverty. In such cases the peripheries sustain the centre rather than centre sustaining the periphery. Complementarities are for the centre. Backward regions lose resources and manpower. The core will continue to experience a circular upward reinforcing trend of favourable effects and the periphery will have opposite experience.

Prime activities remain in the core which becomes the suction point while the subsidiary activities remain in the periphery which become exploited area. Market forces increase inequalities over the area and between the people/activities. The vicious circle continues. Myrdal is very bitter about corruption in less developed countries in the name of developing the poor. The politicians make false pretences about their being interested in development.

Divergence and Convergence

If industries and prime economic activities are centralised, there will be divergence in per capita income: people of developed regions earn fabulous incomes while most people of the backward regions/activities earn mere subsistence incomes or even less. Territorial division of labour leads to divergence. Spread effects in some regions and backwash effects in most regions lead to divergence. There is great property building and income propagation in certain pockets only. Capital flows, innovations, technical progress, further generation of external economies, favourable elasticity cases, government interventions, factor flows and factor-development all take place in the developed regions.

Convergence in the per capita income *is a goal and not merely an objective in regional economics*. Countervailing actions in favour of backward regions are to be taken so that peripheries are not sucked. Dispersal of activities is called for. The theory of comparative costs should *not be bypassed but made friendly to the backward regions by ensuring that the backward regions possess all advantages for favourable locational shifts.* Heartlands have to do a lot for the hinterland. There has to be "pulling down" and "top down" strategies for developed regions and "bottom up or pulling up" strategy for the backward regions.

X. EPILOGUE

Regional economics *has definitely contributed to the three fields of "pure theory", "policy issues" and "analysis of the state of affairs and "future planning" issues.* However, it would be wrong to say that everything in it is innovative. Much of the wisdom is borrowed from the "general economics". A problem with regional economists and regional geographers had been that they felt compelled to criticise the classical and neo-classical approaches *in all* cases.

If the intention of the regional economists and regional planners is to suggest that there should be regional resource inventories and prime moving activities be geared to solve the regional problems, one can have no dispute with the approach. The problem lies in their inventing a few jargons and presenting them as new theories. Not only these theories (except of the type of Weber) were of limited coverage but many of them faulty also.

It is true that *regional planning does not assume that there should be socialist planning.* Here lies its importance. The agro-climatic zonal planning that is proposed for India is a good example. Regional planning would bring the physical and economic conditions in tune with each other.

Regional Economics is what Regional Economists do and as such it also evolved gradually with the central issue of developing the backward regions in conformity with the environment. The aggressive postures of some regional economists towards "general economists" are not true. For one thing regional economists ignored money and finance.

Regional *economics* does not include such things as regional geography or regional sociological studies; Regional "Science" would do that. Isaard (himself an economist) made a very wild charge that classical economists used to wander in the wonderland of no space! This was not correct as even Adam Smith discussed in his "Wealth of Nations" the problems of backward region—and the region was India's Bengal. Malthusian theory of population was related to problem areas and areas where "visionaries" lived. Rent theory of Ricardo was location-specific. Mill and Marshall discussed price theories related to space like prices will be uniform over the entire areas, if transport costs are ignored. If not, then prices will be equal in 'concentric circles" of centrally located function. The old international trade theory was based on location economics and in turn developed the economics of location. *It was the foundation of regional economics.* In old days there used to "equality in poverty" and as such the problems of depressed regions and oppressed groups of people were not discussed in sixteenth century but Adam Smith had reserved all his sarcastic remarks for the industrialists. It was Malthus who propounded the theory of "unequal distribution" and everyone knows that Ricardo discussed the problems of distribution with reference to difference regions or how else can we explain their taking up the issues of mobility and migration. Mobility and migration take place over the space. In J.B. Say's system there is no "general over-production". It is sub-sectoral and regional. If there is over-production *somewhere*, it is the result of under-production *somewhere else*. If both remains unsold and the persons engaged in the production of earthen pitchers cannot have all the cloth they need, then either they should produce more or should produce something else also. Over production is a condition when all producers in sum produce *"too little"*: In this type of discussion of sub-sectoral activities, the *territorial* division of labour was discussed. Geographers paid more attention to cartographic analysis; sociologists to anthropological issues; economists were more concerned with regional problems of the targeted groups as also overall development. Regional economics developed as inequalities between sectors, functions, regions and groups widened not *because of economics but despite it*. Regional economics deals with (but not with all the ramifications) savings, investment, capital returns, employment generation and income propagation with reference to different areas. The hierarchal relations of settlements at the lower level and the meso regions and states are analysed and well quantified.

Part II

REGIONAL DISPARITIES IN INDIA: MEASUREMENTS AND FACTORS

6

Political Economy of Regional Imbalances

—Tushar Kanti Das & Lopamudra Mishra

Introduction

India, a federation, is divided into several states and union territories and balanced growth of all the states and union territories is essential for its political sustainability, economic viability and growth. However, it comprises the regions of extreme diversity. This diversity is with respect to size, natural resource endowments, population density, economic organisation, infrastructural facilities, industrial and commercial structure and availability of institutional finance. Regional imbalances are present mainly due to unequal natural endowments and lack of infrastructural facilities which is the basis for sustained economic growth. Infrastructure is defined as capital of a society or social capital that is embodied in such forms as to help direct production activities. An attempt has been made in this article to study the regional imbalances prevailing in the fifteen major states of India by taking the infrastructure of these states in terms of the per capita income from the four sectors of the economy.

2. Sectoral Incomes

The entire economy is divided into four sectors. They are:

(i) Primary Sector,
(ii) Secondary Sector,
(iii) Tertiary Sector,
(iv) Finance and Services Sector.

Agriculture, forestry and logging, fishing and mining and quarrying are under the primary sector. As part of the national pattern, the share of agriculture in the State Domestic Product of each state have steadily declined except in the case of two major states, namely, Punjab and Rajasthan, which experienced some sporadic increases at constant (1980-81) prices.

The secondary sector is comprised of manufacturing, construction and electricity, gas and water supply. Punjab has experienced a noticeable gain in terms of SDP share originating in manufacturing, so has Haryana. Bihar, which has experienced a fall in SDP originating in agriculture, has seen a significant rise in its share of manufacturing. Gujarat, Karnataka and Uttar Pradesh are the other states which have experienced distinct improvements in their SDP share originating in manufacturing but at the cost of their agricultural shares. In the case of Maharashtra, manufacture share in SDP has experienced a decline in terms of current prices in between the period 1980-81 to 1995-96, while that of West Bengal has declined both in terms of current and constant prices, throughout the 15-year period. Other major states to show declines in manufacturing share are Andhra Pradesh, Tamil Nadu, Orissa and Rajasthan. Like manufacturing, construction and electricity, gas and water supply are also crucial infrastructure. Macro-economic development and these sectors are highly interdependent and it is not possible to achieve high growth in one, without keeping pace with the other.

Transport, storage and communication, trade, hotels and restaurants are in the tertiary sector. The demands of this sector are likely to grow up further with economic and population growth. Rapid industrialisation, urbanisation and agricultural development together increase freight and passenger transport and higher real incomes stimulate leisure-related travel, which in turn lead to the development of hotels and restaurants.

The fourth, *i.e.* finance and services sector is comprised of banking and insurance, real estate, ownership of dwellings and business services, public administration and other services. A diversified and efficient financial sector is necessary for promoting savings in the form of financial assets and transferring them to the investors. A well functioning financial sector can promote greater amount of investment which can help to achieve a faster growth rate of the economy.

'Objective Function' of the States

India is an union of states. These are widely diversified from the point of available infrastructural facilities. The following three points are outlined on the availability of infrastructural facilities in different states.[1] First, the infrastructural facilities available in high income states like Maharashtra and Gujarat are better than the low income states like Orissa and Bihar. The roads and transport facilities etc. available in high income states are better than the low income states. In such a situation, the central transfers in any form coming to the states, the low income states will spend a part of it on infrastructural development unlike the high income states. Second the market for a particular product does not exist in a low infrastructural facilities available region as it is not well-developed. So, the profit maximising private sectors are not at all interested to invest in these areas as the infrastructural facilities available is poor. Here, the government is the last resort to initiate the process of investment in low infrastructural facility available state. The government here has no rival as no one is coming forward to invest in these areas. On the other hand, in high infrastructural facilities available states, the markets are well developed. Private investors are very much interested to invest in infrastructures, as they can create a market for their own products by attracting the people into that area. So investments in infrastructures become rival in a high infrastructure facilities available state. Again between economic and social infrastructure the private investors will prefer to invest in economic rather than in social infrastructure. This is because investment in social have long gestation lags sometimes even larger than in case of economic infrastructure.

The states in India differ from one another significantly in many physical, social and economic aspects. There is a growing evidence to show inter-regional disparities among the states. Inter-regional disparities in various dimensions of development have remained undiminished in spite of overall development during the last five decades.

Regional Multiplier

In an economy, increase in investment leads to an increase in income and increase in income leads to an increase in savings. Saving is a residual, while it is the investment which is the crucial factor. The marginal propensity to consume determines the relation between an increment of investment and the appropriate increment of income. This will induce the increment of saving necessary to maintain the equality of saving and investment. This relationship between the increment of investment and that of income is determined by '*k*' or what is known as the 'multiplier'. This can be represented by the formula $dY = k.\ dI\omega$ where $\left(1 - \frac{1}{k}\right)$ is equal to the marginal propensity to consume. The marginal propensity to consume declines with increasing income. Here the increments of investment become necessary for securing given increments of income at increasing levels of income. As the marginal propensity to consume is likely to be not far short of unity, in the case of poor communities, the multiplier has a high value in their case. It is easier for the community to attain full employment with small investment. Thus, a paradoxical situation arises. In the poorer community, on the one hand, it is easy to get full employment and on the other, the fluctuations caused by changes in its net investment is smaller. The richer the community, it is more difficult to secure full employment. The fluctuations in its total employment due to fluctuations in its net investment are more likely in a richer community. This results in instability in employment. Unless offset by an increased investment there is an increasing tendency towards involuntary unemployment.

V.K.R.V. Rao[2] outlined the following conditions under which the multiplier principle operates. They are:

(*a*) involuntary unemployment,
(*b*) an industrialised economy where the supply curve of output slopes upwards the right but does not become vertical after a substantial interval,
(*c*) excess capacity in the consumption goods industries, and
(*d*) comparative by elastic supply of the working capital required for increased output.

The widening regional disparities in India is due to the failure of regional policies to counter the pulls of external economies exerted by the developed regions.[3] In achieving the objective of reducing the disparities in development it is not only the financial flows that determines the growth; side by side the social, economic, political and administrative environment too have their roles to play. In the absence of the desirable environment, the absorption capacity of the financial flows from outside will be less. Again, the levels of government's expenditure and private expenditure in the corporate and household sectors are likely to be higher in high sectoral income states and lower in low sectoral income states. This may tend to widen the inter-state income disparities. Apart from the volume of expenditure, the size of the regional multipliers also may tend to widen the regional disparities. Regional multiplier refers to the number of times the regional income will increase as a result of a unit of expenditure in a region. It is expressed as a numerical coefficient. The size of regional multiplier depends on the region's import propensity. The larger the import propensity, the smaller is the value of the multiplier. The problem of inter-state economic disparities in India is qualitatively different from that in the developed federations. In India, the size of the less developed areas is much bigger. The financial capacity of the central government and the better off states is limited. The state governments are directly responsible not only for social services but also for economic activities in agriculture, irrigation, power, industry, roads and road transport and so on. Thus, on the one hand, the fiscal needs of the backward areas are greater and on the other, the fiscal capacity to deal with the situation is much smaller. Therefore, solutions have to be found which are suitable to the peculiarities of the Indian situation.

Variables for Ranking of States

The present study is confined to ranking of fifteen major states of India. They are Andhra Pradesh, Assam, Bihar, Gujarat, Haryana, Karnataka, Kerala, Madhya Pradesh, Maharashtra, Orissa, Punjab, Rajasthan, Tamil Nadu, Uttar Pradesh and West Bengal. The ranking of these fifteen major states has to be undertaken by taking the four sector variables. From the four sectors thirteen variables are identified and the per capita income for the thirteen variables are taken for the fifteen major states at constant (1980-81) prices. The variables are the per capita income from

(*i*) Agriculture,
(*ii*) Forestry and Logging,
(*iii*) Fishing,
(*iv*) Mining and Quarrying,
(*v*) Manufacturing,
(*vi*) Construction,
(*vii*) Electricity, Gas and Water Supply,
(*viii*) Transport, Storage and Communication,
(*ix*) Trade, Hotels and Restaurants,
(*x*) Banking and Insurance,
(*xi*) Real Estate, Ownership of Dwellings and Business Services,
(*xii*) Public Administration,
(*xiii*) Other Services.

Data

The data used in the present study are all secondary data taken from the "National Accounts Statistics of India: 1950-51 to 1995-96" published by Economic And Political Weekly Research Foundation. Originally these data are compiled by the directorates of economics and statistics/state statistical bureaus of respective state governments at both current and constant prices and made available for the users by the Central Statistical Organisation (CSO). However, to make things comparable we have taken the variables only at constant prices (1980-81 prices).

Methodology

Consistent with the objective of the study, there are four techniques for the ranking of fifteen major states of India. They are:

(*i*) Principal Component Analysis,
(*ii*) Factor Analysis,
(*iii*) Cluster Analysis, and
(*iv*) Discriminant Analysis.

In the present study principal component analysis (PCA) is used to rank the fifteen major states of India. This method of Principal Component Analysis which is similar to Factor Analysis is widely used for developing composite index of development. The principal component analysis transforms a set of correlated variables to a new set of uncorrelated variables. The objective of the analysis is to find out the first few components which account for most of the variations in the original data. If they do, the first few components will be intuitively meaningful, will help to understand the data better and will be useful in subsequent analysis where we can operate with a smaller number of variables. The 'component scores' are the desired composite indices of development. If the first principal component alone explains more than 50 per cent of the total variance then one set of component scores is enough to analyse the development. The principal component analysis is also used to rank the states in accordance with composite index of development.

The aim of the method of principal component is the construction out of a set of variables, xj's ($j = 1, 2, ...k$) of new variables (P_i) called principal components, which are linear combinations of the x's:

$$P_1 = a_{11}x_1 + a_{12}x_2 + \dots + a_{1k}x_k$$
$$P_2 = a_{21}x_1 + a_{22}x_2 + \dots + a_{2k}x_k$$
$$\vdots$$
$$P_k = a_{k1}x_1 + a_{k2}x_2 + \dots + a_{kk}x_k.$$

It should be noted at the outset that the method of principal components can be applied by using the original values of the

Xj's or their deviation from the means $X_j = x_j - \bar{x}_j$ or the standardised variables (measured as the deviations of the x_j's from the means and subsequently divided by the standard deviations)

$$Z_j = \frac{X_j}{S_{xj}}.$$

However, it may be noted that the values of the principal components will be different depending on the way in which the variables are used (original values, deviations or standardised values).

The *a*'s called loadings are chosen so that the constructed principal components satisfy two conditions:

(*a*) The principal components are uncorrelated (orthogonal);

(*b*) the first principal component P_1 absorbs and accounts for the maximum possible proportion of the total variation in the set of all *x*'s, the second principal component absorbs the remaining variation on the *x*'s (after allowing for the variation accounted for by the first principal component) and so on.

The Method

Stage-I. The problem is to obtain estimates of the *a*'s (loadings) with which we will be able to transform the *x*'s into orthogonal artificial variables, the principal components. In the first place these co-efficients are estimated. Next, some tests are conducted to decide whether the estimates, *a*'s are statistically significant. Finally, some rule of decision is established to decide how many of the principal components (how many of all the possible *p*'s) to retain into the analysis. The maximum number of principal components is equal to the number of *x*'s. However, only a small number of *p*'s is usually retained in the analysis.

Stage-II. Having found the *a*'s, computed values of *p*'s (principal components) and taking the decision about the maximum number of principal components to retain in the analysis, the next step is to regress *Y* on these principal components.

$$Y = \hat{\gamma}_1 P_1 + \hat{\gamma}_2 P_2 + \ldots \hat{\gamma}_m P_m$$

Stage-III. From the $\hat{a}$'s and $\hat{\gamma}$'s we may find the $\hat{b}$'s of the original model transferring back from the p's into the standardised x's.

Estimation of the Principal Components Model

Assume that with the above procedure we have retained r (where $r < k$) out of all the principal components. For simplicity let $r = 2$ and $k = 4$, so that

$$P_1 + l_{11} Z_1 + l_{12} Z_2 + l_{13} Z_3 + l_{14} Z_4$$

$$P_2 = l_{21} Z_1 + l_{22} Z_2 + l_{23} Z_3 + l_{24} Z_4$$

(where the z's are the standardised values of the original x's).

We regress 'Y' on the chosen (extracted) principal components:

$$Y = \gamma_1 P_1 + \gamma_2 P_2 + V$$

(Where 'v' is a random variable satisfying the usual assumptions) from which we obtain the OLS estimates of $\hat{\gamma}_1$ and $\hat{\gamma}_2$.

Ranking of States

By following the principal component analysis, the fifteen major states of India are ranked on the basis of the infrastructural facilities taken in terms of the per capita income obtained from the four sectors of the economy. As pointed earlier thirteen variables are taken in the present analysis. The states are ranked on the basis of their aggregate scores over the thirteen identified variables. The states are ranked in descending order of their scores obtained from the sectoral variables. The ranking of the states are done during the different time periods. They are in 1980-81, 1985-86, 1990-91 and 1993-94.

Principal component analysis has been carried out for all the bench mark years to form the 'composite indices of development' after standardisation of the variables. The values of variance explained by first principal component for the four time periods 1980-81, 1985-86, 1990-91 and 1993-94 are respectively 65.4 per cent, 65.8 per cent, 67 per cent and 63.2 per cent, respectively. Therefore, it would be proper to calculate component scores based on the first principal component alone and compare the development of states for different benchmark years. The ranks so obtained and the value of first principal component for different years and different states so obtained

Table 6.1

Ranking of Major States of India by Per Capita Income of Four Sectors of the States (Principal Component Analysis)

1980-81			1985-86			1990-91			1993-94		
Rank	States	Scores	Rank	States	Scores	Rank	States	Scores	Rank	States	Scores
1	Maharashtra	5.1800	1	Maharashtra	5.6208	1	Maharashtra	5.3845	1	Maharashtra	5.1134
2	Punjab	4.4243	2	Punjab	3.8290	2	Punjab	3.6122	2	Punjab	3.0447
3	West Bengal	1.7150	3	Gujarat	1.8205	3	Haryana	2.0961	3	Gujarat	1.9813
4	Haryana	1.4543	4	Haryana	1.8034	4	Gujarat	1.7302	4	Tamil Nadu	1.5879
5	Gujarat	1.3100	5	West Bengal	1.3064	5	Tamil Nadu	1.4603	5	Haryana	1.4983
6	Kerala	0.9840	6	Tamil Nadu	0.7491	6	West Bangal	0.8820	6	Kerala	1.0428
7	Tamil Nadu	0.5828	7	Kerala	0.0867	7	Kerala	0.0812	7	West Bengal	0.8712
8	Karnataka	–0.3169	8	Karnataka	–0.2421	8	Karnataka	–0.0566	8	Karnataka	0.2373
9	Assam	–0.8012	9	Andhra Pradesh	–1.0289	9	Andhra Pradesh	–0.7562	9	Andhra Pradesh	–0.9245
10	Andhra P.	–0.9034	10	Assam	–1.4900	10	Rajasthan	–1.5279	10	Rajasthan	–1.5824
11	Uttar Pradesh	–2.0105	11	Uttar Pradesh	–2.0851	11	Uttar Pradesh	–1.7930	11	Assam	–2.0169
12	Rajasthan	–2.2433	12	Orissa	–2.1912	12	Assam	–2.2469	12	Uttar Pradesh	–2.0245
13	Orissa	–2.3835	13	Rajasthan	–2.2380	13	Madhya Pradesh	–2.4370	13	Madhya Pradesh	–2.5235
14	Madhya P.	–3.0551	14	Madhya Pradesh	–2.2888	14	Orissa	–2.6933	14	Orissa	–2.7362
15	Bihar	–3.9363	15	Bihar	–3.6519	15	Bihar	–3.7355	15	Bihar	–3.5688
Variance Explained (In Percentage)		65.4			65.8			67.0			63.2

are represented in Table 6.1. The ranks assigned to different states at different time periods can be compared. Over the years some states have moved up while others moved down. There are also states who did not change their positions.

Experience with developed states indicate that huge investments in infrastructure can be domestically manageable by growing economies because of the existence of constant interaction between infrastructure and economic growth, which in turn can provide more resources for investment in infrastructure. But development of infrastructural facilities were seen in 'relative' terms. In some states, the improvement of infrastructural facilities exceeds the improvement of some other states. Better infrastructural facilities available states indicate comparatively more per capita sectoral income in these states. Among the fifteen major states, if a state move up, we say it is an improvement in the sectoral income which is due to the infrastructural development.

All the fifteen major states are ranked into High Income States (HIS), Middle Income States (MIS) and Low Income States (LIS) in four different time periods *i.e.*, 1980-81, 1985-86, 1990-91 and 1993-94. As fifteen states are taken for ranking, we can classify them into three groups on the basis of the component scores and each group having five states. The ranks assigned to different states in 1980-81, 1990-91 and 1993-94 are presented in Table 6.2.

Over the different periods, Maharashtra, Punjab, Karnataka and Bihar have not changed their original position. West Bengal, which was in the high income category states in 1980-81 and 1985-86, came to the middle income category states during 1990-91 and 1993-94. Its position was third in 1980-81 and came to the seventh position in 1993-94. Tamil Nadu had improved its position and came to the fourth position. Similarly, Rajasthan, which was initially in the low income category states had improved its position and came to the tenth position. But Assam, which was in the middle-income category states, moved to the low income category states over the years. Similarly, Haryana, Uttar Pradesh and Orissa have moved to the lower ranks over the years. But Gujarat, Andhra Pradesh and Madhya Pradesh have improved their positions.

Table 6.2
Ranking of States on the Basis of Sectoral Income

States	*Ranks Assigned to Different States in Different Years*			
	1980-81	*1985-86*	*1990-91*	*1993-94*
HIS				
Maharashtra	1	1	1	1
Punjab	2	2	2	2
West Bengal	3	5	6	7
Haryana	4	4	3	5
Gujarat	5	3	4	3
MIS				
Kerala	6	7	7	6
Tamil Nadu	7	6	5	4
Karnataka	8	8	8	8
Assam	9	10	12	11
Andhra Pradesh	10	9	9	9
LIS				
Uttar Pradesh	11	11	11	12
Rajasthan	12	13	10	10
Orissa	13	12	14	14
Madhya Pradesh	14	14	13	13
Bihar	15	15	15	15

Conclusion

The ranking of the states on the basis of the principal component analysis for the four bench-mark years showed that states like Maharashtra and Punjab have highest overall sectoral income. On the other hand, Bihar maintained the last position for all the time periods on which the present analysis is based.

Tenth Finance Commission (TFC) had grouped the fourteen major states into high income states (HIS), middle income states (MIS) and low income states (LIS) taking into account the per capita income. This ranking of states is presented in Table 6.3. Here Assam is taken as a special-category state. But when the major states are ranked in accordance with the sectoral income, Maharashtra gets the first rank rather than Punjab as recommended by the Tenth Finance Commission. Tamil Nadu which is a middle income state according to TFC is a high sectoral income state in 1993-94. Likewise, Rajasthan which is a middle sectoral income state becomes a low income state according to TFC. Except this, all the other major states rearrange themselves within the groups, which are assigned to them.

Table 6.3

Ranking of States Presented by the Tenth Finance Commission*

High Income States	*Middle Income States*	*Low Income States*
Punjab	Tamil Nadu	Madhya Pradesh
Maharashtra	Karnataka	Rajasthan
Haryana	West Bengal	Orissa
Gujarat	Kerala	Uttar Pradesh
	Andhra Pradesh	Bihar

* Assam has not been taken into account as it is a special category state.

Per capita income of the state concerned is only one indicator of development. This does not bring out the structural transformation and improvement in quality of life which are reflected by the development of a specific sector. So the per capita sectoral incomes in a state is a more prominent indicator of development as compared to per capita income. Therefore, the ranking of the states on the basis of per capita sectoral incomes by dividing the entire economy into four sectors and taking into account thirteen variables is better than the Tenth Finance Commission's ranking on the basis of only per capita income. Again, the high sectoral income states are more developed because of high regional multiplier than the low sectoral income states.

Notes and References

1. Das, T.K. (1997), *Nature and Impact of Federal Transfers on Indian States (1960-61) to 1990-91).* Thesis submitted to the Sambalpur University for Ph.D. Degrere, pp. 35-37.
2. Rao, V.K.R.V. (1952), "Investment, Income and Multiplier in an Underdeveloped Economy" in *The Economics of Underdevelopment*, Ed. by Singh and Aggrawal.
3. Das, T.K. (1997), *op. cit.*

Adelman, I. and Morris, C.T. (1973), *Economic Growth and Social Equity on Developing Countries*, Stanford University Press, Stanford, California.

Aldenderfer, Mark, S. and Blashfield, Roger, K. (1984), *Cluster Analysis* in the series Quantiative Applications in the Social Sciences, SAGE University Paper, USA.

Chatfield, C. and Collins, A.J. (1980), *Introduction to Multivariate Analysis*, Chapman and Hall, London.

Das, T.K. (1977), *Nature and Impact of Federal Transfers on Indian States*, Thesis submitted to Sambalpur University for Ph.D. degree.

Das, T.K. (1997), "Infrastructural Development of Major States of India", *IEA Ist Amrit Jubilee (80th) Conference Volume*, Osmania University, Hyderabad, pp. 665-73.

Dutta, Ray Choudhury, Uma (1992), "Inter-State and Intra-State Variations in Economic Development and Standard of Living", *Economic and Political Weekly*, December 5, pp. 2651-55.

EPW Research Foundation (1997), *National Accounts Statistics of India 1950-51 to 1995-96*, Union Press, Mumbai.

Herrick, B. and Kindleberger, C.P. (1983), *Economic Development*, McGraw Hill Inc.

Jackson, J. Edward (1991), *A User's Guide To Principal Components*, Wiley & Sons Inc., New York, USA.

Kim, Jae-on and Mueller, Charles, W. (1978), *Factor Analysis: Statistical Methods and Political Issues* in the series Quantitative Applications in the Social Sciences, SAGE University Paper, USA.

Klecka, William R. (1980), *Discriminant Analysis* in the series Quantitative Applications in the Social Sciences, SAGE University Paper, USA.

Kundu, Amitabh (1980), *Measurement of Urban Process: A Study in Regionalisation*, Popular Prakashan, Bombay.

Parikh, K.S. (Ed.), (1997), *India Development Report*, Oxford University Press.

Rao, Hemlata (1984), *Regional Disparities and Development in India*, Ashish Publishing House, New Delhi.

Rao, V.K.R.V., "Investment, Income and Multiplier in an Underdeveloped Economy" in Singh and Agrawal (eds.) *The Economics of Underdevelopment*.

7

Global Regional Development Experience: Lessons for Policy Planners in India

—P.G. Marvania

Introduction

The regional disparities of development seems to be an universal phenomenon. Countries, irrespective of their size and level of development, have problem of uneven regional development. In many countries, the economic divide has generated socio-political tensions. Both, market and centrally planned economies have followed the policies to reduce the developmental disparities among their sub-regions.

India, too, is a federation of states. The development disparities are quite high among the Indian states. Data pertaining to the per capita SDP and its index are given in Table 7.1 and 7.2. A close perusal of the data indicates, not only the disparities are high but, over the period such disparities have accentuated.

The Indian planners have made conscious efforts to remove the regional disparities. For achieving this goal, they have laid greater emphasis on industrialisation of the backward region. It was assumed that the percolation impact would help in reducing the regional disparities of development.

In this paper an attempt is made to review experiences of other countries in regard to their regional development. Also, contemporary regional development policies of India is discussed. And the possible lessons for our planners have been outlined at the end of paper.

Developed Countries

One of the persistent policy trends in both, developed market economy and centrally planned countries, has been the spatial redistribution of settlements and activity. This trend can generally be characterised by two main emphasis, that is, containment of growth of large cities and development of depressed or underdeveloped regions. Policy measures to achieve these have been varied, ranging from industrial dispersal policies to certain of growth centres and new towns.

In the developed market economy countries policies aimed at limiting the growth of very large cities and controlling urban sprawl have been mainly intended to direct growth to designated locations to decentralise economic activity in space. These countries have adopted a variety of measures including legal prohibitions and financial disincentives to capital investment in large cities as in the cases of Denmark, the FRG and the UK, and financial and other incentives aimed at promoting the development of designated underdeveloped areas and centres. Some countries notably France, and the Netherlands have adopted strategies to achieve optimal spatial distributions of settlements and activity.

The developed countries have consciously formed strategies for initiating development of depressed regions therein. The UK has applied instruments like subsidies, tax allowances and a system of vocational controls for guiding activities to depressed regions.

Italy has used a comprehensive approach to development of Mezzogiorno with emphasis on incentives to stimulate industrialisation-led economic growth and creation of social and physical infrastructure and diversified economic base.

Finland has emphasised similar policies in pursuits of the development of its north-region which suffered from rural exodus during the rapid expansion of urban areas in the southern part of the country during 1960s. By subsidising locations in the north, Finland had attempted to develop the region economically and to create conditions for the balanced national demographic development.

Canada has made efforts to develop medium sized cities within the framework of regional development strategies particularly in the eastern areas of the country. Given the relatively underdeveloped state of great parts in Canada and its low population diversity, the trend in human settlement development has, to a large degree, been determined by the policies that have directed investment to extractive industries which opened up resource frontiers and brought about rapid expansion of settlement and activity.

Belgium, Denmark, Ireland and the Netherlands have sought to advocate regional development by way of administrative decentralisation and vesting more authorities to local governments and creating separate regional authorities.

Centrally planned economies followed a thoroughly planned pattern of production sites and settlements. The period since second war has been one of the rapid urbanisation and industrialisation, although the pace of both showed in the second half of 1970s. The centrally planned economy countries have followed fourfold strategy of development and distribution of activities and settlements: First, the concentration of investment for rapid industrialisation in centres where the required supporting infrastructure was already available or could be created quickly mainly in the country's large cities. Second, the planned growth and expansion of established centres. Third, the containment of the growth of expanding centres, stimulation of the growth of small centres and creation of new centres, particularly in underdeveloped regions. Fourth, the development of rural centres, based on establishment of agro-processing industries.

It is evident from the above that centrally planned countries have attempted to establish a human settlement hierarchy linked to a system of production. This structure is designed to allow for the controlled growth of urban centres through deliberate policies of promoting investment at centres designated for growth and limiting investment in others. The same approach has been used to limit the expansion of large towns and to encourage the development of small and medium-sized towns.

It is fairly clear that world over policy makers in the developed countries have made efforts to reduce spatial imbalance and development. Now let us briefly examine the results of these intervention strategies for balanced regional development in these countries.

The empirical studies have indicated that in the developed market economies, the process of spatial concentration during the phase of rapid industrialisation has ultimately transformed into intra-regional and inter-regional dispersion during the phase of post-industrial maturity (Williamson, 1965; Kuznets, 1966; El Shakhs, 1972). However, this does not mean that the problem of regional imbalances of development has been completely eradicated from the developed countries. The problem is less conspicuous in these countries. Depressed regions do exist in the advanced economies (Robinson, 1969). Not only that but to what extent policies have helped in reducing this problem is not clear (Richardson, 1973).

The centralised economy countries were able to enforce spatial settlement and activity planning quite effectively. Whereas, experiences of developed-market economy—countries in their efforts to contain urban and industrial polarisation at and around certain favoured locations and areas and promote more balanced regional development have been mixed.

In the Western-Europe, with exception of some Mediterranean countries, 70 per cent or more of population growth in the 1960s and 1970s took place in towns with 50,000 or fewer inhabitants and a large number of metropolitan areas reported population losses and decentralisation of economic activities in the sense that their growth trends had shifted in favour of small-sized cities (Drewett and Ross, 1981).

The trends of shifting of activities away from the large metropolitan cities have been observed in most developed countries. In these countries, job opportunities in the manufacturing in the large metropolitan cities have been declining rapidly. The structural changes which have taken place in the manufacturing sector have made smaller cities more attractive locations for fresh investments. To certain extent, the government policies of providing incentives and disincentives for containment of size of large urban metropolitan cities and development of lagging regions have facilitated dispersal process.

It has been found that during the period of 1960 to 1980, 30 out of 78 metropolitan areas in the UK, experienced population losses, 27 out of 53 in the FRG and 23 out of 84 in Italy had similar experiences (Peter Hall, 1983). In the USA, 137 (47 per cent) cities experienced either absolute or relative decline in their population (Nigel Harris, 1984).

In developed countries, socio-economic infrastructure is spread over entire space of the country. This has been the outcome of their early beginning of industrialisation. This vastly diffused network of infrastructure has helped in dispersing settlements and activities across the space.

However, the visible growth of industrial locations in these countries has been in the form of concentrated—dispersed locations and areas in the proximity of large towns and between them along transport corridors. The Washington-Baltimore belt in the USA, London-Lancashier belt in the UK, Los Angeles-California corridor in the USA, Amsterdam to Ruhr in the North-west Europe, Tokaido region in Japan, Tokyo-Yokohama and Osaka-Kobe regions in Japan, and regions around London, Paris, New York, Tokyo, are examples of such industrially concentrated dispersal in the developed countries.

Case of Developing Countries

Regional disparities of development are quite glaring in the developing countries. The tendencies of concentration of settlements and activity at and around certain favoured locations and areas are very powerful barring a few countries like Korea, Taiwan and Brazil. The regional disparities observed in these countries can be described by the following parameters:

(*i*) Regional disparities of income and social infrastructure;
(*ii*) Rural-Urban disparities in living standard;
(*iii*) Urban-Primacy; and
(*iv*) Migration.

(i) Regional Disparities of Income and Social Infrastructure

It has been observed that, in general, regional disparities in the less developed countries are far wider than those in the developed countries (Williamson, 1965). A more recent study of 18 developing countries has corroborated the above hypothesis (Gilbert and Goodman, 1976). In the developing countries, certain favoured locations and areas have been continuously attracting investment, manpower and entrepreneurs. This process of polarisation has not shown any sign of reversal (UNCRD, 1976; Unikel, 1976; Gugler and Flanagan, 1978).

This, continued polarisation of activity and settlements have been attributed to two facts: First, the historical distribution of socio-economic infrastructure and second, contemporary sectoral policies.

The inherited socio-economic infrastructure in the most developing countries was spatially skewed and was designed to subserve the colonial eco-politico interests. Later, during the post-war period, the same had important bearings in the fostering of growth of industrial activity and of settlement patterns (Morse, 1975; Cross, 1979).

The inward looking policies pursued by these countries accentuated polarisation at locations which were favourably placed. The product-mix and technologies in these countries underwent rapid transformation giving rise to such industrial activity, which were more profitable to undertake at or around metropolitan centres. Such growth tendencies resulted into creation of concentrated urban complexes with better socio-economic infrastructure facilities in relation to other regions. The transport network at these locations, facilitated further, the concentration process. Hence, no local or foreign entrepreneur would be willing to forgo the locational advantages provided by 'Urban Complexes' and select a location very far from such complexes. This was further helped by pursuance of sectoral policies aimed at faster economic and export growth (Richardson, 1981; Renaud, 1979; Gilbert and Gugler, 1987).

It has been also observed that there has been no tendency toward greater spatial equality in the most developing countries. The very significant revelation about spatial disparities in these countries is that, per capita income of different countries have been found to be unrelated to the level of spatial disparities. Rather, spatial imbalances of development were more a function of national economic organisation. The small-sized countries like South Korea and Taiwan and a large country like Brazil have less regional disparities than other developing countries. These countries have been able to achieve that due to their more outward looking policies and linking their economies with the rest of the world (Gilbert and Gugler, 1987).

(ii) Rural-Urban Disparities in Living Standard

There are major differences apparent between the living standards of urban and rural people in the developing countries with some exception of socialistic countries where conscious efforts have been made to reduce them.

The rural areas in developing countries contain a high proportion of poor people, are provided with minimum of social services and also existing social services therein are qualitatively inferior, the level of socio-economic infrastructure is very minimal and has very little job opportunities which can be considered as well remunerated. The rural-urban per capita income differential too is very high. The services like education, medical health-hygiene, housing and drinking water supply are at very low level in the rural areas in almost all developing countries (UNECLA, 1971; Gish, 1972; Sharpston, 1972; Gilbert, 1974; Friedmann and Douglas, 1976).

(iii) Urban Primacy

The debate regarding role of primacy in the development process has still remained inconclusive. Also, primacy is not limited to developing countries only. It has been found existing in them in relatively high degree. The existence of primacy has not been confined to any single characteristic of a country, it has been especially common in those countries that are small, highly centralised and of medium income group (Berry, 1961; Mehta, 1964; Browning, 1972; Mills, 1986).

Even though there are conflicting evidence regarding the relationship between urban primacy and the level of development, it does affect the functional distribution of settlements and activity centres. The overpowering impact of primacy does not foster a system of cities which is functionally essential for balanced regional development.

The developing countries like Philippines, Thailand in Asia, Bolivia, Costa Rica in Latin America and most countries in Africa has problem of single city dominance (Renaud, 1979).

(iv) Migration Trends

In developing countries, interaction of factors like high population pressure on cultivable land, lack of remunerative job opportunities in rural areas and a hope of job and better life amenities have led to constant flow of rural-urban migration. And this, continued flow of rural-urban migration, has led to growth of slums in the cities of developing countries. The same has put severe strains upon the scanty infrastructure of urban places and has given rise to social and political problems in some of them. This led to government action either through direct control on population mobility (as in China) and indirect measures of improving economic base of rural areas (as in Malaysia, Brazil and India).

The direct control measures were used in China with administrative success but individuals had to pay heavy price and economy suffered from misallocations of labour. The less stringent controls were applied in Indonesia and Philippines in mid-1960s and 1970s to prevent growth of their capital cities. But in both these cases the controls proved hard to enforce, gave birth to social evil like corruption and could not slow down urban growth significantly. In some parts of Africa, a practice of expulsion of unemployed migrants from cities was in practice (*i.e.* Congo, Niger, Tanzania and Zaire) but it did not make any visible impact on the problem of rural-urban migration (World Bank, 1984). Thus, studies have revealed the failure of direct control measures of population mobility in checking the continued flow of rural-urban migration.

The indirect measures like development of rural areas as in the case of Indonesia, Brazil and Malaysia, met with a little success and that too had proved excessively costly in terms of public expenditure. On the evaluation of performance of this type of strategy of redistribution of population, it was observed intensification of activity to already settled area was more efficient than to relocate settlements elsewhere (World Bank, 1984).

Another approach to lessen pressure on large cities was to promote small and medium sized cities and to set up new towns in the lagging regions through incentives. This has been experimented in countries like Peru, India, Thailand, South Korea etc. But it could not be very successful except in the case of South Korea. But the South Korean case was exception in the sense that besides this package of promoting small towns through incentives, a set of whole lot of other policy packages also played a vital role in the realisation of the goal of redistribution of population and activity (World Bank, 1984).

The rural-urban migration, which is largely the outcome of spatial inequalities of development, could not be checked very successfully either by direct or by indirect measures. In either case, the cost in terms of expenditure or social evils was quite high as compared to benefits.

From the above presented evidence, it is abundantly clear that the state of spatial inequalities of development needs a careful attention. Also, there is a wider scope for policy manoeuvrings in these countries because of their low level of industrial development in particular and economic development in general.

The experiences of regional development policies, either in explicit or in implicit form, can be summarised as follow.

First, in the developed countries, spatial disparities of development do exist but they are not so acute because the gap between living standards in rural and urban areas in these countries is not very wide.

Second, the dispersal of industrial activity in the hinterland has taken place in developed countries only after the polarisation tendencies have weakened. And, the dispersal is usually in axial form or in corridor form.

Third, in the developing countries the regional disparities of development are quite visible. The gaps of income and quality of life in developed regions and backward regions are quite wide. Incidence of poverty, unemployment and poor quality of life in the backward region is quite high. High population pressure and market imperfections are some of the reasons for persistence regional disparities of development.

Regional Development in India

The regional development policy adopted in India can be

summarised as follow. The basic approach to deal with the issue of regional imbalances in development was based upon growth pole/centre type of strategy. For this purpose backward areas were identified based on the criteria prescribed by Pande Committee (1969). These areas were subject to special fiscal and other monetary benefits as suggested by the Wanchhoo Committee (1969). It was pre-supposition that the incentive packages would help to attract industrial investment in the backward regions. Besides, a multi-agency policy to alleviate rural poverty and improve quality of life was adopted. Most of these programmes suffered due to paucity of resources and also due to lack of proper co-ordination and leakages. Both, the central and state governments took initiatives to formulate appropriate policies and they also undertook sole responsibility to implement them. The policies of reducing regional development, relied heavily on industrialisation of backward regions through incentives. Moreover, the policies failed to resolve inherent conflicts in the sectoral and spatial equity goals of development.

Evaluation of Regional Development Policy and Performance

The performance of regional economic development strategy has been a most favoured subject of researchers in India. Some of them have attempted to measure the extent of inequalities and causes behind them (Rao, 1984; Tewari, 1984, 1988; Awasthi, 1991; Nair, 1986; Dholakia, 1985).

One of the serious criticism levelled against the approach of planned development was that it was inadequately conceived and its role was limited to allocation of investment over sectors and sub-sectors and failed to evolve a comprehensive and effective action plan for the spatial development despite its recognition of existence of such inequalities. The glaring disparities in economic growth in general and industrial growth in particular was the outcome of this faulty strategy (Misra *et al.*, 1974 ; Kashyap, 1979; Sekhar, 1983).

There is almost unanimity among researchers that spatial intervention policies have helped more to the developed than to the backward regions. Various instruments like licensing, tax benefits, cash subsidies, physical infrastructure facilities, monetary benefits, concessional credits and supply of key raw materials at concessional rates to attract industries in backward areas, have been used relatively more by developed states and regions than by the backward. Also direct public sector investment to create growth foci have failed to generate development multiplier effect and foster linkages for the sustained development of the hinterland region. As a result, inter-regional and intra-regional development imbalances continued widening during 1960s and 1970s (NCDBA, 1980; Mohan, 1983; Sekhar, 1982).

Further, by examining empirical evidence, some of the researchers arrived at conclusion that government policies in the post-independence period have been somewhat misconceived as far as balanced regional development through industrialisation was concerned. Almost all policies have marginally affected the locational dynamics of industries even after more than 35 years of planning. The regional distribution of industries by and large presents the same picture of spatial concentration of industries as was under British rule (Pathak, 1980; Bhat, 1981; Kundu and Raza, 1982; Wadhwa and Kashyap, 1983).

Some researchers however maintains that the spatial inequalities in the level of economic development in general and industrial development in particular would have been greater in case of absence of the government intervention (Pathak, 1975; Gupta, 1973; Sandesara, 1982; Nair, 1982; Pathak, 1971).

As a matter of fact, it is really difficult to assess that to which extent inter and intra-regional dispersal of development had been due to policy inducement and due to spontaneous forces of the market.

It has been observed that during 1960s and 1970s the disparities of income among states have been widened. It has been pointed out that the forces at work to diversify different state economies in various ways were in operation in such a manner which had brought about an increase in inequality during 1960s and 1970s. Now it has been expected that in 1990s these very forces may turn out to be instrumental in bringing down the state income inequalities in India (Dholakia, 1985).

The per capita income disparities among the 14 major states of India are presented in Tables 7.1 and 7.2. Disparities are quite wide and has got accentuated over the period of time. In early 1960s, traditionally industrial states of Maharashtra and West Bengal used to occupy the top two positions and Bihar and Orissa were on the last two positions respectively. And gap of income between the top and the bottom states was of Rs. 203 (at current prices) only.

Table 7.1
Comparable Statistics of Per Capita State Domestic Product

(at current prices, in Rupees)

No.	*State*	*1960-61*	*1970-71*	*1984-85*	*1995-96*
1.	Maharashtra	419	811	3493	15244
2.	Gujarat	380	845	3224	11036
3.	Tamil Nadu	344	616	2254	9868
4.	West Bengal	386	729	2493	7851
5.	Uttar Pradesh	244	493	1618	5983
6.	Andhra Pradesh	314	586	2267	10933
7.	Madhya Pradesh	274	489	1836	6597
8.	Karnataka	292	675	2431	8933
9.	Bihar	216	418	1517	4097
10.	Rajasthan	271	629	1907	6958
11.	Orissa	226	541	1902	6079
12.	Kerala	278	636	2378	8007
13.	Punjab	226	1067	4093	15504
14.	Haryana	359	932	3249	13770
	All India	306	633	2355	9517

Source: National Accounts Statistics of India 1950-51 to 1995-96, EPW, Mumbai.

However by 1970-71, small and agriculturally prosperous states of Punjab and Haryana occupied first two positions. And from among four traditionally industrialised states—Maharashtra, West Bengal, Tamil Nadu and Gujarat—only Maharashtra and Gujarat could comfortably maintained their higher ranks. Bihar came down to the last rank and Punjab on the first rank. The gap widened to Rs. 649 between the per capita SDP of the top and the bottom states.

Table 7.2

Index of Per Capita State Domestic Product

No.	State	1960-61	1970-71	1984-85	1995-96
1.	Maharashtra	136.9	128.1	148.3	160.2
2.	Gujarat	124.2	133.5	136.9	116.0
3.	Tamil Nadu	112.4	97.5	95.7	103.7
4.	West Bengal	126.1	115.2	105.9	82.5
5.	Uttar Pradesh	79.1	77.9	68.7	62.9
6.	Andhra Pradesh	102.6	92.6	96.3	90.5
7.	Madhya Pradesh	89.5	77.3	78.0	69.3
8.	Karnataka	95.4	106.6	103.2	93.9
9.	Bihar	70.6	66.0	64.4	43.0
10.	Rajasthan	88.6	99.4	81.0	73.1
11.	Orissa	73.6	85.5	80.8	63.9
12.	Kerala	90.8	100.5	99.7	84.1
13.	Punjab	125.2	168.6	173.8	162.9
14.	Haryana	117.3	147.2	138.0	144.7
	All India	100	100	100	100

Prepared from Table 7.1.

By mid-1980s, a group of six states, having their per capita SDP above the national average has been stabilised. These states include Punjab, Haryana, Maharashtra, Gujarat, West Bengal and Karnataka almost in the same descending order of the rank of their per capita SDP. Similarly a group of five states, *i.e.* Rajasthan, Orissa, Madhya Pradesh, Uttar Pradesh and Bihar have stabilised for the bottom five positions. The order, with marginal changes continues, even through mid-1990s. By then the per capita SDP gap between that of top and bottom states, has widened to the extent of Rs. 11407 (at current prices).

Data presented in Table 7.3 reflects the spatial variations of incidence of poverty in terms of population living below poverty-line. The pattern of spatial variations of incidence of poverty, seem to be associated with pattern of sectoral development. Industrially well-developed states, except Tamil Nadu, have incidence of poverty below the national average. Besides, it is observed that the states whose economy was based upon either well-developed agriculture sector or agro-based industries and good amount of village and cottage industries or relatively well-developed agriculture along with predominant manufacturing sector, have the lowest percentage of population living below poverty-line. As is the case of states of Punjab, Haryana, Kerala and Gujarat. Some of the predominantly agrarian less industrialised and highly populated, large sized states like Orissa, Bihar, Madhya Pradesh., Uttar Pradesh have high levels of percentage of population living below poverty-line.

Table 7.3

Population Living Below Poverty Line

(Per cent)

No.	*State*	*1977-78*	*1983-84*	*1987-88*
1.	Maharashtra	50.6	34.9	29.2
2.	Gujarat	38.9	24.3	18.4
3.	Tamil Nadu	52.8	39.6	32.8
4.	West Bengal	52.2	39.2	27.6
5.	Uttar Pradesh	49.7	45.3	35.1
6.	Andhra Pradesh	43.6	36.4	31.7
7.	Madhya Pradesh	50.6	46.2	36.7
8.	Karnataka	50.8	35.0	32.1
9.	Bihar	56.3	49.5	40.8
10.	Rajasthan	33.6	34.3	24.4
11.	Orissa	65.1	42.8	44.7
12.	Kerala	48.4	26.8	17.0
13.	Punjab	16.4	13.8	7.2
14.	Haryana	25.2	15.6	11.6
	All India	48.3	37.4	29.9

Source: Compiled from 'Basic Statistics (States), Vol. II, September 1989 and 1992; CMIE, Bombay'.

The Indian scenario of experience of regional development can be summarised as follow. There exists wide variations in the per capita SDP, among the Indian states. These disparities have accentuated over the period of time. The per capita SDP, urbanisation and growth of manufacturing sectors are highly associated with each other. The states with high per capita SDP, have high level of urbanisation and also high proportion of manufacturing sector.

Besides, the impact of sectoral growth is more prominent than the impact of policy intervention as indicated by the growth of different sectors at the state level and their impact on the regional development process. Moreover, the visible expansion and growth of industrial locations have taken place near metros or large cities and along several national transport routes, joining large cities.

When we combine global and Indian experience of regional development following lessons could be drawn.

1. The disparities of development are almost existing in all countries irrespective of their development status. And experiences of intervention are quite mixed ones. Hence, planners have to be cautious while intervening. Automatic convergence may take a long time. Hence, 'where', 'when' and 'how' to intervene must be carefully planned out.
2. Excessive reliance on industrialisation to reduce spatial disparities of development is an inefficient strategy. As seen from the experience, industrial development is fostered speedily in proximity of metros and along the transport corridors, hence backward regions falling within such space should get priority of incentive packages.
3. For other backward regions, emphasis should be on assessing their sectoral advantage. Such sectoral advantages should be identified first and then they should be subject to promotional measures. This would lessen the excessive reliance on industrialisation as a measure to bring about spatial equity of development.

References

Berry, B.J.L. (1961), "City Size Distribution and Development", *Economic Development and Cultural Change*, 9, 973-87.

Browning, H.L. (1972), "*Primacy Variation in Latin America*", Ref. in Gilbert and Gugler, 1987, p. 118.

Cross, M. (1979), *Urbanisation and Urban Growth in Caribbean*, Cambridge University Press.

Drewett, R. and Ross, A. (1981), "General Urbanisation Trends in Western Europe" in Klassen L.H. *et al., Dynamics of Urban Development*, Farnborough, Grower, 1981.

El-Shakhs, S. (1972), "City Systems, Primacy and Development", *Journal of Developing Areas*, 7, 1972, 11-36.

Friedmann, J. and Douglass, M. (1978), "Agropolitan Development: Towards a New Strategy for Regional Planning in Asia" in Lo Fu-Chen and Salih K. (eds.), *Growth Pole Strategy and Regional Development Policy*, Pergamon, Oxford.

Gilbert, A. (1974), "Industrial Location Theory: Its Relevance to an Industrialising Nation" in Hoyle, B.S. (ed.), *Spatial Aspects of Development*, 271-90.

Gilbert, A. and Gugler, J. (1987), *Cities, Poverty and Development: Urbanisation in the Third World*, ELBS, London.

Gish, O. (1971), *Doctors Migration and Health*, Bell.

Gugler, G. and Flanagan, W.G. (1978), *Urbanisation and Social Change in West Africa*, Cambridge University Press.

Kuznets, S. (1966), *Modern Economic Growth: Rate, Structure and Spread*, Yale University Press.

Mehta, S.K. (1964), "Some Demographic and Economic Correlates of Primate Cities: A Case for Revaluation", *Demography*, 1, 1964, 136-47.

Mills, E.S. and Becker, C.M. (1986), *Studies in Indian Urban Development*, Oxford University Press.

Moore, R.M. (1975), "The Development of Urban System in the America in 19th Century", *Journal of Inter American Studies and World Affairs*, 17, 1975, 4-26.

Renaud, B.M. (1979), *National Urbanisation Policies in Developing Countries*, World Bank Staff Working Paper No. 347, Oxford University Press.

Richardson, H.W. (1973), *Regional Growth Theory*, Macmillan, London.

—— 1981, "National Urban Development Strategies in Developing Countries", *Urban Studies*, 18, 1981, 267-83.

Robinson, E.A.G. (ed.) (1969), *Backward Areas in Developed Countries*, Macmillan, London.

Sharpston, M.J. (1972), "Uneven Geographical Distribution of Medical Code: A Ghananian Study", *Journal of Development Studies*, 9, 205-22.

Unikel, L. (1976), "El desarrollo urbano de Mexico: diagostico e implicaiones futuras; El colegio de Mexico", ref. in Gilbert, A. and Gugler, J., 1987, p. 28.

UNCRD (1976), *Growth Pole Strategy and Regional Development in Asia*, UNCRD, Nagoya, Japan.

UNECLA (1971), *Income Distribution in Latin America*, UN Economic Commission for Latin America, New York.

Williamson, J.G. (1965), "Regional Inequality and the Process of National Development: A Description of Patterns", *Economic Development and Cultural Change*, 13, 1965, 3-43.

World Bank (1987, 1992, 1993), *World Development Report*, Oxford University Press, New York.

8

An Inter-Temporal Analysis of Inter-State Income Disparities

—Ashutosh Sinha

Introduction

Regional disparities in terms of growth and development form one of the basic structural characteristics of the Indian economy. This is indicative of the fact that some regions of the economy have registered a high rate of growth over time and have been successful in attaining a higher level of development as compared to other regions which have experienced low rate of growth over time and have consequently, not been able to reach higher developmental levels. This uneven development pattern of the Indian economy may be attributed to a host of factors *viz.*, nonuniform spatial distribution of resources, market imperfections, unequal level of development of productive forces and coexistence of favourable, less favourable and even unfavourable social conditions, in different regions of the economy.

Soon after India became independent, the gravity of the problem of regional imbalances in the economy was realised by planners and policy makers and attempts have since been made for the redressal of the problem. This has become reflected in the different Five Year Plans of the Planning Commission, which is responsible for the transfer of Plan resources to states and the Awards of the Finance Commissions which help in the transfer of Non-Plan resources to states. The policy of Balanced Regional Development (BRD) has thus been followed, right since the inception of planning for development in India. There have of course, been changes in the strategy for achieving the objective of BRD, like the first two Five Year Plans adopted an integrated approach while the later plans have opted for a differential strategy in the quest for BRD. However, a distinct shift from the policy of BRD came as a response to the process of liberalization of Indian economy. Liberalisation of Indian economy, which began in a small way during the Sixth Five Year Plan period (1980-85) and which received impetus during the Seventh Five Year Plan period (1985-90), has finally gained momentum in the last decade of the millennium. It would, therefore, be imperative to examine the trend of regional disparities in India in the changed scenario. The present paper makes an attempt to study the growth pattern of regional disparities in India, based on per capita net state domestic product and net state domestic product, both at current prices, of the 26 states of the union for the period 1984-85 to 1993-94. Although states of the Indian union do not always represent a national economic region, on practical considerations, such an exercise based on the statistics of the states seems reasonable.[1] The study has been divided into five sections including the introduction. The second section undertakes a brief survey of the relevant literature; the third section deals with the data and methodology of the work; the fourth section presents the interpretation of results; and the fifth and final section forms the concluding part of the work.

Review of Literature

Pandit's[2] study, on the eve of independence revealed the existence of disparities in distribution of industries, and also their perpetuation. Williamson's[3] study reports an increase in disparities in the decade of 1950s, while O.P. Mahajan's[4] study based on state income data reveals convergence for the same period. Nair's[5] study covering a period of three decades from 1950-51 traces a 'U' shaped curve of disparities over time. Ashok Mathur's[6] study for 1950s, 60s and 70s reports a similar temporal behaviour of disparities which initially decline, only to rise later. Dev,[7] Bhalla and Tyagi[8] also report divergence in India in their respective studies. Some recent contributions notably, those of Akkina,[9] Sahay and Cashin,[10] Nagaraj *et al.*[11] have claimed evidence of convergence in India. While Sahay and Cashin, report absolute convergence, the other two studies indicate conditional convergence.

Data and Methodology

For the study of the present type lack of adequate and uniform data is always a problem. To study regional imbalances, the data for the per capita net state domestic product and net state domestic product, both at current prices, have been collected from various issues of the Economic Survey of the government of India. The data have been collected for the 26 states, for the period 1984-85 to 1993-94.

Sen[12] and Atkinson[13] have emphasized the importance of using more than one inequality measure for arriving at a reliable estimate of inequality. Keeping this in mind as many as four measures of inequality *viz.*, Coefficient of Variation, Standard Deviation of Logarithms, Theils Index and Hirschmans Index have been chosen for analysis. For the period under study, values of all the inequality measures have been computed for each year. Apart from Theils Inequality Index and Hirschmans Index which are based on net state domestic product and measure total inequality, the remaining inequality measures are based on the per capita net state domestic product.

Further, regression analysis has been undertaken through ordinary least squares (OLS) procedure and log-lin model has been used for the purpose. The various inequality measures have been regressed on time postulating the following relationship:

$$\ln_e I_t = b_1 + b_2 t + U_t$$

Where, I = Inequality Measure (Index),

t = time,

U_t = stochastic error term,

and b_1 and b_2 are regression coefficients.

Moreover, with the aid of the above model, instantaneous (at a point in time), as well as compound (over a period of time) rates of growth have been computed for each inequality measure. This may help in evaluating relative changes as far as inter-state disparities are concerned.

Finally the unit root test of stationarity[14] has been done for all the inequality measures.

Table 8.1
Indices of Inter-State Income Disparities in India (1984-85 to 1993-94)

Years	*Coefficient of Variation* *	*Standard Deviation of Logarithms* *	*Theils Index* **	*Hirschmans Index* **
1984-85	34.78	0.308	0.506	0.1971
1985-86	36.15	0.314	0.507	0.1981
1986-87	35.43	0.315	0.504	0.1970
1987-88	36.63	0.323	0.511	0.1997
1988-89	36.14	0.314	0.510	0.1984
1989-90	37.47	0.328	0.516	0.2011
1990-91	36.66	0.332	0.525	0.2034
1991-92	39.55	0.354	0.514	0.2002
1992-93	40.69	0.375	0.526	0.2048
1993-94	42.42	0.388	0.534	0.2071

Notes: * Based on per capita net state domestic product at current prices.

** Based on net state domestic product at current prices.

Source: Values computed on the basis of the data available in the various issues of the Economic Survey, government of India.

Interpretation of Results

As stated in the previous section, the values of the different inequality measures for the period 1984-85 to 1993-94 have been computed and presented in Table 8.1. A glance at the table reflects the increasing trend in the level of disparities, irrespective of the inequality measure considered. However, the increasing trend is not altogether smooth and some years offer decline in disparity.

Table 8.2
Regression of Inequality Measures on Time
(1984-85 to 1993-94)

Model: $In_e\ I_t = b_1\ bt_2 + U_t$

Inequality Measures	*Constant*	*Regression Coefficient*	*0 R^2*	*F Ratio*	*D.W. Stat.*	*D.F. Stat.*
Coefficient of Variation	3.518	0.019 (6.309*)	0.83	39.80*	1.43	0.33
Standard Deviation of Logarithms	–1.232	0.025 (6.634*)	0.85	44.01*	0.72	–9.46*
Theils Index	–0.694	0.006 (5.605*)	0.80	31.41*	2.31	–0.38
Hirschmans Index	–1.634	0.005 (5.706*)	0.80	32.56*	2.39	–0.47

Notes: Figures in parantheses are '*t*' values;
* Significant at 1% level;
** D.F. Statistic has been computed using the model:
$\Delta I_t = a_1 + a_2 I_{t-1} + U_t$[15]

For a clearer picture, the regression has been run, as per the specifications discussed in the previous section and results have been summarized in Table 8.2. The values of the Coefficient of Determination (R^2) are high for all the inequality measures, ranging from 0.80 to 0.85, revealing high explanatory power of the independent variable. For all the inequality measures, the regression coefficient (b_2) holds positive values and the '*t*' values are significant at 1 per cent level. All the '*F*' Values are significant at 1 per cent level. This all is indicative of the fact that over time income disparities across the states are on the rise.

Table 8.3
Growth Pattern in Inequality Measures
(1984-85 to 1993-94)

Inequality Measures	*Instantaneous Rates of Growth*	*Compound Rates of Growth*
Coefficient of Variation	1.94%	1.96%
Standard Deviation of Logarithms	2.45%	2.48%
Theils Index	0.57%	0.57%
Hirschman's Index	0.50%	0.50%

Note: Both the growth rates, instantaneous as well as compound have been derived from the regression results of Table 4.2.

Moreover, with the aid of regression results presented in Table 8.2, the instantaneous and compound rates of growth for all the inequality measures have been computed and presented in Table 8.3. All the values observed in the table are positive which clearly establish that there is growth in inter-state disparities over time. The values of growth rates, both instantaneous and compound for Coefficient of Variation, Standard Deviation of Logarithms are relatively high, in comparison to Theils Index and Hirschmans Index, which may be attributed to the fact that the latter are based on net state values while the former are based on per capita net state values.

The Durbin-Watson (D-W) Statistic holds satisfactory values for Coefficient of Variation, Theils Index and Hirschmans Index. The Dickey-Fuller (D-F) Statistic computed for unit root test of stationarity holds satisfactory values for Standard Deviation of Logarithms only, which indicates that long-run tendency of divergence cannot be forecasted with certainty from the data.

Concluding Observations

The above analysis based on different inequality measures clearly establishes that inter-state income disparities in India are rising during the period of study. This finding bears significance as for the last fifteen years, there has been a perceptible change in governmental policy towards liberalization and issue of balanced regional development has taken a backseat. Schemes like Freight Equalisation[15], which were specially designed for taking care of the problem of regional disparities have been withdrawn from core sectors. Same has happened to other subsidies to industries in the backward regions. Most importantly the Seventh Five Year Plan has made only a passing reference to balanced regional development and the Eighth Plan has virtually ignored it. Keeping in view the findings of the study it would be appropriate to suggest that efforts need to be strengthened for balanced regional development and in the present era of liberalization it calls for formulation of policy to ensure efficiency along with reduction of regional imbalances in India.

Notes and References

1. Singh, A.K., "Inter-State Differences in Levels and Rates of Growth of Income in India: 1951-81" in Mishra, G.P. (ed): *Regional Structure of Development and Growth in India*, Vol. I, Ashish Publishing House, New Delhi.
2. Pandit, S.A., *Regional Distribution of Industries in India*, Bombay, 1949.
3. Williamson, J.G., "Regional Inequality and the Process of National Development: A Description of Patterns", *Economic Development and Cultural Change*, Vol. XIII, No. 4, Part II, July, 1965.
4. Mahajan, O.P., *Economic Planning and Regional Development in India*, ESS, New Delhi, 1992.
5. Nair, K.R.G., *Regional Experience in a Developing Economy*, Wiley Eastern Ltd., New Delhi, 1982.
6. Mathur, Ashok, "*Regional Development and Income Disparities in India: A Sectoral Analysis*", April, 1983.
7. Dev, S.M., "Growth of Labour Productivity in Indian Agriculture: Regional Dimensions", *Economic and Political Weekly*, Vol. XXI, June 21-28, Bombay, 1996.

8. Bhalla, G.S. and Tyagi, D.S., "Spatial Disparities in Agricultural Development in India" in Nadkarni, M.V.; Seetharamu, A.S.; Azia, A. (ed): *India the Emerging Challenges*, Sage Publications, 1991.
9. Akkina, K.R., "Convergence and the Role of the Infrastructure and Power Shortages on Economic Growth Across States in India", Paper presented at the Midwest Economic Association Meetings. Chicago, March 1996.
10. Sahay, R. and Cashin, P., "Regional Economic Growth and Convergence in India", *Finance and Development*, March, 1996.
11. Nagaraj, R.; Varaudakis, A. and Veganazones, H.A., "Long Run Growth Trends and Convergence Across Indian States", Technical Paper Development Centre, 1997.
12. Sen, A.K., *On Economic Inequality*, Oxford University Press, New Delhi, 1974.
13. Atkinson, A.B., "On the Measurement of Inequality" in Atkinson, A.B. (ed): *Wealth, Income and Inequality*, Penguin, 1973.
14. For the unit root test of stationarity regression is run in the form: $\Delta I_t = a_1 + a_2 t - 1 + U_t$; (where Δ is the first order differencer, t the trend variable, I the inequality measure (index), a_1 and a_2 are parameters, U is the stochastic error term) and Dickey-Fuller (DF) Statistic has been computed.
15. Sinha, A., "*Freight Equalisation and Its Impacdt on Regional Development in India.*" Unpublished Ph.D. Thesis, Varanasi, 1992.

9

Inter-State Disparities in India's Social Sector

—*Ms Neena*

Sustainable development cannot take place without investment being made in people. It is now widely believed that improvement in the quality of people as productive agents must be a central objective of policies. The neo-classical concepts of human resource development, human capital and the theories of indigenous growth were first to highlight the relevance of social sector. The UNDP also stressed the process of enlarging people's choices (Prabhu, 1996). Development economists are concentrating more and more basic human needs and 'first things first,' rather than objectives of development. (Hicks and Streeten, 1979, Streeten, 1981).

Even the growth of physical capital formation depends considerably on human capital formation. The slow growth of the social sector can be a serious impediment to the growth of a region. For balanced development of an economy, the availability of social services to all is extremely essential. In case of India, there are wide disparities not only in the levels of state per capita incomes but also in the development of social infrastructure.

This paper aims at analysing the regional disparities in the social sector in India and attempts to examine the relationship between economic development and development of social sector in the states. Data have been mainly taken from various reports of CMIE. The paper has been divided into three sections. Section I deals with inter-state disparities in the level of economic development. In Section II, the disparities in demographic features, health facilities, literacy and educational facilities have been discussed. Section III, an attempt has been made to analyse the interaction and correlation between various indicators of human development. The relationship between economic development and development of the social sector has also been discussed.

SECTION I

In this section the disparities in the levels of economic development in terms of per capita income, structure of Net State Domestic Product and the levels of poverty have been discussed.

Per capita income is still a good overall indicator of a region's level of development. Differences in per capita Net State Domestic Product, and their growth rates do reflect disparities in the levels of development of different states (Table 9.1). Throughout the period 1980-81 to 1994-95, Punjab had the highest per capita income. Top four states in terms of this indicator are Punjab, Maharashtra, Haryana and Gujarat. These states continuously maintained their positions. Tamil Nadu, which had ninth rank in terms of per capita income in 1980-81 as well as 1990-91, improved to fifth position in 1994-95.

The growth rate of per capita Net State Domestic Product was very low during 1970-71 to 1980-81 for most of the states (less than 1 per cent) (Table 9.2), except for Punjab, Haryana, Maharashtra and Jammu & Kashmir. Rajasthan experienced negative growth during.this period (–1.9 per cent). During the decade of 1980-81 to 1990-91, all the states except Jammu & Kashmir experienced more than 2 per cent growth in their per capita NSDP. Highest growth was experienced by Rajasthan followed by Assam, Punjab, Haryana, Maharashtra, Bihar and Gujarat. Even the relatively poor states attained high growth

Table 9.1

Per Capita N.S.D.P. at Factor Cost (at Current Prices (Rs.)

States	*1980-81*	*Rank*	*1989-90*	*Rank*	*1990-91*	*Rank*	*1994-95*	*Rank*
Andhra Pradesh	1380	11	3973	7	4722	8	7155	8
Assam	1200	15	3179	13	3427	14	5999	11
Bihar	878	17	2122	17	2539	16	3816	17
Gujarat	1951	4	5404	4	6060	4	10578	4
Haryana	2370	3	6265	2	6936	3	12158	3
Himachal Pradesh	1698	5	4005	6	4813	5	7784	7
Jammu & Kashmir	1649	6	3453	9	NA	—	4244	16
Karnataka	1596	8	4075	5	4737	7	8082	6
Kerala	1494	10	3389	11	3843	11	6983	9
Maharashtra	2447	2	6184	3	7409	2	13112	2
Madhya Pradesh	1183	16	2878	16	3814	12	5845	12
Orissa	1231	13	3066	15	3180	15	5157	15
Punjab	2675	1	7081	1	8281	1	14188	1
Rajasthan	1222	14	3219	12	3983	10	5220	14
Tamil Nadu	1498	9	3894	8	4428	9	8941	5
Uttar Pradesh	1286	12	3072	14	3553	13	5331	13
West Bengal	1612	7	3923	10	4750	6	6877	10
All India	1625		4284		5015		9285	
Relatively rich states	2443		6361		7276		—	
Relatively poor states	1142		2638		3286		—	

Source: Basic Statistics Relating to Indian Economy, Centre for Monitoring Indian Economy (CMIE) Issues: September 1993, March 1997.

in comparison with near stagnation and even decline during the previous decade.

Table 9.2
Per Capita Net Domestic Product at Factor Cost (CARG %)

States	*1970-71 to 1980-81*	*1980-81 to 1990-91*
Andhra Pradesh	1.01	2.87
Assam	0.42	4.13
Bihar	0.93	3.08
Gujarat	0.97	2.96
Haryana	1.91	3.97
Himachal Pradesh	0.89	2.58
Jammu & Kashmir	1.55	0.08
Karnataka	0.70	2.56
Kerala	0.35	2.36
Maharashtra	2.16	3.79
Orissa	1.02	2.75
Punjab	2.60	3.42
Rajasthan	–1.94	4.50
Tamil Nadu	0.05	2.75
Uttar Pradesh	0.66	2.39
West Bengal	0.99	2.07
All India	0.96	3.26

Source: Basic Statistics Relating to Indian Economy, Vol. 2, CMIE, 1994.

The changes in the sectoral shares of agriculture, industry and services sectors in State Domestic Product overtime is a good indicator of structural changes brought by the process of development. At all India level the share of agriculture declined from 48 per cent in 1970-71 to 29 per cent in 1994-95, while that of industrial sector increased from 21 per cent to 28 per cent and services sector from 31 per cent to 48 per cent during the same period (Table 9.3). The structure of NSDPs shows that the share of agriculture declined in almost all the states, but even now agriculture accounts for a major share in most of the states. The only exceptions being Maharashtra, Tamil Nadu, Gujarat, West Bengal, Karnataka and Andhra Pradesh. These also happen to be the major industrially developed states. But even in these states, it is the services sector which accounts for

Table 9.3

Sectoral Shares in Net State Domestic Product of Various States *(Percentage)*

States	1970-1971			1980-81			1989-90			1994-95		
	Agriculture	Industry	Services	Agriculture	Industry	Services	Agriculture	Industry	Services	Agriculture	Industry	Services
AP	57	9	35	46	18	37	41	18	41	40	17	43
Assam	61	9	29	54	12	34	41	26	33	42	23	35
Bihar	58	10	32	54	17	28	44	23	32	48	24	28
Gujarat	48	16	36	38	29	32	26	35	39	29	34	37
Haryana	65	10	25	54	19	26	44	23	33	45	23	32
HP	51	6	37	50	19	31	40	22	38	36	22	42
J & K	56	5	38	51	14	35	47	14	39	47	16	37
Karnataka	54	15	30	43	26	31	34	29	37	39	22	39
Kerala	49	12	38	39	25	36	34	24	41	37	21	42
Maharashtra	28	26	45	28	35	37	23	36	41	21	35	44
Orissa	65	8	26	55	16	29	48	20	32	51	20	29
Punjab	58	8	34	49	19	32	45	22	33	47	20	33
Rajasthan	61	8	31	50	20	30	50	18	32	50	18	32
Tamil Nadu	39	19	41	25	34	40	17	33	49	21	34	45
UP	60	9	31	52	16	32	41	21	38	43	20	37
West Bengal	43	17	39	32	32	36	35	28	57	35	28	37
All India	48	21	31	38	26	36	31	29	40	29	28	43

Source: Basic Statistics Relating to Indian Economy, CMIE, 1994, 1997.

Table 9.4
State-wise Poverty Rate and Number of People Living Below Poverty Line *(Lakhs)*

States	*1983-84*	*Rank*	*1987-88*	*Rank*	*1993-94*	*Rank*
Andhra Pradesh	29.9 (169.5)	5	27.2 (167.8)	5	22.2 (154.0)	2
Assam	40.9 (83.7)	10	36.8 (85.4)	9	40.9 (96.4)	13
Bihar	62.5 (465.9)	16	53.4 (439.8)	16	55.0 (493)	17
Gujarat	33.3 (120.8)	6	32.3 (128.6)	7	24.2 (105.2)	3
Himachal Pradesh	16.4 (7.4)	2	15.5 (7.6)	2	28.4 (15.9)	8
Jammu & Kashmir	24.1 (15.4)	4	23.2 (16.4)	4	25.2 (20.9)	5
Karnataka	38.5 (152.6)	8	38.1 (162.3)	10	33.2 (156.4)	9
Kerala	40.8 (109.9)	9	32.1 (92.2)	6	25.4 (76.4)	6
Madhya Pradesh	50.1 (279.4)	13	43.4 (265.9)	12	42.5 (298.5)	15
Maharashtra	43.5 (291.8)	11	40.1 (294.2)	11	36.9 (305.2)	12
Orissa	65.3 (181.8)	17	55.6 (168)	17	48.6 (160.6)	16
Punjab	16.3 (29.1)	1	12.7 (24.6)	1	11.8 (25.1)	1
Rajasthan	35 (130.3)	7	34.6 (141.2)	8	27.4 (128.5)	7
Tamil Nadu	52.4 (266.4)	14	45.1 (243.2)	15	35.0 (202.1)	10
Uttar Pradesh	47.2 (557.5)	12	41.0 (537.0)	13	40.9 (604.5)	14
West Bengal	52.7 (317.1)	15	44.0 (276.7)	14	35.7 (254.6)	11

Source: CMIE, 1997, State Profiles.

major share in their State Domestic Products and not the industrial sector, throughout the period 1970-71 to 1994-95. Even in case of Punjab and Haryana which have high per capita incomes, Industrial Sector has the third position and accounts for only about 20 per cent of State Domestic Products. Thus all the states are in the transition phase and no state has been able to attain maturity in the process of development, as indicated by the structural changes.

Existence of poverty even in the richest states also indicates insufficient development. But the comparison among states shows positive correlation between underdevelopment and poverty. Punjab has the lowest proportion of people living below the poverty line (Table 9.4). The proportion of poor people has declined from 16.3 per cent in 1983 to 12.7 per cent in 1987-88 and 11.8 per cent in 1993-94. In the year 1993-94, the second position was held by Andhra Pradesh (22.2 per cent) followed by Gujarat (24.2 per cent) and Haryana (25.1 per cent). Highest poverty has been observed in Bihar (55 per cent), Orissa (48 per cent), Madhya Pradesh (42.5 per cent), Uttar Pradesh (40.9 per cent) and Assam (40.9 per cent). In this context two important trends have been observed. First, development has not been strong enough in any state to completely wipe out poverty. Secondly, though the proportion of people living below poverty line has declined but the absolute number of poor people has increased in most states, after 1987-88. In some states, even the proportion of poor people has increased. In case of Haryana, the proportion of poor people increased from 16.6 per cent in 1987-88 to 25 per cent in 1993-94. In Himachal Pradesh it increased from 15.5 per cent in 1987-88 to 28.4 per cent in 1993-94. In Bihar it has increased from 53.4 per cent in 1987-88 to 55 per cent in 1993-94. Economic reforms policies seem to be especially harsh towards poor people.

SECTION II

The demographic features of an economy are a strong reflection of the level of social and economic development. Cheneny and Syrquin (1975) identified the changes in demographic patterns as one of the stylized facts of development.

Total population of India has increased from 54.8 crores in 1971 to 84.4 crores in 1991 (*i.e.* by 53.95 per cent) (Table 9.5).

Among the major states the highest growth has been experienced by Rajasthan, 70.54 per cent (2.82 per cent annual growth rate), Haryana, 65 per cent (2.42 per cent per year), Madhya Pradesh, 58 per cent (2.28 per cent per year), Jammu & Kashmir, 58.7 per cent (2.51 per cent per year) and Uttar Pradesh, 57.53 per cent (2.27 per cent per year). Population of most of the states has been growing by more than 2 per cent. Only exception are Kerala (1.50 per cent), Tamil Nadu (1.62 per cent) and Orissa (1.88 per cent). Orissa which is the poorest state, also has very high death rate and infant mortality rate. High poverty is the reason of relatively slow growth of population of this state. The poor states of Bihar, Orissa, Madhya Pradesh, Uttar Pradesh and Assam have high death rates and birth rates.

Life expectancy is highest for the state of Kerala followed by Punjab, Haryana, Karnataka and Tamil Nadu. Whereas the poor states of Uttar Pradesh, Madhya Pradesh, Assam and Bihar have low life expectancy (Table 9.6).

Infant mortality rate is lowest in case of Kerala. It has declined from 47 per thousand live births in 1976-77 to 16 in 1991 (Table 9.7). In case of Punjab, it has declined from 105 in 1976-77 to 53 in 1991. Despite this, there is a big gap between top ranking and second state. Tamil Nadu and Maharashtra are the other states which have relatively low infant mortality. Madhya Pradesh and Orissa, on the other hand, have very high infant mortality rates (124 and 117 respectively in 1991).

Health and medical facilities and education are the most important constituents of social sector. There are wide disparities among states in public health expenditure, health facilities and literacy.

In 1990-91, the per capita health expenditure was highest for the state of Sikkim (Rs. 238.70) followed by Mizoram (Rs. 238.40) and Goa (Rs. 235.15) (Table 9.8). At other states which had high per capita health expenditure include Nagaland (Rs. 159.58), Meghalaya (Rs. 143.6) and Himachal Pradesh (Rs. 144.79). Hilly states have low population density and hence have to spend more on health facilities. Punjab which is the richest state spent only Rs. 98.47 per capita on health and Haryana was still lower (Rs. 59.67). In Kerala it was Rs. 79.47. In case of poorest states of UP, Bihar and Orissa, it was Rs. 39.58, Rs. 46.80 and Rs. 55.31 respectively.

Table 9.5
Population

(Lakhs)

States	*1971*	*1972*	*1973*	*1974*	*1975*	*1976*	*1977*	*1978*	*1979*	*1980*	*1981*	*1982*
AP	435	444	453	463	473	482	492	503	513	524	535	546
Assam	146	151	155	160	165	170	176	181	187	193	199	205
Bihar	564	576	589	602	615	628	642	655	670	684	699	714
Gujarat	267	274	280	287	294	302	309	317	325	333	341	349
Haryana	100	103	105	108	111	114	117	120	123	126	129	132
Karnataka	293	300	307	315	322	330	338	346	354	362	371	380
Kerala	213	217	221	225	229	233	237	242	246	250	255	259
MP	417	427	436	446	456	467	477	488	499	511	522	534
Maharashtra	504	515	527	538	550	562	575	588	601	614	628	642
Orissa	219	223	227	232	236	241	245	250	254	259	264	269
Punjab	136	139	142	145	148	151	154	158	164	164	168	172
Rajasthan	258	265	273	281	289	298	306	315	324	333	343	353
Tamil Nadu	412	419	425	432	439	446	454	461	469	476	484	492
UP	883	903	924	946	967	990	1013	1036	1060	1084	1109	1135
West Bengal	443	452	462	472	482	492	502	513	524	535	546	557
HP	35	36	36	37	38	39	40	40	41	42	43	44
J&K	46	47	49	50	51	53	54	55	57	58	60	62
Manipur	11	11	12	12	12	13	13	13	14	14	14	15
Meghalaya	10	10	11	11	11	12	12	12	12	13	13	14
Nagaland	5	5	5	6	6	6	6	7	7	7	8	8
Sikkim	2	2	2	2	2	2	3	3	3	3	3	3
Tripura	16	16	17	17	18	18	19	19	20	21	21	22
UT Delhi	41	43	45	46	48	50	53	55	57	59	62	65
All India	5482	5605	5730	5862	5994	6131	6269	6410	6545	6702	6852	7012

(Contd.)

States	1983	1984	1985	1986	1987	1988	1989	1990	1991	CAGR(%)	%age increase during 1970-91
AP	558	569	582	592	603	614	624	635	665	2.06	52.87
Assam	212	218	220	225	230	235	241	246	224	2.63	53.42
Bihar	730	746	767	783	800	817	835	853	864	2.19	53.19
Gujarat	358	367	372	379	386	393	399	406	413	2.25	54.68
Haryana	136	139	146	149	153	156	159	162	165	2.61	65.00
Karnataka	389	398	408	416	424	432	440	448	450	2.26	53.58
Kerala	264	269	275	280	285	289	294	298	291	1.50	36.62
MP	547	559	574	586	589	610	622	635	661	2.28	58.51
Maharashtra	656	671	689	701	713	724	735	746	746	2.15	48.02
Orissa	274	279	285	290	296	301	306	311	317	1.88	44.75
Punjab	175	179	183	186	189	192	194	197	197	2.02	44.85
Rajasthan	363	374	385	395	406	417	427	439	440	2.82	70.54
Tamil Nadu	500	508	520	529	537	544	552	559	559	1.62	35.68
UP	1161	1188	1214	1239	1265	1291	1319	1346	1391	2.27	57.53
West Bengal	569	581	595	606	618	629	641	652	681	2.08	53.73
HP	45	46	47	47	48	49	50	51	52	2.01	48.57
J&K	63	65	66	68	69	70	72	73	73	2.51	58.69
Manipur	15	16	12	16	17	17	17	18	18	2.39	63.64
Meghalaya	14	14	15	16	16	16	17	17	18	2.92	80.00
Nagaland	8	8	9	9	10	10	11	11	12	4.41	140.00
Sikkim	3	3	3	4	4	4	4	4	4	4.13	100.00
Tripura	22	23	23	23	24	25	25	26	28	2.67	75.00
All India	7129	7290	7463	7614	7776	7916	8068	8248	8357	2.19	53.95
Delhi	67	70	73	75	78	81	84	85	88	3.97	114.63

Source: Basic Statistics Relating to Indian Economy: CMIE, 1988, 1990, 1993.

Table 9.6
Expectation of Life

State/UT		*1971-81*	*1981-86*	*1986-91*	*1991-96*	*1996-2001*
1. Andhra Pradesh	Male	53.90	56.10	59.10	61.40	63.40
	Female	57.60	59.98	62.23	64.48	65.93
2. Assam	Male	49.19	52.74	55.74	58.74	61.14
	Female	48.29	51.98	55.23	58.48	61.18
3. Bihar	Male	53.71	55.21	58.21	60.81	62.81
	Female	50.71	52.90	57.00	60.09	62.78
4. Gujarat	Male	53.14	55.34	58.34	60.94	62.94
	Female	55.92	58.30	61.49	62.74	65.59
5. Haryana	Male	59.89	61.41	63.41	65.21	66.21
	Female	57.21	59.59	61.97	64.22	65.94
6. Karnataka	Male	57.88	60.15	62.15	64.15	65.55
	Female	59.11	61.06	63.31	65.30	66.55
7. Kerala	Male	64.19	65.23	66.23	67.23	68.23
	Female	68.95	69.87	71.12	72.37	73.62
8. Madhya Pradesh	Male	51.04	53.24	56.24	59.24	61.50
	Female	49.25	51.46	54.71	57.96	60.81
9. Maharashtra	Male	57.65	59.85	61.90	63.90	65.45
	Female	58.65	60.66	62.91	65.06	66.31
10. Orissa	Male	51.93	54.13	57.13	60.13	62.13
	Female	49.59	51.90	55.15	58.40	61.15
11. Punjab	Male	62.84	64.31	65.61	66.61	67.61
	Female	62.69	64.34	65.30	66.55	67.80
12. Rajasthan	Male	52.30	54.80	57.80	60.50	62.50
	Female	52.73	55.44	58.69	61.34	63.59
13. Tamil Nadu	Male	56.05	58.25	60.85	62.85	64.85
	Female	55.63	57.85	60.80	63.05	65.20
14. Uttar Pradesh	Male	48.86	51.14	54.14	57.14	60.09
	Female	44.60	46.89	59.64	52.84	56.09
15. West Bengal	Male	55.45	56.95	59.95	61.95	63.95
	Female	54.65	56.28	59.53	61.94	64.19

Source: CMIE: India's Social Sectors, February 1996.

Table 9.7
Infant Mortality Rate ('000 Live Births)

States	*1976-77*			*1980-81*			*1990-91*		
	Rural	*Urban*	*Combined*	*Rural*	*Urban*	*Combined*	*Rural*	*Urban*	*Combined*
Andhra Pradesh	136	62	125	90	38	83	77	56	73
Assam	116	95	115	112	91	111	83	42	81
Bihar	—	—	—	109	59	105	71	46	69
Gujarat	147	106	138	112	64	98	73	57	69
Haryana	123	53	113	92	58	85	73	49	68
Jammu & Kashmir	—	—	—	94	44	86	—	—	—
Karnataka	89	64	83	80	41	71	87	47	77
Kerala	49	37	47	32	30	32	17	16	16
Madhya Pradesh	157	88	148	131	78	112	125	74	117
Maharashtra	126	63	108	78	49	68	69	38	60
Orissa	151	85	147	135	77	130	129	71	124
Punjab	111	78	105	77	51	71	58	40	53
Rajasthan	150	92	142	114	72	108	84	50	79
Tamil Nadu	114	79	103	93	53	80	65	42	57
West Bengal	—	—	—	85	48	77	—	—	—
Uttar Pradesh	174	119	168	152	77	140	—	—	—
Himachal Pradesh	—	—	—	87	32	84	76	38	75

Source: Basic Statistics Relating to Indian Economy, CMIE, February 1988, February 1996.

Table 9.8
Per Capita Public Health Expenditure

(Rs.)

States	*1975-76*	*1980-81*	*1985-86*	*1990-91*	*CARG 1981-92*
Andhra Pradesh	11.71	23.43	51.58	53.71	–0.47
Assam	12.17	20.48	52.85	48.43	–0.16
Bihar	7.53	12.33	31.11	46.80	4.59
Goa	38.54	66.46	148.74	235.15	3.87
Gujarat	16.18	26.73	58.54	65.37	0.17
Haryana	18.52	32.93	69.42	59.67	–2.75
Himachal Pradesh	28.20	46.04	96.45	144.79	2.68
Jammu & Kashmir	37.19	51.30	108.25	123.22	–0.01
Karnataka	14.13	24.41	56.46	68.88	1.59
Kerala	14.72	25.06	50.61	79.97	2.83
Madhya Pradesh	10.98	18.96	42.72	48.94	0.70
Maharashtra	16.90	30.04	70.25	66.06	–0.87
Manipur	34.24	61.01	126.48	96.09	–4.08
Meghalaya	29.93	46.60	107.75	143.19	2.44

(Contd.)

Table 9.8 (Contd.)

(Rs.)

States	*1975-76*	*1980-81*	*1985-86*	*1990-91*	*CARG 1981-92*
Mizoram	78.04	116.55	226.65	238.40	–1.58
Nagaland	86.81	117.48	278.24	159.55	–5.48
Orissa	12.01	21.94	42.19	55.31	0.47
Punjab	18.61	34.12	68.89	98.47	1.81
Rajasthan	13.78	22.57	43.54	62.72	1.44
Sikkim	0.00	119.00	185.38	238.70	–1.77
Tamil Nadu	13.56	18.95	48.38	74.78	4.99
Tripura	22.82	40.19	91.28	103.19	0.65
Uttar Pradesh	9.51	16.16	35.69	39.58	0.19
West Bengal	11.05	19.38	40.32	61.56	2.78
All India	12.77	21.94	48.75	58.99	1.11
Relative rich states	17.43	31.18	69.88	70.81	–0.56
Relatively poor states	10.00	17.02	37.37	47.10	1.40
Cov.	82.71	75.14	70.36	61.38	

Source: Basic Statistics Relating to Indian Economy, CMIE, 1993.

Table 9.9
Number of Primary Health Centres

States	*April 80*	*No. of Health Centres per Lakh of Population*	*April 91*	*No. of Health Centres per Lakh of Population*
Andhra Pradesh	420	.80	1293	1.94
Assam	150	.78	479	2.14
Bihar	575	.84	2494	2.89
Gujarat	253	.77	911	2.21
Haryana	189	1.50	395	2.39
Karnataka	271	.75	1173	2.61
Kerala	167	.668	911	3.13
Madhya Pradesh	465	.91	1182	1.79
Maharashtra	441	.72	1650	2.21
Manipur	27	1.93	70	3.81
Meghalaya	22	1.69	81	4.50
Mizoram	16		38	
Nagaland	157	2.14	33	2.75
Orissa	314	1.21	1029	2.97
Punjab	129	.79	2048	10.40
Rajasthan	232	.70	1373	3.12
Sikkim	12	4.0	23	5.75
Tamil Nadu	383	.80	1429	2.56
Tripura	28	1.33	50	1.79
Uttar Pradesh	877	.81	3638	2.62
West Bengal	326	.61	1544	2.27
Delhi	8		8	
All India	5499		22441	
Relatively rich states	659		4093	
Relatively poor states	2463		9710	

Source: Basic Statistics Relating to Indian Economy, CMIE: September 1993.

The number of primary health centres in India increased from 5499 in 1980 to 22441 in 1991 (Table 9.9). In 1980, there was less than one health centre per lakh of population in most of the major states except Haryana and Orissa. That means each primary health centre served more than one lakh of population. Only in case of hilly states the number of health centres per lakh of population was relatively high. The number of health centres per lakh of population has increased in almost all the states in 1991. It was highest in case of Punjab, and was relatively low in case of Andhra Praesh, Madhya Pradesh and Uttar Pradesh.

Literacy rate has increased from 28.3 per cent at all India level in 1961 to 29.5 per cent in 1971 and 36 per cent in 1981 (Table 9.10). There was major improvement in the decade of 1981-91, when it increased to 52 per cent in 1991. Kerala tops the list with highest literacy of 84.8 per cent followed by Maharashtra, (64.9 per cent), Gujarat (61.3 per cent) and Punjab (58.5 per cent). Among the smaller states, Mizoram has the highest literacy rate followed by Himachal Pradesh (63.9 per cent), Nagaland (61.7 per cent), Tripura (60.4 per cent) and Manipur (59 per cent). States with low literacy rates are Bihar (36.5 per cent), Rajasthan (38.6 per cent), Uttar Pradesh (41.6 per cent) and Andhra Pradesh (44 per cent). Punjab which has highest per capita income, ranked fourth among the major states. Among the North-Eastern and hilly states it is only Meghalaya which is lagging in terms of literacy (49 per cent in 1991).

The index of infrastructure, which is a composite measure based on various economic and social indicators is an important overall measure of the level of infrastructure development (CMIE, 1997). The indicators included in this index are, per capita electricity consumption, villages electrified railway route length, surfaced roads, unsurfaced roads, handling roads, grass irrigated area as percentage of grass cropped area, bank branches per lakh of population, post offices per lakh of population, telephone lines per hundred persons, primary schools per lakh of population, hospital beds per lakh of population and primary health centres per lakh of population. At the all India level, this index increased from 10.3 per cent in 1980-81 to 134.4 in 1990-91 and further increased to 142 in 1993-94 (Table 9.11). The states in case of which index was higher than the national value, were Himachal Pradesh (183), Madhya

Table 9.10

Literacy: 1961, 1971, 1981, 1991
Literates as Percentage of Total Population

States	*1961*	*Rank*	*1971*	*Rank*	*1981*	*Rank*	*1991*	*Rank*
Andhra Pradesh	24.6	16	24.6	11	29.7	10	44.1	12
Assam	33.0	6	28.2	8	—	—	52.9	9
Bihar	21.8	12	19.9	14	26.0	13	38.5	15
Gujarat	36.2	3	35.8	4	43.8	4	61.3	3
Haryana	24.1	11	26.9	9	35.8	8	55.9	7
Karnataka	29.8	8	31.5	7	38.4	7	56.0	6
Kerala	55.1	1	60.4	1	69.2	1	89.8	1
Madhya Pradesh	20.5	14	22.1	12	27.8	11	44.2	11
Maharashtra	35.1	4	39.2	3	47.0	2	64.9	2
Orissa	25.2	9	26.2	10	34.1	9	49.1	10
Punjab	31.5	7	33.7	5	40.7	6	58.5	4
Rajasthan	18.1	15	19.1	15	24.1	14	38.6	14
Tamil Nadu	36.4	2	29.5	2	45.8	3	54.6	8
Uttar Pradesh	20.7	13	21.7	13	27.4	12	41.6	13
West Bengal	34.5	5	33.2	6	40.9	5	57.7	5

(Contd.)

Table 9.10 (Contd.)

States	*1961*	*Rank*	*1971*	*Rank*	*1981*	*Rank*	*1991*	*Rank*
Other States								
Himachal Pradesh	24.6	2	32.0	3c	41.9	3	63.9	2
Jammu & Kashmir	13.0	6	18.6	7	26.2	8	—	—
Manipur	36.0	1	32.9	2	41.5	5	59.9	5
Meghalaya	—	—	29.5	5	33.4	7	49.1	7
Nagaland	20.4	4	27.4	6	42.0	2	61.7	3
Sikkim	14.2	5	17.7	8	33.9	6	56.9	6
Tripura	24.3	3	31.0	4	41.8	4	60.4	4
Mizoram	—	—	53.8	1	59.5	1	82.3	1
Union Territories								
Delhi	62.0	1	55.6		61.1			
All India	28.3		29.5		36.0		52.0	
Cov.	38.91%		35.06%		28.76%		21.92%	

Source: Basic Statistics Kelating to Indian Economy, CMIE, September 1988, 1993.

Table 9.11

Index of Growth in Infrastructure: 1980-81 to 1993-94

States	*1980-81*	*1981-82*	*1983-84*	*1984-85*	*1985-86*	*1986-87*	*1987-88*	*1988-89*	*1989-90*	*1990-91*	*1991-92*	*1992-93*	*1993-94*
AP	102.7	105.2	109.1	113.3	117.9	121.1	122.8	131.0	136.0	134.4	137.1	139.6	142.2
Assam	102.3	100.5	108.2	116.5	120.1	124.6	129.6	133.2	136.2	144.6	141.4	141.6	140.8
Bihar	105.7	109.7	108.6	113.2	113.7	119.5	124.4	127.7	130.4	126.8	158.4	167.2	163.0
Gujarat	102.9	106.9	110.5	116.0	115.9	116.9	120.0	122.3	126.2	137.9	140.1	144.4	145.6
Haryana	104.6	108.3	107.4	108.9	109.7	115.3	123.2	116.6	124.9	124.9	129.1	130.8	133.5
HP	105.4	107.2	113.9	118.2	122.3	128.0	136.6	150.0	180.1	169.1	174.6	179.3	183.0
J & K	103.4	103.6	107.8	111.3	113.6	122.7	131.7	129.6	131.1	127.7	120.6	135.3	138.4
Karnataka	105.2	108.6	112.7	119.7	121.1	127.8	129.6	142.2	143.4	146.4	149.2	151.3	155.9
Kerala	100.6	100.6	99.4	105.8	107.7	114.1	116.6	123.1	125.0	128.3	130.2	129.8	136.3
MP	104.5	102.4	118.4	124.4	127.5	136.2	139.3	147.4	152.5	155.2	162.4	175.0	181.0
Maharashtra	100.6	105.6	106.8	109.0	109.9	111.2	113.9	117.2	119.7	126.0	124.8	127.8	129.0
Orissa	110.4	111.6	110.4	118.6	122.8	129.1	136.2	144.3	150.8	152.3	158.1	176.4	178.3
Punjab	102.7	105.8	107.8	109.1	111.6	145.0	148.8	147.9	150.7	149.1	153.4	156.0	158.1
Rajasthan	102.1	107.2	109.5	116.4	118.1	125.5	131.0	141.1	150.7	148.1	157.8	158.7	164.4
Tamil Nadu	100.2	103.9	106.0	110.4	112.4	115.9	118.1	126.2	129.8	129.5	132.5	134.3	136.9
UP	105.7	110.1	112.5	118.2	120.7	127.3	132.2	135.0	141.1	141.1	143.5	148.1	149.3
West Bengal	101.9	104.1	106.4	110.1	106.6	115.2	116.8	120.5	123.2	120.3	119.9	128.5	129.5
All India	103.1	104.8	107.0	112.0	113.7	120.4	124.4	128.9	133.1	134.1	136.6	139.9	142.0

Source: "Profile of States", CMIE, March 1997.

Pradesh (181), Orissa (178.3), Bihar (163.0), Rajasthan (164.4), Punjab (158.5), Karnataka (155.9). The index was relatively lower in case of Maharashtra (129), West Bengal (129.5), Haryana (133.5), Kerala (136.3), Tamil Nadu (136.9), Jammu & Kashmir (138.4) and Assam (140.8). Inter-state variation has increased during 1980-81 to 1993-94 in this indicator. This index shows that in case of infrastructural facilities, which are primarily provided by government and public sector institutions, more attention is being given to the poor states. But the performance of poor and backward states shows that development cannot be attained merely through the provision of social and economic infrastructure. The removal of social and institutional barriers and the quality of governance play a very important role.

SECTION III

Thus there are high regional disparities in the levels of economic development in India, as indicated by per capita income, structure of state economies and poverty. There is no indication of disparities being narrowed down over time. Scenario in terms of poverty ratio is particularly disturbing. Poverty seems to have increased after mid-eighties. Very high population growth particularly in poor states and economic reforms seem to be the two main factors. The earlier declining trend was reversed, in absolute or relative terms, after 1987-88, in case of Assam, Bihar, Himachal Pradesh, Jammu & Kashmir, Madhya Pradesh, Uttar Pradesh and Haryana. The high inflation of eighties also adversely affected the poorest sections of the society.

Highest poverty has been found in case of Bihar, Orissa, Madhya Pradesh, Uttar Pradesh and Assam. These are the states which are having very high growth rates of population. Thus there must be structural and institutional barriers operating in these states which are responsible for the vicious circle of poverty. Though government has taken significant steps in providing socio-economic infrastructure, as indicated by the growth of infrastructure index. but their impact on these relatively poor states is yet to be seen.

States with high literacy rates had relatively low population growth rates, particularly during the decade of 1981-1991. These states are Kerala, Tamil Nadu and Punjab. Literacy and per capita income are the important factors influencing, infant mortality and life expectancy. Kerala is the only state which ranks low in terms of per capita income but tops in terms of literacy, life expectancy, very low infant mortality, and lowest population growth rates. Punjab, Maharashtra and Tamil Nadu, which are relatively rich states also have high life expectancy, low infant mortality. Population growth rates are also declining in case of Tamil Nadu and Punjab, Haryana and Karnataka, which also have relatively high per capita income, and high life expectancy but do not fare well in terms of other indicators like infant mortality and are middle ranking in terms of literacy.

Per capita health expenditure and number of health centres per lakh of population have increased in all the states and are higher in case of economically better-off states. But there seems to be no direct link between these indicators on one hand and infant mortality, life expectancy and population growth rates on the other hand.

The experience of various states shows that the links between social sector and economic development are not strong enough. There are two basic reasons for this. First, even the richest states of Punjab, Haryana and Maharashtra cannot be classified as economically developed states. They are also in the transition stage. Secondly, the social as well as economic development is not hindered only by the inadequacy of socio-economic infrastructure. Other factors which play a very important role are the quality of services, quality of governance, and the level of acceptance of these services among the masses.

Notes and References

1. Chenery, H.B. and Syrquin, M. (1975), *Patterns of Development, 1950-70*, Oxford University Press, London.
2. Hicks, N. and Streeten, P. (1979), "The Indicators of Development: The Search for a Basic Needs Yardstick", *World Development*, Vol. 7.
3. Prabhu, K.S. (1996), "*Social Sectors in Economic Development: Some Issues*", paper presented at 79th Annual Conference, Indian Economic Association.
4. Streeten, P. (1981), *First Things First*, Oxford University Press.
5. UNDP (1996), *Human Development Report*, Oxford University Press, New York.

10

Impact of Finance Commission Transfers on Inter-State Economic Disparities

—*Amitabh Shukla & S.K. Khare*

Introduction

The finances of the federal government and their inter-relationship is known as Federal Finance. There is no guarantee that if the federal government and the state governments follow the principle of public finance in their fiscal operations, known as the principles of federal finance indpendently, the principle will be followed in the combined sphere. The federal government may equalise the aggregate sacrifice of marginal unit of taxation to the aggregate benefit of marginal unit of expenditure and so also the state governments also follow the same principle with regard to taxation and expenditure but the equality of sacrifice and benefit for each unit of money for different governments is likely to be different—lower for rich states and higher for poor states. The same unit of taxation may result into higher sacrifice for the poor state and less sacrifice for the rich states. Similarly, the same unit of money expenditure result into higher benefit to the poor state and less benefit to the already rich state. Therefore, from the national viewpoint the richer states should be taxed more and resultant revenue should be spent on poor states. This function can be performed by the federal government alone such that the principle of public finance for the nation as a whole, is not violated.

The Indian federal government seeks to fulfil its function of the public finance by effecting transfers through three channels:

(*i*) Planning Commission,
(*ii*) Finance Commission, and
(*iii*) Central Ministries.

The present paper seeks to analyse the transfers through second channel only, *i.e.* the transfers recommended by the Finance Commission known as statutory transfers.

The basic objectives underlying the statutory transfers are:

(*i*) vertical equality,
(*ii*) horizontal equity, and
(*iii*) promotion of fiscal discipline and efficiency in the utilization of resources.

Out of these, the objective of horizontal equity or redressal of inter-state equity has always been the main objective kept in the mind by various Finance Commissions. Sir Otto Niemeyer's award in 1936 for the first time stated this objective very explicitly. Since then, without exception, all the Finance Commissions have reiterated that equalisation is the avowed objective of the federal transfers. However, critics have levelled serious charges against the Finance Commission with regard to the fulfilment of the objective of equity in practice.

Economists have made use of different statistical measures to examine the inter-state equity aspect of the Finance Commission. Below are discussed various such studies.

Brief Review of Earlier Studies

D.M. Najundappa, (1974)[1] in his study entitled, *Inter-Governmental Financial Relations in India,* holds the faulty criterion of 'population' and 'collection', used for the distribution of taxes, responsible for inequitable transfers. He has constructed an integrated index of general development based on variables such as agriculture and irrigation, power, transport and communication, storage, education and health, industrial structure and development, credit and banking and social change to be the basis of distribution of taxes. Each variable is to be assigned weightage as per the priority assigned in the national plan. As a safeguard against any lethargy in tax raising which this basis may introduce, it has been suggested that tax effort should be considered for determining grants.

P.K. Jha, (1978-79)[2] in his paper entitled *Federal Finance and the Backward States: The Case of Bihar,* goes on to comment that the transfers through the Finance Commission have been adverse to backward states in general and to Bihar in particular as the per capita transfers to Bihar have always (upto sixth F.C.) been less than the national per capita transfers. Also its percentage devolution under Fifth and Sixth Finance Commissions were less than its population.

G. Thimmaiah, (1985)[3] in his study entitled *Burning Issues in Centre-State Relations* in order to analyse the equity aspect of Finance Commission transfers has found rank correlation between average per capita transfers and each of the three indicators of backwardness—per capita SDP at constant prices, poverty and PQLI (Physical Quality of Life Index) for first eight Finance Commissions. Due to statistically insignificant coefficients he concluses that Finance Commission transfers have not favoured the backward states.

George, K.K. (1986)[4] in the paper entitled *Statutory Transfers and Inter-State Disparity* has found rank correlation coefficients between

(*i*) per capita SDP and per capita transfers,
(*ii*) per capita SDP and per capita tax transfers, and
(*iii*) per capita SDP and per capita excise duty.

The coefficients have been found to be positive for the first three Five Year Plans and the annual Plans. However, they, (coefficients) have been found to be negative for the period covered by the Sixth and the Seventh Finance Commission, implying that states with lower incomes were favoured by the Commission.

Bagchi, Amaresh, Sen, Tapas and V.B. Tulasidhar, (1987-88)[5] in their paper entitled *Issues Before the Ninth Finance Commission* have found rank correlation coefficient between

(*i*) per capita SDP (1973-76) and statutory transfers (1979-84) for 14 major states,
(*ii*) per capita SDP and total revenue,
(*iii*) per capita SDP and own tax revenue,
(*iv*) per capita SDP and tax revenue, and
(*v*) per capita SDP and grants have been found.

Rank correlation coefficient between per capita state income and statutory transfer was found to be significantly negative. Rank correlation between SDP and total revenue was less than the rank correlation coefficient between SDP and own revenue, reflecting the equalising effect of federal transfers. The negative rank correlation coefficient between SDP and taxes has been found to be stronger in comparison to rank correlation between SDP and grants.

Amresh Bagchi, (1990)[6] in his paper entitled *Some Central Issues* has made use of coefficient of variation (C.V.) to compare equity aspect of Ninth Finance Commission with that of previous Commission. The C.V. under the Ninth Finance Commission of per capita devolutions is higher compared to C.V. under the Eighth Finance Commission implying that transfers have been more equitable under the Ninth than under the Eighth Finance Commission.

Objectives of the Presdent Study: To examine the impact of resource transfers on inter-state disparity for a decadal period between the years 1980-81 and 1990-91, a period which is not too for removed in the past. The specific objectives of the study are as follows:

(*i*) To find out the financial transfers from the centre to the Indian states and to study inter-state variation in transfers.
(*ii*) To express transfers to states as percentage of their expenditure and to find the impact of such transfers on states per capita S.D.P.

The findings of the study will reflect the impact of statutory transfers on inter-state disparity for a relatively current period.

Methodology

In order to study the inter-state disparity, following statistical measures have been used:

(*i*) Rank Correlation Coefficient (RHO) has been found between percentage of central transfers in total expenditure of states and their per capita S.D.P.

(*ii*) Coefficient of variation (C.V.) of state expenditurg financed by Finance Commission transfers.

The coefficient of correlation and the coefficient of variation each has been found for 1980-81 and 1990-91 to examine how, over the last decade, the Finance Commission transfers have been able to fulfil its objective of reducing inter-state disparity.

Findings

(i) For the Year 1980-81

Percentage of central transfers in total expenditure to low income states*, except Rajasthan, is more than percentage transfers to all the states. Percentage of central transfers in total expenditure to high income states** is less than the percentage transfers to all states. This proves that low income states have benefited more than the high income states by the Finance Commission transfers. Examining the ranks of percentage of central transfers, in total expenditure of state it is found that low income states have got higher ranks and high income states have got low ranks.

Rank correlation coefficient between percentage of central transfers in total expenditure and per capita SDP*** Average of per capita SDP of 6 years period from 1989 to 1995 is negative implying that Finance Commission transfers have favoured low income states but the strength or coefficient (0.4820) is not strong.

---

* Bihar, Madhya Pradesh, Rajasthan and Uttar Pradesh.

** Gujarat, Maharashtra, Punjab and West Bengal.

*** Average of per capita SDP of 5 years period from 1984 to 89.

(ii) For the Year 1990-91

Percentage of central transfers in total expenditure of low income states is more than the percentage transfers to all states. Percentage of Central transfers in total expenditures to rich states is less than the percentage transfers to all states. This proves that low income states have benefited more than the high income states by the Finance Commission transfers.

Examining the states ranks of percentage of central transfers in total expenditure, it is difficult to discern a clear cut trend because a low income state like Madhya Pradesh is ranked 16th and a high income state like Maharashtra has got 12th rank.

Rank correlation coefficient between percentage of central transfers in total expenditure of states and per capita SDP* is negative implying that Finance Commission transfers have favoured low income states but the strength of coefficient (0.5454) is moderate. However, the strength in 1990-91 is more than in 1980-81. This goes to prove that transfers are marginally more equalising in 1990-91 than in 1980-81.

Coefficient of variation (C.V.) of State expenditure financed by Finance Commission transfers is 38.19 percentage in 1980-81 and the coefficient of variation of state expenditure in 1990-91 is 62.44 percentage. This implies that the percentage of central transfers in total expenditure of states is more widely dispersed in 1990-91 than in 1980-81. However, the dispersion is favourable to the low income states.

---

* Average of per capita SDP of 6 years period from 1989 to 1995.

Table 10.1

State-wise Expenditure, Central Transfers, Percentage of Central Transfers in Their Expenditure and Ranks of Percentage of Central Transfers in State Expenditure for the Year 1980-81

States		*Total Expenditure in Lakhs of Rupees*	*Share in Central Taxes in Lakhs of Rupees*	*Statutory Grants in Lakhs of Rupees*	*Central Transfers Effected Under Finance Commission in Lakhs of Rupees*	*Percentage of Central Transfers in Total Expenditure*	*Ranks of Percentage of Central Transfers in Total Expenditure*
1.	Andhra Pradesh	116113	29575	—	29575	25.47	13
2.	Assam	35744	9832	—	9832	27.50	11
3.	Bihar	92853	42385	—	42385	45.64	3
4.	Gujarat	90326	18967	—	18967	20.99	19
5.	Haryana	40072	6123	—	6123	15.27	21
6.	Himachal Pradesh	18776	2170	4054	6224	33.14	8
7.	Jammu & Kashmir	27326	2897	4082	6979	25.53	12
8.	Karnataka	89490	19773	—	19773	22.09	18
9.	Kerala	66760	15141	—	15141	22.67	17
10.	Madhya Pradesh	101616	30288	—	30288	29.80	9

11.	Maharashtra	191704	33640	—	33640	17.54	20
12.	Manipur	7048	752	2800	3552	50.39	1
13.	Meghalaya	5992	719	1767	2486	41.55	5
14.	Nagaland	9155	350	4134	4484	48.97	2
15.	Orissa	54052	15998	3774	19772	36.57	7
16.	Punjab	54953	8221	—	8221	14.96	22
17.	Rajasthan	68753	17452	—	17452	25.38	14
18.	Sikkim	2982	28	670	698	23.40	16
19.	Tamil Nadu	115225	29176	—	29176	25.32	15
20.	Tripura	8721	1193	2575	3768	43.20	4
21.	Uttar Pradesh	171609	63222	—	63222	36.84	6
22.	West Bengal	111521	30989	—	30989	27.78	10
	Total	1480781	378891	23856	402747	27.19	

Source: Report on Currency and Finance, 1981-82, p. 117.

Table 10.2

State-wise Expenditure, Central Transfers, Percentage of Central Transfers in Their Expenditure and Ranks of Percentage of Central Transfers in State Expenditure for the Year 1990-91

S. No.	States	*Total Expenditure in Lakhs of Rupees*	*Share in Central Taxes in Lakhs of Rupees*	*Conditional Grants in Lakhs of Rupees*	*Centres Contribution in Calamity Relief in Lakhs*	*Central Transfers Through Finance Commission in (5) = (2)+(3)+(4)*	*%s of Central Transfers in Expenditure (6)=(5) as a % of (1)*	*Ranks of % Central Transfers in Expend.*
		(1)	(2)	(3)	(4)	(5)	(6)	(7)
1.	AP	550478	114709	4607	6450	125766	22.84	18
2.	Arunachal	25814	8208	5765	150	14123	54.71	3
3.	Assam	192040	48764	20561	2250	71575	37.27	10
4.	Bihar	488771	161585	18553	2625	182763	37.39	9
5.	Goa	27540	5329	3366	75	8770	31.84	13
6.	Gujarat	408192	28026	—	6375	34401	8.42	25
7.	Haryana	193307	18590	—	1275	19865	10.27	24
8.	HP	90147	18796	11375	1350	31521	34.96	12
9.	J & K	124905	32462	21099	900	54461	43.60	7

10.	Karnataka	397109	66035	—	2025	68060	17.13	21
11.	Kerala	282495	48626	5569	2325	56520	20.00	19
12.	MP	474611	108935	14145	15000	138080	29.09	16
13.	Maharashtra	875367	98986	—	3300	102286	11.68	12
14.	Manipur	30716	11200	7492	75	18767	61.09	11
15.	Meghalaya	31077	8036	5888	150	14074	45.28	6
16.	Mizoram	30483	9970	7475	75	17520	57.47	2
17.	Nagaland	42191	12378	9226	75	21679	51.38	5
18.	Orissa	219053	69409	14620	3625	87654	40.01	8
19.	Punjab	251991	24824	728	2100	27652	10.97	2
20.	Rajasthan	347994	75887	19532	9300	104719	30.09	14
21.	Sikkim	12815	2518	1759	225	4502	35.13	11
22.	Tamil Nadu	564129	100292	591	2925	103808	18.40	20
23.	Tripura	49703	15613	10119	225	25957	52.22	4
24.	UP	953836	230565	43674	6760	280999	29.45	15
25.	West Bengal	512811	104404	13482	3000	120886	23.57	17
	Total	7177575	1424147	239626	72635	1736408	24.19	•

Source: Report on Currency and Finance 1981-82, p. 117.

Notes and References

1. Nanjundappa, D.M. (1974), *Inter-Governmental Financial Relations in India,* Sterling Publishers Pvt. Ltd., New Delhi.
2. Jha, P.K. (1978-79), "Federal Finance and the Backward States: The Case of Bihar", *Indian Economic Journal,* Vol. 26, pp. 74-83.
3. Thimmaiah, G (1985), *Burning Issues in Centre-State Financial Relations,* Ashish Publishing House, New Delhi.
4. Sinha, R.K. (1986), *Centre-State Financial Relations in India: Various Aspects, Irritants, Framework for Action,* Deep and Deep Publications, New Delhi.
5. Bagchi, Amaresh; Sen, Tapas and Tulasidhar, V.B. (1987-88), "Issues Before the Ninth Finance Commission: A Background Note", National Institute of Public Finance and Policy Papers and Publication, Vol. 9, Pt II, paper I.
6. Bagchi, Amaresh (1990), "Ninth Finance Commission Award II. Some Central Issues", National Institute of Public Finance and Policy Papers and Publications of Staff Members, pp. 1263-1268.

11

Ecological Balance: A Prerequisite for Balanced Development

—*Shridhar Pandey*

Introduction

In the world there is nothing greater than man as the man is the epitome of God's Creation. But man is only a part of the nature. It is now widely and commonly held that the relationship of man with nature is such that nature can survive without man but man cannot survive without a supportive nature or "biosphere" as is now called. Therefore, by protecting nature man is still first and foremost protecting himself. But here in this view of relationship between man and nature the environment is endowed with no intrinsic value. Rather the action stems from the awareness that by destroying his surroundings man may be endangering his own existence or at the very least, depriving himself of the conditions for a good life on earth. Thus nature is taken only indirectly based on a position that may be called "humanist" or rather "anthropocentrist." Here nature is thus only human environment the periphery and not the centre.

Obviously this view of environment is narrow and hence unsatisfactory. A satisfactory concept of environment may be one which is suggestive of the basic principles of ecology, *viz*., maximum diversity and least interference. Tolerance or "live and let live" is the basic principle. If we consider the meaning of the word "eco" which came from "aeiko" that means "home or natural habitat", our principle would be more meaningful. Home is not just the people but the entire surrounding including all animate and inanimate objects. Ecology thus should be a "study of home or natural habitat" as a whole. It encompasses the structure and function of the natural environment as a whole.

Dangers to Eco-System and the Need for Ecological Balance

Rising economic activities based on modern technology pollute environment and environmental pollution poses a threat to the very existence of the homo sapiens. Modern industrial production disturbs and hinders the regenerating capacity of nature. It has been found that steel takes 95 years to decompose, ordinary plastic 220 years, aluminium 465 years while glass could take upto a million years to become bio-degradable, and for the manufacture of a tonne of paper, according to a study conducted by VATAVARAN, a non governmental organisation in India, we need to hack down 17 fully grown up trees, vastly devastative of biosphere.

The surest solution to the danger to our environment would be to ban the use of steel, plastic, aluminium, glass and paper. But since this is not a very practical one, it is necessary to find a possible compromise solution. The present style and form of development are highly detrimental to ecological balance and the very eco-system. Take the example of paper manufacturing in our own country. The forests are being devastated to manufacture paper products in India. The production level of paper in the country is 28 lakh tonnes at present (1997) which is expected to reach the 50 lakh tonne mark by 2000 A.D. To meet the current demand, an estimated 8.5 crore grown-up trees would have to be felled every year which is eroding the country's forest cover by approximately one per cent annually. If waste paper is reconverted into pulp and this pulp is used to substitute part of the total requirement of wood in the production of paper, just imagine the number of trees it will save! That is why ecological consciousness is now becoming a reality. The result has been the creation of a market for eco-friendly products. People are now increasingly realising the dangers of environment pollution. Many of us feel that if environmental pollution is not checked earnestly within a short span of some years there will be total disaster. This impending danger called for maintaining ecological balance. We have to learn to live with nature.

Ecological Consciousness in Ancient India

India had realised this fact from very ancient times. Karl Marx might have ridiculed Indians as worshippers of trees, snakes, monkeys, mouses and insects some one and a half century ago when the dangers of Industrial Revolution were not very clear insofar as environmental pollution is concerned. But it is now widely recognised that as in the case of computers, in maintaining ecological balance, too, Indians have been the fore-runners. The world is now accepting the truth that ecological consciousness in India has its roots deep into the ancient times. That is why trees and non-human beings all have been given an important place in human environment and nature has been elevated to the status of the mother in our country. What the West is realising today India had realised thousands of years ago. It is pertinent in this connection to quote here the observation of the Report of the Royal Industrial Commission (1916-18) under the chairmanship of Sir Henry Holland: "At a time when the West of Europe, the birth place of modern industrial system", was inhabited by uncivilized tribes, India was famous for the wealth of her rulers and for the high artistic skills of her craftsmen (p. 6). And all this in complete harmony with nature when the West was aware of the significance of ecological balance.

A New Awareness

Thus, contrary to the position in India, in the West, traditionally ecology has been of little relevance to those interested in human affairs. The position, however, has changed in recent years, till recently natural resources were considered a free good to be exploited and urge for unlimited growth prevailed. But today three fundamental ecological principles are being increasingly and widely recognised:

1. Human economic activity is a sub-system that operates within a larger but finite eco-system. Any disturbance to eco-system, whether depletion or pollution, would eventually damage the life support system.
2. With fast expansion of economic activity and human numbers causing use of increasing amounts of natural resources and producing ever increasing volumes of waste, the limits of eco-systems are being exceeded now.
3. Some development programmes cause long-term and even irreversible environmental changes. For instance deforestation results in soil erosion and prevention of forest regeneration.

As a result of this new awareness, ecologists are now being called upon to play a vital role in various development programmes aiming at economic development with sound environmental management. For there is a crucial and potentially positive link between environmental quality and economic growth. Humanity must learn to live within the limitations of the physical environment as both a provider of inputs and a sink for waste. We must face our responsibility to other species of the world and the need to protect bio-diversity.

The Challange Ahead

We must also find a way to enable all people now and in the future, to enjoy clean water, clean air and fertile soil. The world today faces a tremendous backlog in providing these basic amenities to the poor and the disadvantaged. One billion people, mostly in developing countries, do not have access to clean water, 1.7 billion people do not have access to sanitation and 2.3 million children die annually because of diseases associated with the lack of water and sanitation. To this situation we are adding about 90 million people to the global population every year mostly again in developing countries.

This raises huge challenges for policy makers as they seek

to reconcile the needs and aspirations of the growing population with the limitations of the natural world. Three particular challenges are most significant which call for our urgent and immediate attention:

1. *Production of food* which as agro-economists agree is likely to be a much more difficult task now. As the world's population expands from 6.5 billion now to 9 billion over the next 35 years, food consumption would double. But many of sources of earlier growth in agricultural production are no longer available. The challenge today and in later years will be not only to raise yields but to do so in a less damaging way than in the past. Already the environmental problems of intensification of agricultural production are serious in many areas such as chemical and biological run off, water logging, salinization, water pollution and the like.

2. *Urbanization and pollution* which go together. Ninety per cent of the world's increased population will be located in urban areas posing formidable problems of social and institutional changes, infrastructure investment and pollution control. Making clean waters available to everybody in the next 35 years will require extending services to 3.7 billion more urban residents and preventing pollution from worsening in some fast-growing countries will require that pollution per unit of industrial output fall by 90 per cent between now and 2030 A.D.

3. *Human encroachment* which is likely to be intensified with the increase in population and human activities. Pressure on fragile eco-system would surely increase. Already in the past decade 7-10 per cent of tropical forests and wet lands have been destroyed, important acquifers have been depleted and coastal zones have been polluted at a unprecedented rate. Without better policies the coming decades will witness even worse damages.

Thus without better environmental stewardship, development will be undermined and without accelerated development in poor countries, environmental policies will fail. Evidence is all around us. In sub-Saharan Africa, "Slash and burn" approaches to agriculture, in the face of rising population growth, are creating vicious circles of soil degradation and impaired productivity. In cities like Sao Paulo, Mexican City, Delhi, Bombay, Calcutta and Bankok the polluted air and water are posing a serious health threat. Industrial country emissions of "green house" gases, threatening a 2-4 centigrade rise in global temperatures over the next century, show little sign of abatement.

On the contrary over the next 35 years the world's population will grow by 3.7 billion 90 per cent of which will take place in developing countries largely in cities pushing population densities in many places to an extreme. World consumption of energy and manufactured goods will triple even under more efficient patterns of use. For developing countries, this increase will be fivefold. The Brundtland Commission Report contemplates a 5 to 10 fold increase in manufactured output by the middle of the next century. Similarly, the World Development Report 1992 of the World Bank envisages that Northern economies will grow by a factor of 3 and Sourthern economies by a factor of 5 by 2030 leading to a global economy that is 3.5 times larger than today's. Even with these differential growth rates, this scenario will greatly increase the already enormous danger to environment. If emissions per unit of output remains unchanged tens of millions of people will die prematurely each year as a result of pollutants, water shortage will become intolerable and tropical forests and other natural habitats will shrink dramatically. As both reports also acknowledge, if environmental destruction increases at the same rate as GDP the damage will be appalling. As far as the human species is concerned, it could prove terminal. Hence the call to make development environmentally "sustainable."

The Difficulties

The term "sustainable development" was brought into common use by Brundtland Commission (World Commission on Environment and Development) 1987. Calling for development that "meets the need of the present generation without compromising the needs of future generations" the Brundtland Commission Report highlighted the need to simultaneously address development and environmental imperatives. Since then substantial work has been undertaken in an effort to draw out the operational implications of the concept of sustainable development. But certainly we will fail in our efforts unless better progress is made to integrate the viewpoints of three disciplines:

1. That of the economists whose methods seek to maximise human welfare within the constraints of existing capital stock and technologies. Economists are currently relearning the significance of natural capital.
2. That of the sociologists who emphasise that the key actors are human beings whose pattern of social organization is crucial for devising viable solutions to achieving sustainable development.
3. That of the ecologists who stress preserving the integrity of ecological sub-system viewed as critical for the overall stability of the global eco-system. The unit of account are physical not monetary and the prevailing disciplines are biology, chemistry, geology and the natural sciences generally.

While economists, sociologists and ecologists would all agree that the other's concerns matter, they do not see these concerns through each other's eyes. An economist for instance may surely readily acknowledge the importance of social and environmental factors but would interpret these concerns through an economist's lens. Social concerns tend to be reduced to questions of inequality and poverty reduction and environmental concern to question of natural resource management. Many such very important concerns as social cohesion, cultural identity and eco-system integrity are all absent.

Economic analysis *vis-a-vis* environment has its sure limitation. True that convinced by the economic importance of bio-diversity, economists start treating it as a hard core economic commodity where one can maximise one's utility out of the natural bio resources within one's given pocket money. They, thus construct demand curve for natural bio-diversity on the basis of willingness to pay (WTP) or willingness to accept (WTA) criteria and supply curve on the basis of restoration cost of undisturbed state of ecological resilience. Their calculation is through the measuring rod of money and they always try to reach at the optimal number of plant and animal species. This objective of optimality even in case of biodiversity should not be questioned but the *modus operandi* of optimality derivation must be sound and logical. It is obvious that every human activity and corresponding economic welfare is at the cost of some species or the other. Therefore, the optimal number of life forms will not be liked by the conservation biologists who prefer conservation of every life form at any cost and do not allow themselves to fall prey to the economic logic. Here even if one presumes that economic analysis is essentially in an anthropocentric instrumentalist utilitarian approach and it is the human welfare which matters not the plants or animal species welfare the question still remains unanswered that how an economic agent at microlevel can put value for biological resources where even eminent biological experts can't say with certainty about the precise value of that resource, write Lallan Prasad and Rashmi Agrawal in *Economics of Environment and Natural Resource Management*.

As ecologists take on a larger role in economic decision-making they bring a system wide perspective a long-term view that underscores prevention and a package of ecological practices that reinforce sound socio-economic development.

The challenge for ecologists is how best to measure and predict what happens to the relevant natural system or eco-system when development takes place. As ecologists become increasingly drawn into development process they are helping to shape the new more environmentally aware development agenda. For them the strategy is threefold:

1. Encouraging the integration of ecological considerations into economic and sectoral development policies.
2. Devising anticipatory and preventive strategies for development projects.
3. Demonstrating that sound ecological policies also benefit development.

Ultimately ecologists will be effective in influencing policy only if they can demonstrate that sound ecological policies will promote, not hinder, sustainable economic development. This requires a partnership with economists both in estimating the economic cost of damaged eco-system and economic benefits of conserving such systems.

Even so the structure of government decision-making often works against the best policies being adopted. This is particularly true of such developing countries as India where governments are very prone to choose soft options and too eager to show quick results ignoring the long-term considerations. This explains why the environment departments in the country is unable to persuade, for instance, forestry department to develop forests on a sustainable basis or the agriculture department to regulate the use of chemical fertilizers and pesticides which are causing health hazards.

Environment and Development

However, the views about development and environment and about the relationship between the two have undergone significant changes in recent years. In the past, development policies tended to be viewed as those that promoted growth in human activities while environmental policies were seen as those that tried to restrict it. But of late the idea of "environment as constraint" has given way to an acceptance of "environment as partner". It is now increasingly realised that there is a very close and unvoidable link between environment and development so much so that without sound environmental policies, development will be undermined and without development environmental protection will fail. That is why development policy makers now increasingly recognise that failing to take cost of environmental damage into account will prove to be inefficient and often ineffectual in raising incomes and well-being. Similarly environmentalists realise that for many problems especially those in developing countries the answer lies in greater and faster not slower growth in incomes, alongwith sound environmental policies. Think that over one billion people live in acute poverty suffering grossly from inadequate access to the resources to give them a chance for a better life. Attacking this problem is not only a moral imperative, it is also essential for a sound environment.

It is true that rising economic activity can cause environmental problems. But it can also help address them. Three patterns are clearly noticable:

1. Some environmental problems decline as income increases. Once individuals no longer worry about day-to-day survival, they can devote resources to profitable investment in conservation.
2. Some such problems initially deteriorate but then improve as incomes rise. Most forms of air and water pollution fit into this category.

3. Some Problems keep growing as incomes increase. Carbon and nitrogen oxide emissions are current examples.

This explains why the environmental debate has shifted away from a concern over physical limits to growth towards a concern about incentives for human behaviour and policies to overcome market and policy failures.

Thus our understanding of the links between economic development and the natural environment has undergone a profound change in recent years. It is true that intense controversies were witnessed about the key propositions of a sustainable development laid out in the World Commission on Environment and Development (Brundtland Commission) Report, 1987 and in the Rio de Janeiro Earth Summits Agenda 21 in 1992 at the time. But now there is a broad acceptance of the propositions even among the mainstream economic policy makers. Some more important of such propositions are the following:

1. There is a crucial and potentially positive link between economic development and environment.
2. The costs of inappropriate economic policies on the environment are very high.
3. Addressing environmental problems requires that poverty be reduced.
4. Economic growth must be guided by prices which incorporate environmental values.
5. The governments must actively strive to ensure pollution-free environment and the people must be made conscious of the dangers of atmospheric pollution.
6. Since environmental problems pay no respect to boarders, global and regional collaboration is needed to complement national and regional actions.

Current Trends

Of late the social workers, the intellectuals and scientists and even political leaders all over the world have become conscious of the dangers to the earth's environment. In recent years many natural and social science disciplines have investigated and suggested remedial measures to check the hazards of environmental pollution.

Many institutions have been established to protect the earth from pollution such as Scientific Committee on Problems of the Environment (SCOPE) established in 1969 by the International Council of Scientific Unions (ICSU), Man and Biosphere (MAB) Programme started in 1971 by UNESCO; World Climate Research Programme (WCRP) launched in 1981 by the UN Environment Programme (UNEP) the World Meteorological Organisation (WMO) and ICSU etc.

In short, countries all over the world are now increasingly showing a willingness to act now to prevent atmospheric pollution and check the build-up of "green house" gases in the atmosphere which could trigger a significant warming of the Earths surface. June 1992 Earth Summit in Rio de Janeiro where more than 150 countries signed a treaty aimed at stabilising "green house" gases mainly carbon di-oxide (CO_2) which is by far the largest contributor to the "green house effect" is an evidence of such a willingness. Many countries such as Swedan, Finland and Netherlands have imposed carbon taxes, that is, taxes on the carbon content of fossil fuel.

Though most environmental problems continue to intensify and in many countries there are few grounds for optimism especially the developed and the OECD (Organization of Economic Co-operation and Development) countries, in a growing number of other countries awareness is leading to action as policy makers begin to bring their mind, money and political capital into line with their rhetoric. About 100 countries have now prepared national environmental strategies and tangible changes in addressing environmental issues are apparent in about half this number. Sixty-eight countries are currently receiving financial and technical support from the World Bank for environmental policy reforms and associated investments. Active World Bank loans for these purposes currently total more than $11 billion and, if co-financing and the countries' own financing are added in these investments, total more $ 25 billion.

A "new environmentalism" is emerging as policies are being adopted that differ from those traditionally implemented by industrial nations. Many developing countries also are beginning to weigh the various options because although industrial countries account for around 43 per cent of total CO_2 (Carbon dioxide) emissions from fossil fuel consumption, the developing world also is now fast contributing an increasing proportion. The "new environmentalism" characterised by greater rigour in factoring

World Bank Financing for the Environment

Year	Amount (billion US dollars)	No. of Projects financed
1986	0.1	01
1987	0.2	05
1988	0.8	10
1989	1.0	16
1990	2.0	33
1991	3.0	45
1992	4.2	70
1993	6.3	94
1994	9.1	119
1995	10.0	136
1996	11.0	153

Source: World Bank Environment Report Quoted in Finance and Development, December 1996.

environmental costs and benefits into policy-making puts local people at the centre of environmental stratagies, diagnoses and addresses behavioural causes of environmental damage and recognises the political dimensions of environmental reforms.

Concluding Observation

Protecting the "green" aspects during rapid growth, however, remains a tough challenge. Countries' institutional capacity to make, implement and enforce difficult decisions is a key consideration. Even the best solutions require the support of well functioning markets and property rights along with firm political will on the part of the government. Priorities have to be set, resource limits acknowledged and systematic processes put in place to help make tough choices. Current experiences and policies even if limited demonstrate that it is possible to protect the environment, promote growth and enhance competitiveness at the same time. Most developing countries, Bharat, *i.e.* India included, can benefit from both the positive and negative lessons of rapid growth elsewhere. If they can take economic and environmental actions now they could become the "green tigers" of the future.

The significance of the role of ecologists and environmental education here thus becomes apparent. Interactions between social and natural scientists and social reformers must be more frequent and close. Environmental education should be a life long process. It should aim not only at imparting knowledge and understanding of entire animate and inanimate surroundings but also at improving our near and distant surroundings, skills, attitudes, values necessary to understand, appreciate and improve our biosphere and troposphere. Better education is essential as it enables the adoption of more sustainable practices in agriculture, industry and household management and helps accelerate the transition from subsistance agriculture to intensive agriculture and off farm employment. Providing increased access to education has been found in Thailand to be the single most important policy for reducing pressure on forests.

Notes and References

1. Zuvekas, Clarence, *Economic Development*, Macmilllan, London.
2. Pandey, Shridhar, *Economic Development* (Hindi), Moti Lal Banarasi Das, Patna.
3. *The Statesman*, Calcutta, Dak Ed., May 10, 1997.
4. Commoner, Barry, "Environment—World Problem", *Span*, May 1971.
5. Dubos, Rene, "Is Man Over-adopting to the Environment?", *The American Review*, Autumn, 1972.
6. Strong, Maurice F., "Environment—An International View", *The American Review*, June, 1972.
7. *The Statesman*, Calcutta, Dak Ed., June 9, 1987.
8. *The Second Citizen's Report*, 1985, New Delhi.
9. *The Statesman*, Calcutta, Dak Ed., May 4, 1997.
10. *Finance and Development*, Dec. 1972 (Bjorn Larsen and Anwar Shah) "Combating the Greenhouse Effect".
11. *Finance and Development*, December, 1996.
12. *Finance and Development*, December, 1993.
13. Steer, Andrew, "The Environment for Development", *Finance and Development*, June, 1992.
14. UN Conference on Environment and Development (The Earth Summit) 1992.
15. Pandey, Shridhar, "Urbanization and Environment in India", *Nava Arthiki*, Autumn November, 1993.
16. *Nava Arthiki*, Vol. 5, No. 1 (Spring November, 1995) article by Shridhar Pandey.

12

A Study on Regional Disparities in Rates of Growth of Productivity and Instability in Indian Agriculture

—K. *Pochanna*

Food sector accounts for about 40 per cent of the national income in India and provides livelihood to over one-half of the total population. The food crops constitutes the major dietary intake of the people of the Indian economy. The increase in food grains production and yield are important means to accelerate the economic growth. In India, increase in food grains may be due to area expansion as well as vertical growth in terms in yields. Since, in India, 70 per cent of cultivated area still depends upon monsoon, hence, the performance of food grains economy is depends upon suitable weather and climatic conditions. Therefore, it is imperative to give attention to agricultural growth and stability which are extremely important in the process of economic development. There are several studies on Indian agriculture in relation to growth and instability at the regional level. Studies by Ashok Mitra (1967), Sen Gupta and Sandasyak (1968), Sharma (1973) and Yogender K. Alagh (1979) have dealt with regionalisation of agriculture in the Indian economy. Studies by Sen (1973), Ch. Hanumanth Rao (1973), Mehra (1981), Hazel (1982) and Ray (1983), Parthasarathy (1985), Mahendra Dev (1987) and C.H. Rao (1988) had also examined the links between growth and variability in productivity. Given the constraints of available data all the above studies have attempted either using the state or a district as a spatial unit of analysis.

Keeping these aspects in view, an attempt is made in this paper to study on Regional Disparities in rate of growth of productivity and instability using the state as a unit of analysis. The specific objectives of the study are:

1. to estimate the trend of food grains yield (growth rates) at national level and state level to determine area specific growth pattern;
2. to examine the inter-state variation in the performance of yield growth rate, and
3. to study the relationship between yield growth and instability at national level and across the states.

The paper is divided into five sections, the first section deals with importance and relevance of the disparities. The second section presents data and methodology of the study. The third section examines the performance of yield growth at national level and across the state by using state as a unit of analysis. The fourth section examines nexus between the growth and instability of food grains economy. The main conclusion and broad policy implications are presented in section five.

II. DATA AND METHODOLOGY

The study is based on the secondary source of data collected from CMIE (Centre for Monitoring Indian Economy Reports). The study is mainly confined to food grains crops. the study reckoned the period from 1970-71 to 1989-90.

Growth of food grains yields were estimated by using log $y = a + bt$ formula (where y = yields, t = time factor, a, b =

constants and coefficients). Fluctuations are measured by coefficient of variation around the trend line (CVTL) which is defined as below:

$$\text{CVRL} = \sqrt{\frac{\Sigma (y - \hat{y}1)^2/n-2}{\overline{Y}}}$$

where

$\Sigma (y - \hat{y}1)^2/$ = Sum of the squared residuals of the regression of V on t, *i.e.*, yield on time. Where y is the estimated value of the linear trend time $y = a + bt$

n = Number of observations and

$\overline{Y}$ = Mean of Y

To access the impact of bio-chemical technology on amplitude of fluctuation, the study period is divided into two sub-periods, *viz.*, 1971-80 as period I, 1981-90 as period II. Period I termed as a GRP (Green Revolution Period) and Period II termed as post-GRP. Regarding the choice of inclusion of the drought years, there are two views, Mehra and others (1981), Hazel (1982) and some other scholars in their studies excluded the two drought years, 1965-66, 1966-67, while studying the fluctuations over a period of time one has to consider both bad and good years. Jain's study (1986) showed contradictory results regarding the nexus between growth and fluctuation in Indian agriculture depending on whether the drought years are included or excluded. Even in the post new technology period also, there are abnormal years such as 1972-73 which showed more than 8 per cent decline in food grains production from its previous year (Sawant, 1983). It is clear from discussion that there is no adequate justification for dropping out the abnormal years. In the present study we did not exclude any abnormal year. Dummy variables were included to differentiate the period 1970-71 to 1979-80 with subsequent period (1980-81 to 1989-90).

Table 12.1
Growth Rates Trends in Food grains Yield: All India and the States

Sl. No.	States	Period I (1971-80)	Period II (1981-90)	Period III (1971-90)
1.	Andhra Pradesh	3.14*	2.8*	3.47*
		(4.15)	(3.331)	(12.59)
2.	Assam	–0.86**	0.53	0.68*
		(–1.65)	(0.99)	(3.04)
3.	Bihar	–3.85	3.7*	3.1**
		(–0.46)	(3.44)	(1.54)
4.	Gujarat	2.90	–2.7	1.0*
		(1.31)	(–0.86)	(1.02)
5.	Haryana	2.8*	1.83	3.44*
		(2.03)	(0.95)	(5.90)
6.	Himachal Pradesh	0.08	1.14	0.6**
		(.091)	(0.78)	(1.48)
7.	Jammu & Kashmir	1.31*	-0.72	1.07*
		(2.26)	(–0.53)	(2.83)
8.	Karnataka	2.29*	0.81	0.5**
		(2.61)	(0.81)	(1.43)
9.	Kerala	0.59**	1.05*	1.01*
		(1.55)	(5.39)	(9.37)
10.	Madhya Pradesh	–2.11**	2.59*	1.89**
		(–1.40)	(4.01)	(3.61)
11.	Maharashtra	8.62*	1.39	3.15*
		(4.44)	(0.83)	(4.04)
12.	Orissa	–1.5	2.4**	1.24*
		(–1.01)	(1.65)	(2.21)
13.	Punjab	3.18*	2.9*	3.35*
		(5.83)	(6.83)	(19.93)
14.	Rajasthan	0.03	2.2	1.5*
		(0.14)	(1.25)	(2.38)
15.	Tamil Nadu	1.01	3.6*	1.4*
		(0.64)	(3.07)	(3.60)
16.	Uttar Pradesh	1.84	3.7*	3.87*
		(1.15)	(6.43)	(8.80)
17.	West Bengal	0.72	7.81*	1.82**
		(0.83)	(2.03)	(1.63)
18.	India	1.59*	2.91*	2.49*
		(2.19)	(6.39)	(11.42)

Note: Figures in parentheses indicate *t*-values.
* significant at 5 per cent level.
** significant at 20 per cent level.

III. YIELD PERFORMANCE

This section examines state-wise yield performance of the food grain economy of India during the period 1970-71 to 1989-90. The estimated yield (trend) growth rates for food grains are given in Table 12.1. It is clear from the table that growth rate in food grains stood at 2.49 per cent per annum in India as a whole. However, yield performance is not uniformly spread across the states during the period 1970-71 to 1989-90. In terms of magnitude of yield growth rate, Andhra Pradesh, Haryana and Punjab states registered relatively higher growth as compared to other states during the study period. For the country as a whole the growth in yield overwhelming witnessed higher growth rate in Period II, as compared to Period I. The growth rate has increased from 1.59 per cent to 2.91 per cent from Period I to Period II.

Across the states yield performance in terms of magnitude of growth rates exhibits certain interesting observations. During the period I, Maharashtra (8.62 per cent), Punjab (3.18 per cent) and Andhra Pradesh (3.14 per cent) states showed significant trend growth rates. But in Period II the same states experienced deceleration trend growth rates. On the whole in Period II high significant growth rate is demonstrated by the states like West Bengal (7.8 per cent), Tamil Nadu (3.6 per cent) and Uttar Pradesh (3.7 per cent) respectively. During period I, the negative trend growth rate are appeared in states like Bihar (– 3.85 per cent), Madhya Pradesh (–2.11 per cent), Orissa (–1.5 per cent) and Assam (–0.86 per cent) respectively. It is interested to note that the same states have improved their yield performance in Period II and exhibited a positive significant trend growth rates.

To summarise, the India's food grain economy has shown a significant trend growth with higher side in Period II as compared to Period I. Most of the states also exhibited the same trend. However, the dummy variables for estimating shift in growth rate between Period I to Period II shown by and large insignificant. Inter-state-wise analysis reveals that certain states which have endowed favourable agricultural infrastructure facilities experienced a significant positive trend growth with higher side in Period I and Period II. Therefore, to minimise relative yield difference in across the states it is required the penetration of yield promoting inputs into various states.

Regarding in explanation of regional differences in terms of the yield and its determinants relationship in across the states and India as a whole exhibited no marked difference in level of response for yield growth. However, some of the states noticed that the irrigation and fertilizer have provided the leading impulses for yield growth. The estimated regression elasticities has not exhibited statistical significant in most of the states. Hence, the results are not presented in table form. The estimated dummy variable coefficients are not shown systematic evidence to support the hypothesis of differentiation in the relationship between the two periods (*i.e.*, 1971-80 and 1981-90).

Fluctuations in Food Grains

The fluctuation in production of the food grains may be caused by price and non-price factors. The price influence the decision relating to acreage and it also influence the yield, through the use of other inputs to the crops other than land. The non-price factors which contribute to fluctuation in productivity (yield rate) are rainfall and it time lines, climatic conditions, irrigation, use of biological chemical inputs and distribution of land holding, yield variability could also very much depend upon the pattern of investment by which growth is brought about. For instance, irrigation water from perennial sources and the use of pesticides may counteract the vagaries of weather. If increase in yield is brought about through investments in such inputs their growth may be associated with the decline in amplitude of fluctuation. Provision of irrigation water through tanks of rain-fed well may accentuate the fluctuation by increasing the dependence on weather.

Fluctuations are measured by coefficient of variation around the trend line (CVTL). The higher the CVTL the greater the instability and *vice versa*. The estimated CVTL are presented in Table 12.2. The Table clearly reveals that at national level the fluctuation in yield is high in Period I as compared to Period II. A comparison of yield variability across the states clearly exhibits that West Bengal, Jammu & Kashmir, Gujarat and Rajasthan have higher variability in yield as compared to other states during the period 1970-71 to 1989-90. The Table clearly witnessed that the yield instability or amplitude of fluctuation is observed high in most of the states in Period I (GRP) as compared to Period II (post-GRP).

Table 12.2
CVTL of Yield: All India and the States

Sl No.	*States*	*Period I (1971-80)*	*Period II (1981-90)*	*Period III (1971-90)*
1.	Andhra Pradesh	4.07	2.90	3.81
2.	Assam	1.46	1.57	2.72
3.	Bihar	9.57	3.09	10.35
4.	Gujarat	5.02	7.60	9.92
5.	Haryana	4.27	7.04	8.81
6.	Himachal Pradesh	2.74	4.75	5.62
7.	Jammu & Kashmir	1.89	4.30	15.02
8.	Karnataka	2.32	4.73	4.09
9.	Kerala	1.33	0.72	1.61
10.	Madhya Pradesh	3.10	1.65	4.67
11.	Maharashtra	3.00	3.90	6.28
12.	Orissa	3.70	3.94	6.10
13.	Punjab	2.24	2.07	3.29
14.	Rajasthan	4.41	4.13	6.17
15.	Tamil Nadu	3.18	4.13	5.26
16.	Uttar Pradesh	4.39	1.96	15.42
17.	West Bengal	2.75	12.72	2.83
18.	India	2.01	1.48	1.59

Note: CVTL = Coefficient of variation around trend line.

IV. GROWTH AND INSTABILITY

Various studies examined the relationship between growth and instability and most of studies reinforced the positive association between growth and instability. In the present paper link between growth and instability was attempted. In Table 12.3, the direction of growth and CVTL between two periods *i.e.* (1971-80, Period I (GRP), 1981-90 Period II, (post-GRP) were specified by positive (+) and negative (–) trends. Increase and decrease of growth or CVTL refer to positive and negative symbol, respectively. The growth and CVTL moves in the same direction denoted as positive association and growth and CVTL moves opposite direction denoted as negative association. At all India level growth has increased from 1.59 per cent to 2.91 per cent and instability declined from 2.01 to 1.48 between Period I and Period II. The direction between growth and CVTL exhibits a negative association. Among the states the positive association is observed in seven states and remaining states witness a negative association between growth and instability.

Table 12.3
Yield Growth Rates and CVTL Between Period I and Period II

Sl. No.	*States*	*Yield Growth Rate Period I & II*	*CVTL Between Period I & II*
1.	Andhra Pradesh	– ve	– ve
2.	Assam	– ve	+ ve
3.	Bihar	+ ve	– ve
4.	Gujarat	– ve	+ ve
5.	Haryana	+ ve	+ ve
6.	Himachal Pradesh	– ve	+ ve
7.	Jammu & Kashmir	– ve	+ ve
8.	Karnataka	– ve	+ ve
9.	Kerala	+ ve	– ve
10.	Madhya Pradesh	+ ve	+ ve
11.	Maharashtra	– ve	+ ve
12.	Orissa	+ ve	– ve
13.	Punjab	– ve	– ve
14.	Rajasthan	+ ve	– ve
15.	Tamil Nadu	+ ve	+ ve
16.	Uttar Pradesh	+ ve	– ve
17.	West Bengal	+ ve	+ ve
18.	India	+ ve	– ve

Note: Period I (1971-80)
Period II (1981-90)
– ve = Negative
+ ve = Positive

V. CONCLUDING REMARKS

The analysis indicated that at all India level the yield growth performance is consistently increased from Period I to Period II. Across the state level the yield performance shows the inter-regional differences. The association between yield and instability clearly shows a negative direction at national level and in most of the states. This observation is contradictory to earlier studies (indicated that growth observed was marked by instability). The positive association between yield growth and fluctuation is observed in Punjab, Haryana, Andhra Pradesh, Karnataka, Orissa and West Bengal. Hence, stabilisation policies, therefore, have to be further strengthened to minimise the adverse effects of instability in the yield of food grains. It is observed in the analysis of the study that the fertilizer and spread of irrigation are important factors not only to yield growth but also to reduce the fluctuation and ensure stability in yield growth. Therefore, the policy makers attention should be given to strengthen and provide for better availability and penetration of the technological inputs by increasing irrigated area through improving management of irrigation system.

Notes and References

1. Mitra, Ashok, *Levels of Regional Development in India,* Manager of Publications, Census of India, Vol. I, Part-I (A), New Delhi, 1967.
2. Alagh, Y.K. and Sharma, "Growth of Crop Production 1960-61 to 1978-79, Is It Decelerating?", *Indian Journal of Agricultural Economics,* 35 (2), 1980, pp. 104-10.
3. Hazell, P.B.R., "Instability in Indian Food Grains Production", Washington D. C., IFPRI, Research Report 30, 1982.
4. Rao, Hanumanth, Ch., *Technological Change and Distribution Gains in Indian Agriculture,* Macmillan, New Delhi, 1975.
5. Rao, Hanumanth, CH.; Ray and Subba Rao, *Unstable Agriculture and Droughts,* Vikas Publications, New Delhi, 1988.
6. Mehra, Shakuntala, "Instability in Indian Agriculture in the Context of the New Technology", Research Report No. 25, IFPRI, Washington D.C., See a Review by Ashok Mody, *Economic and Political Weekly,* May 29, 1982, p. 907.

7. Mahendra Dev, "Growth and Instability in Food Grains Production—An Inter-state Analysis", *Economic and Political Weekly*, September 26, 1987.
8. Parthasarathy, G., "Growth Rates and Fluctuations of Agricultural Production—A District-wise Analysis in Andhra Pradesh", *Economic and Political Weekly*, Review of Agriculture, June 1985.
9. Ray, S.K., *Growth and Instability in Indian Agriculture*, Institute of Economic Growth, 1982.
10. Sawant, S.D., "Investigation of the Hypothesis of Deceleration in Indian Agriculture", *Indian Journal of Agricultural Economics*, No. 4, October-December 1983.
11. Sen., "Growth and Instability in Indian Agriculture", *Agriculture Situation in India*, Vol. 21, No. 10, January 1967.
12. Sharma, P.S., *Agricultural Regionalisation of India*, New Heights, New Delhi, 1973.
13. Sengupta, P. and G. Sandasyuk, *Economic Regionalisation of India—Problems and Approaches*, Manager of Publications, Census of India, New Delhi, 1968.

13

An Extra Dimension to Regional Inequality

—Padmaja Mishra

Introduction

In regional economic policies the issues of balance and equity are usually dealt with at the inter-regional level. Regional imbalance is usually considered being reflected in the disparity between the average levels of incomes. The most common justification for policies to reduce regional disparities is that such disparities are inequitable. Nobody would deny that the ultimate objective of equity is to bring an equitable distribution of the fruits of development to the people irrespective of where the level. But reduction in disparities in average regional per capita incomes will not necessarily guarantee reduction in inter-personal disparity•though it certainly affects the total income distribution but not in any obvious ways. Two regions with

This paper was presented in the 25th International Conference of Regional Science Association at I.I.T. Kharagpur (1992). It is published with kind permission of the Secretary, Regional Science Association and author, respectively.

same average income can have completely different distribution of income within the regions. It is an empirical guess that the relationship between regional disparity and economic development takes an inverted U shape. This implies that in the early stages of economic development, regional income disparity increases but subsequently regional incomes start to converge (Williamson, 1965, Mehra; 1972). But the critical question is "Does this kind of interregional convergence mean that there is also an interregional convergence in the distribution of the population by income class?" (Fisch; 1984). It is likely that regions differ with regard to regional profiles of population by income class. This can lead to vast differences in regional welfare levels and, therefore, can be an important dimension to regional imbalance. In this context, this paper is addressed to income distribution disparities within the region as regions very often differ with regard to intra-regional distributive scenario which is an important dimension of regional welfare. This aspect of regional imbalance has a special significance in the context of developing countries because of the dynamic association between inequality and economic development. Do all sub-populations behave in the same way during the process of regional average income convergence? Different groups of population within the regions might be getting very different impacts of overall economic development which is not reflected in the average standards of individual regions.

The present paper is organised as follows:

Section 1.1 spells out the objective of the study and introduce the data base used. Section 1.2 gives a decomposition analysis of the overall national inequality. Section 1.3 measures regional disparity using Fisch's approach and the final Section 1.4 summarises and concludes the study.

1.1 Objective of the Present Study and Data Base

The present paper emphasis on intra-regional (*i.e.* intra-state) distributive scenario in India. Dissimilarity of the spatial distribution of population by income classes is considered as one important angle of regional disparity.

The objective of this paper is to calculate indices of regional inequality on the basis of regional differences with regard to intra-regional distributions and, therefore, differences in regional welfare.

The data used for the analysis has been taken from the Household Consumer Expenditure survey conducted by the National Sample Survey Organisation (NSSO) of India. The survey period covered is January 1983—December 1983. Household Consumer expenditure inequality has been used as the proxy for inequality in income or in living standards of the people. The original survey data is given for both rural and urban sectors for each of the states and for all-India as well. We have considered 17 major states only. Those are Andhra Pradesh, Assam, Bihar, Gujarat, Haryana, Himachal Pradesh, Jammu & Kashmir, Karnataka, Kerala, Madhya Pradesh, Maharashtra, Orissa, Punjab, Rajasthan, Tamil Nadu, Uttar Pradesh and West Bengal. The concept of all-India in this paper consists of these 17 major states only. The data for both the sectors have been added for each of the expenditure classes to arrive at the state level distributions. Similarly, the 17 state level distributions have been added to arrive at the national level distribution of population. The problem we faced with the original data is that some states do not have any sample points in some expenditure classes, especially at the lower side of the distribution. Therefore, for uniformity and for practical necessity in doing decomposition analysis, we merged the first four classes in all the cases and arrived at 10 expenditure classes for final analysis.

1.2 Decomposition of National Inequality

The reason for decomposition in the present context is to examine the contribution of inter-state and intra-state inequality towards the overall inequality. As we know, the index of regional disparity is usually constructed on the basis of the disparity between average regional incomes following Williamson's formula for coefficient of variation. This index is a measure of between-region inequality whereas the total inequality in the country is composed of both between-region and within-region inequality. We are decomposing total inequality into its between-region and within-region components.

A number of recent studies have discussed the issue of relating sub-group inequality levels to overall inequality (*e.g.* Cowell, 1980; Cowell and Kuga, 1981; Bourguignon, 1979; Shorrocks, 1980 and 1984; Shorrocks and Mukherjee, 1982; Das and Parikh, 1982 and Blakorby *et al.*, 1981; Mishra and Parikh, 1992). If the total inequality can be expressed as a function of sub-group inequality values when the sub-groups are mutually exclusively and exhaustive, then a variety of ways are found to decompose the total inequality. The particular way of decomposition depends on the nature of the inequality index and the way in which it is decomposed as decomposability of the indices differ from measure to measure. The most attractive type of decomposability has been additive decomposability. An index is additively decomposable if it can be neatly expressed as the sum of a 'between group' term and a 'within group' term.

As additive decomposability is considered to be a superb quality of the indices, these measures are most used for decomposing inequality, especially the Theil's entropy index. Theil's entropy index has been used here to measure and decompose the total national inequality, because of its superb additively decomposable properties. Total inequality is decomposed into between-region and within-region components which has helped us to study the relative significance of inter-regional and intra-regional inequality in total national inequality. This formula for decomposition is given below:

(*a*) Theil's Entropy index (*T*):

$$
\begin{aligned}
T &= \Sigma_j \Sigma_j (e_{ij} / e) \log (e_{ij} / e) / (f_{ij} / f) \\
&= \Sigma_i (e_i / e) \Sigma_j (e_{ij} / e_i) [\log \{(e_{ij} / e_i) / (f_{ij} / f_i)\} \\
&\quad + \log (e_i / f_i) / (e/f)] \\
&= \Sigma_i (e_i / e) [\Sigma_j (e_{ij} / e_i) \log (e_{ij} / e_i) / (f_{ij} / (f_i) \\
&\quad + \Sigma_i (e_i / e) \log [(e_i / e) / (f_i / f)] \\
&= \Sigma_i (e_i / e) T_i + \Sigma_i (e_i / e) \log [(e_i / e) / (f_i / f)] \\
&= T_W + T_B
\end{aligned}
$$

e_{ij} = Total expenditure of *i*th group *j*th class.
e_i = Total expenditure of *i*th group
e = Total expenditure of the whole population.
f_{ij} = No. of units in *i*th group and *j*th class
f_i = Total no. of units in *i*th group

T_i = Theil's entropy index for *i*th group.
T_w = Within - group inequality
T_B = Between - group inequality.

We found the following results from our decomposition.

$$T - T_W + T_B$$
$$0.1920 = 0.1814 + 0.0106$$
$$(94.5\%) \quad (5.5\%)$$

It is important to note that the contribution of within-state inequality has been quite high (more than 90 per cent) in comparison to the between-state inequality (5.5 per cent). Disparity within the states are high compared to the disparity between the states so far as the levels of living are concerned.

1.3 Measure of Regional Disparity

In view of the high significance of intra-regional inequality, we propose to adopt Fisch's approach of measuring regional disparity which is a novel way of considering the degree of imbalance between regions so far as distribution of population by income groups is considered. In the previous section, though we are made aware of the important contribution of intra-state inequality towards national inequality, we did not get any idea on the dissimilarity in regional income distributions. If the regions have different distributional scenario then that can be a very important angle of regional imbalance because intra-regional welfare levels will vary. Fisch's measure of regional disparity intends to consider this aspect. Usually, in the popular literature of regional science, Williamson's coefficient of variation is taken as the measure of regional disparity. This is a unidimensional measure which is based on the difference between regional average incomes and the national average income. It ignores the multidimensional variation between the region's distribution of population by income class and the corresponding national distribution. We can consider this multidimensionality by calculating two "coefficient of movement". One is the national coefficient of latent population movement and the other is the national coefficient of latent income movement. These two coefficients give ideas about the percentage of total population and the percentage of total income that have to move between regions under the existing situation to bring every region's income distribution profile at par with the overall national scenario. Finally, we calculate the national dissimilarity index as a measure of regional disparity by considering the gaps between each region's population distribution over different income classes compared to the national distribution of population. The indices are discussed below.

National Coefficient of Latent Population Movement (LP)

$$LP = (1/2)\ \Sigma_j \Sigma_i \mid P_{ij}\ (t) - e_j\ (t)\ (P)_i\ (t) \mid /\ P\ (t)$$

The symbols are defined as follows:

P_{ij} = No. of households in the *j*th income class in the *i*th region.

$P_j\ (t)$ = $\Sigma_i\ P_{ij}\ (t)$ = The national number of households in the *j*th income classes.

$e_j\ (t)$ = $P_{ij}\ (t)\ /\ P\ (t)$ = The nation's proportion of families in the *j*th income class.

$P_i\ (t)$ = $\Sigma_j P_{ij}\ (t)$ = The *i*th region's total number of families.

$P\ (t)$ = $\Sigma_i\ P_i\ (t)\ \Sigma_j\ P_j\ (t)$ = The nation's total number of households.

It is evident that this measure indicates the proportion of population that has to move between regions in order for the regions to achieve national distribution profile. Because this measure is based on the gap between each region's proportion of population in each income classes and the expected proportion of population (*i.e.* the national proportion of population) in the corresponding income class.

National Coefficient of Latent Income Movement (LY)

$Y\ (\mathrm{t}) = 1/2\ \Sigma_{\mathrm{j}}\ Y_{\mathrm{j}}\ (\mathrm{t})\ \Sigma_{\mathrm{i}}\ \mid\ P_{\mathrm{ij}}\ (\mathrm{t}) - e_{\mathrm{j}}\ (\mathrm{t})\ P_{\mathrm{i}}\ (\mathrm{t})\ /\ Y\ (\mathrm{t})$
where $Y_{\mathrm{j}}\ (\mathrm{t})$ = The average income or *j*th class and
$Y(\mathrm{t})$ is the national income.

This measure indicates the proportion of the national income that has to be reshuffled between the regions with the help of population movement in order for the regions to achieve the nation's distribution of population by income class.

National Dissimilarity Index (D)

$$D(t) = \Sigma_j (1/2) \mid P_{ij}(t) - e_j(t) P_i(t) \mid / P(t) e_j(t) [1 - e_j(t)].$$

This measure relates the total required population to move in the actual situation with the total required population to move in the hypothetical situation of completed regional segregation by income classes (*i.e.* when each region has only one income class) for each region to achieve national distribution of population by income classes.

The calculated value for each of the indices discussed above are as follows:

$$LP = 0.0496$$
$$LY = 0.0293$$
$$D = 0.0511$$

The above values indicate that a very negligible proportion of total population and, therefore, a very small amount of income along with the population have to move between regions to close the gaps between regions as far as population distribution by income classes are concerned. LP = (0.0496) suggests that nearly 5 per cent of the population are the latent movers who have to move to bring regional balance. Alongwith this population nearly 3 per cent of income has to move as indicated by LY (=0.0293). The national dissimilarity index D (=0.05%) indicates the small value of the index for regional disparity. To sum up the findings we can say that there are not much income distribution variations between the states. All the regions/ states under considerations are more or less similar to the nation with regard to within-region distribution.

1.4 Summary and Conclusion

To sum up, the paper tries to point out the regional variation with regard to distribution of population by income classes instead of solely concentrating on regional per capita income as it does not reflect the living standard of the masses in the region. The various coefficients of regional imbalance used here indicate the amount of population and income that have to relocated between regions so that each region's profile of population distribution by income classes will come upto the national profile. A higher value for the coefficient obviously indicate a higher degree of existing imbalance which needs a larger proportion of total population and income to be redistributed among the regions.

The low value for the indices of regional imbalance derived from our empirical study indicate that the Indian states are not very different from each other or from the national picture so far as within-region inequalities are concerned.

But, can we take this result as a true reflection of the reality? The reliability of our results depends both on the data base and the methodology used.

So far as data base is concerned the NSS consumer expenditure survey data used here is the most used one and generally agreed to be reasonably reliable. But so far comparability between the states is concerned, its reliability is less because of non-uniformity in data collection procedures. In case of the present study, we have merged the bottom four classes in all the cases to bring uniformity and to make the decomposition exercise feasible. But in the process, we have lost the most vital information on the inequality at the lower end of the distribution which could have changed the regional disparity indices significantly.

The problem with the indices used here is that the limits of the coefficients are not very well defined. Again, the movement of income and population that we derive do not distinguish between the rank of the income classes. But the required movement from the lowest class to the uppermost class has definitely got more significance from the policy point of view than a movement between two consecutive classes.

Therefore, the conclusion we draw from our empirical analysis has to be interpreted with limitations. The data source and the methodology have to be improved to get a more clear picture. The present paper has only tried to raise the issue of considering intra-regional income distribution as one aspect of regional disparity. The practical importance of considering intra-regional inequality arises with regard to the fact that high degree of poverty can be associated with a high average income. Moreover, in a liberalized economy with a lot of private sector activities, the analysis of marketing areas, especially the purchasing power in different regions, necessarily depend on the income distribution pattern in a region. Therefore, in the context of present liberalisation of Indian economy, within-region distribution studies are useful. Again, from the policy point of view of a federal economy, the central government also needs to be aware of regional situations both with regard to average income and the distribution thereof while allocating federal resources among the states.

Notes and References

1. Blackorby, C., Donaldson, D. and Auersperg M., "A New Procedure for the Measurement of Inequality within and among Population Groups", *Canadian Journal of Economics*, 14, 665-85, 1981.
2. Cowell, F.A., "On the Structure of Additive Inequality Measures", *Review of Economic Studies*, 47, 521–31, 1980.
3. Cowell, F.A. and Kuga, K., "Additivity and the Entropy Concept: An Axiomatic Approach to Inequality Measurement", *Journal of Economic Theory*, 25, 131-43, 1981.
4. Das, T. and Parikh, A., "Decomposition of Inequality Measures: A Comparative Analysis", *Empirical Economics*, 7, 23-48, 1982.
5. Fisch, O. "Regional Income Inequality and Economic Development", *Regional Science and Urban Economics*, 14, 89-111, 1984.
6. Merca, K. *Income Distribution and Regional Development*, Tokyo, University of Tokyo Press, 1975.
7. Mishra, P. and Parik, A., "Household Consumer Expenditure Inequalities in India: A Decomposition Analysis", *Review of Income and Wealth*, 38, 225-36, 1992.
8. Mookherjee, D. and Shorrocks, A.F., "A Decomposition Analysis of the Trend in UK Income Inequality", *Economic Journal*, 92, 886-902, 1982.
9. Shorrocks, A.F., "The Class of Additively Decomposable Inequality Measures", *Econometrica*, 48, 613-25, 1980.
10. Williamson, J.G., "Regional Inequality and the Process of National Development: A Description of the Patterns", *Economic Development and Cultural Change*, 13, 3-45, 1965.

PART III

POVERTY, URBANISATION, ENVIRONMENT AND STRUCTURAL ADJUSTMENT: IMPACT UPON BALANCED AND SUSTAINABLE DEVELOPMENT

14

Poverty Alleviation for Sustainable Development

—Shankar Chatterjee

The word sustainable development has been defined by various institutions and academicians in various ways but the meaning of sustainable development as defined by World Bank clearly implies that in order to achieve sustainable development poverty alleviation is *sine qua non*. In the following few lines World Bank's definition has been quoted.

> ". . . Satisfy the multiple criteria of sustainable growth, poverty alleviation and sound environmental management".
>
> *"To a large degree, environmental management should be seen as a means of attaining the wider objectives of sustained economic growth and poverty alleviation".
>
> *". . . concern about environmental matters. . . . and developing the capacity to implement sound practices for environmental management . . . are (both) needed to reconcile and, where appropriate, make tradeoffs among the objectives of growth, poverty alleviation and sound environmental management"

* "Promoting growth, alleviating poverty, and protecting the environment are mutually supportive objectives in the long run . . . In the short run, however, the objectives are not always compatible . . ."

*"Poverty of people and of countries is thus a major cause of environmental degradation. That makes it essential, if environmental degradation is not to become completely unmanageable, to devise policies oriented toward economic growth, with special emphasis on improving the incomes of the poor. Nevertheless economic growth may also destroy the environment and further jeopardize the already tenuous lives of the poor . . . . Thus although growth is imperative for alleviating poverty, it may also adversely affect the poor and the environment if inadequate attention is paid to the poor and their needs".

*". . . economic growth, the alleviation of poverty, and sound environmental management are in many cases mutually consistent objectives."

The above explanation clearly reveals that poverty and sustainable development cannot move simultaneously. To achieve sustainable development poverty has to be alleviated. Poverty is the result of imbalance between population growth and resource distribution. Any student of science/social science knows that imbalance between any two variables leads to disequilibrium. So to alleviate poverty, control of population growth *vis-a-vis* redistribution of resources are necessary. In our country redistribution of resources is taken care of through poverty alleviation programmes. Therefore, in this paper an attempt has been made to discuss about major poverty alleviation programmes presently going on in the rural areas of India *vis-a-vis* the problem cropped up due to high growth rate of population has also been highlighted.

Poverty in India

In India calories intake has been considered as the criterion of determining poverty. According to this, if a person living in rural area gets less than 2400 calories of food value daily then the person will be treated as poor, the same for the urban area is less than 2100. To ascertain this, income has been taken as a measuring rod. During Sixth, Seventh and Eighth Plan periods, the annual income level for determining poverty (for rural family) was Rs. 3500, Rs. 6400 and Rs. 11000, respectively.

Poverty in India has been estimated regularly by the Planning Commission on the basis of consumer expenditure data generated by the National Sample Survey Organisation (NSSO). From 1960-61) to 1973-74, poverty estimates are available for each year except for the year 1962-63. And afterwards the poverty data are available for the selected years *i.e.*, for the years of 1977-78, 1983-84 and 1987-88. In the meantime, Planning Commission constituted an Expert Group under the chairmanship of Dr. D.T. Lakdawala to consider methodological aspects of estimation of proportion and number of poor in India. According to the Report, percentage of people below the poverty line in 1987-88 has been estimated as 39.3 against the Planning Commission's estimation of 29.9 per cent during the same period. The number of people below the poverty line and the percentage are presented in Table 14.1:

Table 14.1
Population Below the Poverty Line
(As per the Expert Group Report)

S. No.	*Sector*	*1983-84*	*1987-88*
		Population in Millions	
1.	Rural	251.7	229.4
2.	Urban	75.3	83.4
3.	Total	327.0	312.8
		Poverty Ratio (%)	
4.	Rural	45.6	39.1
5.	Urban	42.2	40.1
6.	Total	44.8	39.3

Source: Rural Development Statistics, 1994-95, NIRD, Hyderabad.

The Report of the Expert Group reveals that in some of the states even 50 per cent or more than that of its total population are below the poverty line. This may be seen in Table 14.2.

The above discussion clearly reveals that poverty exists in our country in massive way. Government of India is also aware

Table 14.2
Incidence of Rural and Urban Poverty

(percentage)

S.No.	States/UTs	Rural				Urban			
		1973-74	1977-78	1983	1987-88	1973-74	1977-78	1983	1987-88
1.	Andhra Pradesh	48.4	38.1	26.5	20.9	52.6	46.5	40.1	44.6
2.	Arunachal Pradesh	52.7	59.8	42.6	39.4	37.2	37.6	26.4	17.3
3.	Assam	52.7	59.8	42.6	39.4	37.2	37.6	26.4	17.3
4.	Bihar	63.0	63.3	64.4	52.6	51.8	52.2	50.4	57.7
5.	Goa	46.9	37.6	14.8	17.6	36.9	36.7	27.2	33.7
6.	Gujarat	46.4	41.8	29.8	28.7	49.3	43.1	40.6	39.6
7.	Haryana	34.2	27.7	20.6	16.2	39.6	36.2	23.5	17.8
8.	Himachal Pradesh	27.4	33.5	17.0	16.3	13.2	19.5	9.3	6.2
9.	Jammu & Kashmir	45.5	42.9	26.0	25.7	30.4	31.9	17.1	14.8
10.	Karnataka	55.1	48.2	36.3	32.8	52.0	52.9	43.4	49.1
11.	Kerala	59.2	51.5	39.0	29.1	62.2	59.5	48.7	43.4
12.	Madhya Pradesh	62.7	62.5	48.9	41.9	58.3	62.1	54.6	48.2
13.	Maharashtra	57.7	64.0	45.2	40.8	43.0	40.6	40.6	39.0
14.	Manipur	52.7	59.8	42.6	39.4	37.2	37.6	26.4	17.3
15.	Meghalaya	52.7	59.8	42.6	39.4	37.2	37.6	26.4	17.3

16.	Mizoram	52.7	59.8	42.6	39.4	37.2	37.6	26.4	17.3
17.	Nagaland	52.7	59.8	42.6	39.4	37.2	37.6	26.4	17.3
18.	Orissa	67.3	72.4	67.5	57.6	56.3	53.6	50.6	44.1
19.	Punjab	28.2	16.4	13.2	12.6	27.7	27.6	23.9	12.9
20.	Rajasthan	44.8	35.9	33.5	33.2	53.2	46.4	40.4	39.0
21.	Sikkim	52.7	59.8	42.6	39.4	37.2	37.6	26.4	17.3
22.	Tamil Nadu	57.4	57.7	54.0	45.8	54.5	53.2	49.2	43.9
23.	Tripura	52.7	59.8	42.6	39.4	37.2	37.6	26.4	17.3
24.	Uttar Pradesh	56.4	47.6	46.5	41.1	59.5	57.1	50.3	45.2
25.	West Bengal	73.2	68.3	63.1	48.3	34.5	38.7	32.2	32.8
	UT's								
26.	Delhi	24.4	30.2	7.7	1.3	49.2	33.3	28.3	16.9
27.	A & N Islands	57.4	57.7	54.0	45.8	54.5	53.2	49.2	43.9
28.	Chandigarh	27.7	27.6	23.9	12.9	27.7	27.6	23.9	12.9
29.	D & N Haveli	46.9	37.6	14.8	17.6	36.9	36.7	27.2	33.7
30.	Lakshadweep	59.2	51.5	39.0	29.1	62.2	59.5	48.7	43.4
31.	Pondicherry	57.4	57.7	54.0	45.8	54.5	53.2	49.2	43.9
	All India	56.4	53.1	45.6	39.1	49.2	47.4	42.2	40.1

Source: Planning Commission, Report of the Expert Group on Estimation of Proportion and Number of Poor, July 1993.

about the fact and various poverty alleviation programmes have been launched in the country in a systematic way from early '80s.'.

Poverty Alleviation Programmes in India (Rural)

The poverty alleviation programmes presently going on in the rural areas of India may be classified into two categories *viz.*, self employment programme and wage employment programme. The purpose of these programmes is to bring the families above the poverty line (to enable them to cross the required income level), as mentioned already in different plan periods different income criterion was taken into consideration for determining poverty.

The self employment programme includes Integrated Rural Development Programme (IRDP), Training of Rural Youth for Self Employment (TRYSEM) and Development of Women and Children in Rural Areas (DWCRA). Of these, IRDP is the major programme, TRYSEM and DWCRA are the sub-component of IRDP. On the other hand, wage employment programme consists of Jawahar Rozgar Yojana (JRY) and Employment Assurance Scheme (EAS).

The objective of IRDP is to enable poor families to cross the poverty line by providing them income generating assets through financial assistance by way of government subsidy and term credit from financial institutions. Since inception till March, 1996, 490.47 families have been assisted with total investment of Rs. 25111.04 crores. Even with this huge amount of spending, IRDP could not make much dent to alleviate poverty from rural India. Because, impact of IRDP is assessed on the basis of Concurrent Evaluation Study carried out by the government of India. Up till now five rounds of Concurrent Evaluation studies have been carried out, *albeit*, reports are available upto Fourth Round (Half Yearly). All the Reports evince that a low percentage of beneficiaries could cross poverty line through IRDP (Table 14.3).

This poor performance of IRDP, naturally raises the question why its performance is like this. One of the reasons is that per family investment (subsidy + loan) was low. For example, during Sixth Plan and Seventh Plan, per family investment was Rs. 2876 and Rs. 4569, respectively. Many people believe that in order to make IRDP much more fruitful size of investment should be enhanced. As a sequal of this Family Credit Plan under IRDP has been introduced on a pilot basis from 1991-92 and altogether 213 districts have been covered. As a result of these interventions, the average level of investment (per family) which was Rs. 7889 at the beginning of Eighth Plan has gone upto Rs. 14400 during 1996-97 (upto November, 1996). This may be treated as a right step in this direction.

Table 14.3

Percentage of Families Crossed Poverty Line

Sl. No.	*Concurrent Evaluation*	*%age of People Crossed Poverty Line*
1.	First Round (1985 October-1986 September)	12
2.	Second Round (1987, January-December)	13
3.	Third Round (1989, January-December)	18
4.	Fourth Round (September 1992-February 1993) Half yearly report	15

Source: Various Concurrent Evaluation Reports, government of India.

Wage Employment Programme

The wage employment programme in the country includes Jawahar Rozgar Yojana (JRY) and Employment Assurance Scheme (EAS). JRY has been introduced from April 1989, by merging two employment programmes *viz.*, National Rural Employment Programme (NREP) and Rural Landless Employment Guarantee Programme (RLEGP). JRY has been introduced to all the Blocks of the country. On the other hand EAS has been introduced from 2 October 1993 in 1778 Blocks of the country. During 1994-95, EAS has been extended to another 409 Blocks. However, Prime Minister of India in his Independence Day address on 15 August 1996 announced that EAS would be extended to all the Blocks within two years.

The main objective of both the programmes is to generate additional employment for the unemployed and underemployed persons, both men and women, in the rural areas through the creation of rural economic infrastructure, community and social assets with the aim of improving the quality of life in the rural areas. In case of EAS, the scheme aims at providing assured employment of 100 days of unskilled manual work to the rural poor who are in need of employment and seeking it. A maximum of two adults per family are provided the assurance of 100 days employment.

Impact of JRY and EAS

The Ministry of Rural Areas and Employment, government of India carried out a Concurrent Evaluation Study of JRY during June 1993 to May 1, 1994 covering 470 districts, 933 Blocks and 4700 village panchayats in the country. One of the findings of the study is that roughly a person got 11 mandays of employment during the reference period.[1] Prior to that, Programme Evaluation Organisation (PEO) of the Planning Commission took up a quick study of JRY during 1991-92 in 10 major states of the country. One of the important findings of the study was that JRY could not provide employment to the extent expected as the average number of days for which a person got employment was 11.44 days during 1989-90, 15.68 days in 1990-91 and 12.81 days during 1991-92 (upto September, 1991) respectively.[2]

It is evident from the discussion that JRY created very low number of mandays for a person. With this low number of mandays a person cannot earn minimum level of income for crossing the poverty line.

On the other hand EAS also could not make much dent among the poor people. For example, upto 1995-96, more than 1.97 crore persons have been registered under the scheme and 63.90 crore mandays of employment generated. This vividly reveals that a person got on average 32.4 mandays of employment.[3] With this low number of days of employment a family cannot be expected to cross poverty line.

Population Growth

As mentioned already, poverty and population growth are closely associated. In a developing country like India, high growth rate of population will neutralise poverty alleviation programmes if simultaneously measures are not taken to control population growth. In this analysis, two points are highlighted to explain the impact of population growth.

During 1981-91, rate of growth of population was 23.85 per cent in India. This was very high in comparison to many countries of the world. Moreover, in many states of India, the rate was more than the national average of 23.85. The growth rate is even more than the growth rate of 1951-61 which was 21.51. As already mentioned we are having huge number of population, so a small increase in percentage even sometimes a small decrease in percentage causes increase in the number of population. The case may be clarified by looking at Table 14.1. As is evident from the table, although urban poverty ratio has gone down during 1987-88 over 1983-84 but in numerical term, the number has gone up substantially.

Another example which may be cited here with respect to net availability of food grains, in our country. It shows that in recent years, the same has gone down (Table 14.4).

Table 14.4
Per Capita Availability of Food Grains in India

Sl. No.	*Food Grains*	*1991*	*1992(P)*	*1993 (P)*
1.	Cereals (gms/day)	468.50	434.20	427.40
2.	Pulses (gms/day)	41.60	34.30	37.00

P = Provisional

Source: Rural Development Statistics, 1993-94, NIRD, Hyderabad.

The above reveals that there is urgent need to control population growth otherwise development programmes meant for the people in general and poor in particular will be frustrated.

Conclusion

Before winding up, it can be suggested that for achieving sustainable development, poverty alleviation programmes need to be redesigned in such a way that poor people are benefited to a great extent. On the other hand, there is need to control population growth in the country. To control population growth 'incentive' and 'punishment' may be introduced simultaneously. Incentive for them who will adhere to two children norm and punishment for those who will not adhere the same.

Before conclusion, *The Deccan Chronicle*, a local daily published from Hyderabad (editorial column, August 27, 1997) may be quoted to evince impact of population growth on poverty. According to the daily

> "success in poverty-eradication schemes gets neutralised by the steady increase in population, exemplifying the truth that for every forward step taken in combating poverty India takes three steps backward by failing to control its population. According to the report (report refers here World Bank Report) 164 million Indians lived in poverty in 1951 whereas these number rose to 312 million in 1993-94. The number is rising every day, every hour and every minute. The Indian government and officialdom continue to remain under great pressure to breathe some determination and will into the national population control programmes, but, compared to China, the Indian campaign has not met with encouraging success."

Notes and References

1. *World Bank (1987)*: "Environment, Growth and Devleopment", Development Committee, World Bank, Washington, DC.
2. *World Bank (1988)*: "Environment and Development: Implementing the World Bank's New Policies", Development Committee, World Bank, Washington, DC.
3. *Annual Report 1996-97*, government of India, Ministry of Rural Areas and Employment.
4. *Annual Report 1994-95*, government of India, Ministry of Rural Areas and Employment.
5. *Programmes for Change*, government of India, Ministry of Rural Areas and Employment.

15

Urbanization and Spatial Planning in India: Policy Issues

—*C.R. Pathak*

Introduction

During the post-Independence period, India had urbanised at fast rate upto 1981 while during 1981-91 decade, the rate has slowed down. The Table 10.1 records the trend of urbanization during 1901-91 and also the projected urbanization rates during 1991-2001. The rates of urbanization vary over time and space. It is the quantum increase of urban population *vis-a-vis* total population is of vital concern. Even though by the end of the century only 30 per cent of India's population of one billion would reside in urban areas because of slowing down urbanization process, the moot question is, where to accommodate the 295 million urban people? Could our urban areas be able to contain and absorb gainfully that much population? What would be the role of Metro Cities in the

This paper was published in *Indian Journal of Regional Science* (Volume XXV, No. 2, 1993). It is published with kind permission of the Secretary, RSAI and author.

urbanization process? The expected result will be spatially and structurally imbalanced urban growth—so, what would be the planning policy to tackle the problem?

Level and Trend of Urbanization in India

The 1991 population census has recorded 217.18 mn urban population in the country which accounts for 25.72 per cent of 844.32 mn total population, distributed over 3768 urban agglomerations/towns. At the beginning of this century, the level of urbanization was only 10.84 per cent with only 25.85 mn people in 1827 towns. In 1951, at the starting point of planned economic development, the level was 17.29 per cent with 62.45 mn urban population. The urban population has multiplied by about 8.5 times compared to 3.5 fold increase in total population during this century. Despite such high urban population increase, the level of urbanization has not risen to a high level. Firstly because, the level of urbanization was very low in the earlier part of this century and the tempo was slow (Table 15.1). This phenomenon could be explained by the slow rate of economic development in the country.

The urbanization process being the demographic counterpart of economic development, during the planned economic development period in Independent India the tempo of urbanization would have been expected to be very fast.

Table 15.1 presents the trends and level of urbanization during 1901-91 and also estimates of urban growth upto the end of this century. From the table it is clear that during 1971-81, the urban growth was highest (46.14 per cent) and the rate (36.19 per cent) during 1981-91 was slower than even to that of the decade 1961-71. Has the tempo come down? If so, the decade 1991-2001 will experience farther slow down in the tempo of urbanization. Even then the urban population will reach an alarmingly large figure *i.e.* 295 mn or 30.0 per cent of total population with the assumed urbanization rate of 35.35 per cent during 1991-2001 (revised estimates).

Structure of Urbanization

The urban growth in India had always the size bias. The large

Table 15.1
Trend of Urbanization in India

Census Year	*Number of Towns*	*Total Population (in '000)*	*Urban Population ('000)*	*Urban Population as %age of Total Population (%)*	*Decennial Growth Rate of Urban (%)*	*Annual Exponential Growth Rate*
1901	1,827	238,400	25,855	10.84	—	—
1911	1,815	252,095	25,942	10.29	0.35	0.03
1921	1,949	251,322	28,086	11.18	8.27	0.79
1931	2,072	278,977	33,456	11.99	19.12	1.75
1941	2,250	318,660	44,153	13.86	31.97	2.77
1951	2,843	361,088	62,444	17.29	41.42	3.47
1961	2,355	439,235	78,937	17.97	26.51	2.34
1971	2,590	548,160	109,114	19.91	38.23	3.21
1981	3,378	683,330	159,463	23.34	46.14	3.83
1991	3,768	844,324	217,178	25.72	36.19	3.09
2001*	—	986,099	295,000	30.00	35.35	3.04

Notes: 1. As the 1981 census was not conducted in Assam, the 1991 population figures for India include interpolated figures for Assam.

2. The 1991 census has not been held in Jammu and Kashmir. The 1991 population figures for India include projected figures for Jammu and Kashmir as Projected by the Standing Committee of Experts on Population Projections (October, 1989).

3. The figures have been estimated based on population projection made by the Expert Committee, Planning Commission.

size towns having population 100,000 and above (Class I) accounted for 26 per cent of urban population in 1901 and had gained all through to contain 65 per cent in 1991 (Table 15.2). The Class II towns (with population 50,000 to 99,999) had maintained their share of urban population around 11 per cent, so was the case of Class III towns. The most vulnerable groups are Class IV, V and VI towns whose share have been constantly declining decade after decade. Their share of population is lowest in 1991.

In growth pattern, it also reveals that Class I towns have been growing faster than any other class during this century. The small size towns have had fluctuating growth. As a matter of fact, Class V and VI towns experienced absolute loss and Class IV towns grew only by 10.72 per cent compared to Class I towns which grew by 46.86 per cent. The Class II and III towns have maintained a steady growth since 1921 but still could not keep pace with the rate of urbanization in India (Figs. 15.1 and 15.2).

Table 15.2
Percentage Distribution of Urban Population by Size Class India, 1901-1971

Census Year	*Size Class* I	II	III	IV	V	VI
1901	26.00	11.29	15.64	20.83	20.14	6.10
1911	27.48	10.51	16.40	19.73	19.31	6.57
1921	29.70	10.39	15.92	18.29	18.67	7.03
1931	31.20	11.65	16.80	18.00	17.14	5.21
1941	38.23	11.42	16.32	15.78	15.08	3.14
1951	44.63	9.96	15.72	13.63	12.97	3.09
1961	51.42	11.23	16.94	12.77	6.87	0.77
1971	57.24	10.92	16.01	10.94	4.45	0.44
1981	60.42	11.63	14.33	9.54	3.58	0.50
1991	65.20	10.95	13.19	7.71	2.60	0.29

Urban Frame

In the 1991 census, 4,689 places were identified as common towns against 4,029 in 1981. Out of which 2,996 were statutory

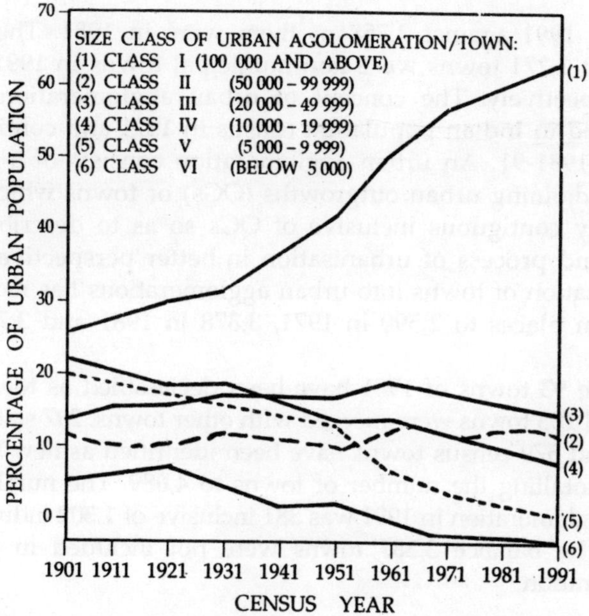

Fig. 15.1 Urban Population of India by Size Class (1901-1991)

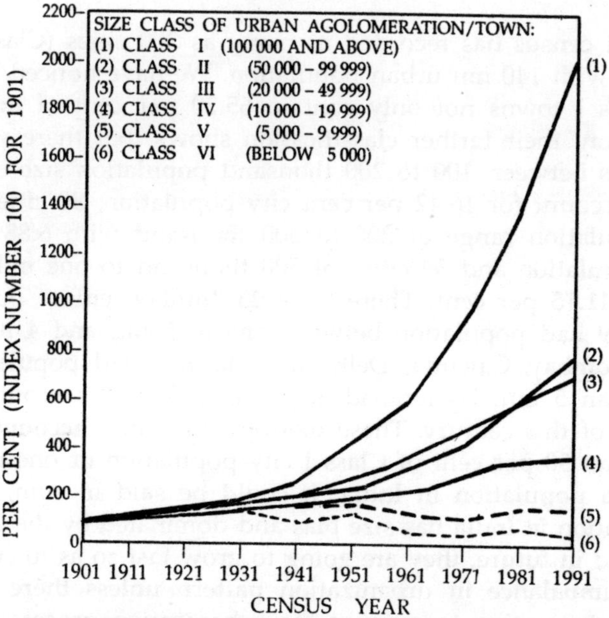

Fig. 15.2 Growth Rate of Urban Population in India by Size Class (1901-1991)

towns in 1991 against 2,758 of them were in 1981. The rest 1,693 and 1,271 towns were non-municipal towns in 1991 and 1981 respectively. The concept of urban agglomeration was introduced in Indian population census in 1971 and continued through 1981-91. An urban agglomeration consists of a town and its adjoining urban outgrowths (OGs) or towns which are physically contiguous inclusive of OGs so as to describe the spread and process of urbanisation in better perspective. The reorganisation of towns into urban agglomerations has reduced the urban places to 2,590 in 1971, 3,378 in 1981 and 3,768 in 1991.

While 93 towns of 1981 have been declassified as towns in 1991, and 103 towns were merged with other towns, 297 statutory towns and 579 census towns have been identified as new towns in 1991 totalling the number of towns to 4,689. The number of urban agglomeration in 1991 was 381 inclusive of 1,302 individual towns. The balance 3,387 towns were not included in urban agglomeration.

Size Class Distribution of Towns

The 1991 census has recorded as many as 300 cities (Class I) in India with 140 mn urban population. We have noticed that the Class I towns not only contain 65.20 per cent of urban population, their farther classification shows that there were 167 cities between 100 to 200 thousand population size class which account for 16.42 per cent city population, 80 cities in the population range of 200 to 300 thousand with 6.88 per cent population and 30 cities of 500 thousand to one million contain 11.15 per cent. There were 23 "million cities" out of which 19 had population between one to 5 mn and 4 mega cities (Bombay, Calcutta, Delhi and Madras) had population more than 5 mn. Hyderabad is going to join this group by the end of this century. These metropolitan cities account for more than 50 per cent of Class I city population or one-third of urban population in India. It could be said in sum, that urbanization in India has size bias and dominated by the large cities and in future, they are going to grow fast so as to create farther imbalance in urbanization pattern unless there is a policy intervention to reorient the urbanization process. The

Urban Population Distribution in India

Year		1981		1991		2001**	
	City Size	Popl. in mn.	Per cent of Total	Popl. in mn.	Per cent of Total	Popl. in mn.	Per cent of Total
1.	Class I	94	60%	140	65%	206	70%
	(*a*) Population in mn. Cities	42	27%	70	28%	98	33%
	(*b*) No. of mn. Cities	12	—	23	—	85	—
2.	Class II & III Medium Size	42	27%	51	24%	74	22%
3.	Class IV, V & VI Small Towns	20	13%	26	11%	15	8%
	Total	156	100%	217*	100%	295	100%

Source: Census of Population—1991 paper 2 and the estimates by Expert Committee.

*Excludes J & K

** Projected Figures.

following statement records the class-wise distribution of urban population during 1981 and 1991 and projected one of 2001.

Spatial Structure of India's Urbanization

The imbalanced size class distribution of urban population has also been reflected regionally. The urbanized states have improved their level of urbanization where as the lowly urbanized states despite high rate of urban growth could not raise their level significantly because of low urban population base. They lack in number of metropolitan cities but still their largest towns mostly commercial-administrative-capital cities, have grown very fast during the post-Independence period.

Percentage Decadal Variation of Urban Population in Each Size Class India, 1901-11 to 1981-91

Decade	*All Classes*	*Class I*	*Class II*	*Class III*	*Class IV*	*Class V*	*Class VI*
1	*2*	*3*	*4*	*5*	*6*	*7*	*8*
1901–11	0.14	5.54	–7.07	4.71	–5.39	–4.23	7.48
1911–21	8.25	16.99	7.09	5.10	0.32	4.66	15.82
1921–31	19.08	25.11	33.50	25.66	17.22	9.30	–11.74
1931–41	32.09	61.83	29.50	28.57	15.78	16.18	–20.23
1941–51	41.49	65.19	23.34	36.00	22.21	21.73	39.21
1951–61	25.85	44.99	41.98	35.62	17.90	–33.33	–68.71
1961–71	37.91	53.51	34.06	30.34	18.22	–10.75	–20.71
1971–81	46.23	54.35	55.73	30.85	27.54	17.82	65.73
1981–91	36.09	46.87	28.14	25.30	10.72	–1.27	–21.70

Out of 25 states and 7 union territories (U.T.), Delhi (89.93 per cent) and Chandigarh (89.69 per cent) are most urbanized and Dadra-Nagar Haveli (8.47 per cent) and Himachal Pradesh (8.70 per cent) are least urbanized. The latter ones interchanged their 1981 rank in urbanization, so was the case of Delhi and

Chandigarh. Table 15.3 shows the urbanization rank of all the states in 1981 and 1991 and their annual exponential growth rate during 1971-81 and 1981-91. Out of 25 states and UTs, 17 had higher than the national level of urbanization both in 1981 and 1991. The rest of the states had lower than the national urbanization level during both the decades. The state of Maharashtra apart from the Union Territories was most urbanized state (38.73 per cent in 1991 and 35.03 per cent in 1981) in both the decades. Gujarat maintained its rank next to Maharashtra.

The spatial pattern of urbanization is also an imbalanced one. The district-wise level of urbanization shows concentration of urban agglomeration near about the metropolitan cities and the industrial magnets and mining areas, set up during the planned economic development period. The urban agglomerations appear in clusters being geographically favoured for commercial-cum-industrial-cum-administrative functions of urbanization during the later half of this century as the colonial cities have grown faster in the post-Independence period. The economically backward districts and states have not been able to participate effectively in the nationwide urbanization process except that there had been population concentration in the capital cities in search of employment opportunity. The urbanization has been induced by social and economic deprivation in the rural areas rather than effective pull generated at those cities, so there is a built-in constraint in thwarting the process of urbanization. Although some lowly urbanized states have made strides recently through rural-urban influx of people, the share of most of the states towards Indian urbanization has not changed during 1981 and 1991.

These spatially imbalanced urbanization process with structural imbalance or hierarchical ordering have not only agglomerated majority of urban people in 300 large cities, but have accentuated urban problems. These cities deserve separate treatment as they are going to shoulder the major share of urban growth in future unless planned otherwise.

Out of 3,768 urban agglomerations/towns in 1991, 300 cities with population 100,000 and above have been categorised into 5 classes. Table 15.4 shows their number, population percentage share of total urban population, sex ratio etc. The table farther reveals that more than 50 per cent of urban population has

Table 15.3
Level of Urbanization and Annual Average Exponential Growth Urban Population in 1971, 1981 and 1991

Rank 1981	States/UT's	Urban Population as of Total Population		Annual Average Exponential Growth Rate in Urban Population		
		1991	1981	1961-71	1971-81	1981-91
	India	25.72	23.34	3.21	3.83	3.09
1.	Delhi	89.93	92.73	4.36	4.58	3.79
2.	Chandigarh	89.69	93.68	6.53	5.96	3.07
3.	Pondicherry	64.05	52.28	8.01	4.66	4.92
4.	Laksha dweep	56.29	46.28	—	—	4.46
5.	Daman & Diu	46.86	36.75	5.54	2.12	4.93
6.	Mizoram	46.20	24.67	9.74	11.71	9.57
7.	Goa	41.02	32.03	8.24	4.66	3.96
8.	Maharashtra	38.73	35.03	3.42	3.36	3.27
9.	Gujarat	34.40	31.10	3.44	3.47	2.90
10.	Tamil Nadu	34.20	32.95	3.27	2.47	1.76
11.	Karnataka	30.91	28.89	3.02	4.10	2.55
12.	Punjab	29.72	27.68	2.25	3.68	2.56
13.	Manipur	27.69	26.42	7.37	9.76	2.98
14.	West Bengal	27.39	26.47	2.50	2.76	2.54

15.	Andhra Pradesh	26.84	23.32	2.92	3.96	3.55
16.	A. & N. Islands	26.80	26.30	6.22	6.38	4.10
17.	Kerala	26.44	18.74	3.05	3.19	4.76
18.	Haryana	24.79	21.88	3.04	4.67	3.58
19.	Jammu & Kashmir	23.83	21.05	—	—	—
20.	Madhya Pradesh	23.21	20.29	3.83	4.45	3.71
21.	Rajasthan	22.88	21.05	3.25	4.62	3.31
22.	Uttar Pradesh	19.89	17.95	2.68	4.74	3.29
23.	Meghalaya	18.69	18.07	2.25	4.95	2.74
24.	Nagaland	17.28	15.52	9.87	8.50	5.58
25.	Tripura	15.26	10.99	4.55	3.29	6.19
26.	Orissa	13.43	11.79	5.09	5.22	3.08
27.	Bihar	13.17	12.47	3.64	4.37	2.65
28.	Arunachal Pradesh	12.21	6.56	—	8.74	9.38
29.	Assam	11.08	9.88	5.01	3.27*	3.27*
30.	Sikkim	9.12	16.15	16.55	9.54	–3.29
31.	Himachal Pradesh	8.70	7.61	3.05	2.98	3.11
32.	Dadra & Nagar Haveli	8.41	6.69	—	—	5.28

* Interpolated using 1971 and 1991 census figures.

Sources: Census of India 1991, Series I, Paper 2, pp. 16 & 51.

concentrated in the 23 metropolises of which more than half are in four mega cities indicating urban population concentration in the large cities. The sex ratio declines as the size class of the cities increases. The sex ratio is least in the Mega Cities (842). Although there is size bias in sex ratio, there is wide variation from one part of the country to the other—being higher in south India to lowest in Maharashtra.

There is wide variation in growth rate among the Class I cities. In 1981-91, 63 cities have grown at rates higher than 50 per cent. The 23 metropolitan cities have grown on an average by 67.76 per cent during 1981-91. Out of the four mega cities Calcutta has been growing at slowest rate, the Delhi being the fastest during 1951-91. Other metropolitan cities have grown significantly of which Bhopal's growth was highest (1,039 growth index, 1951 = 100). The four mega cities account for 52.68 per cent of 76.66 mn metropolitan population.

Table 15.4
Distribution of Class I Urban Agglomerations/ Cities (Population 100,000 and Above) by Different Population Sizes 1991

Population Size	*Number of UAs/Cities*	*Population*	*Percentage Class I UAs/ Cities*	*Sex Ratio*
Class I	300	139,730,050	100.00	882
M1 Less than 200,000	167	22,939,086	16.42	913
M2 200,000-299,999	40	9,606,814	6.88	904
M3 300,000-499,999	40	15,586,157	11.15	906
M4 500,000-999,999	30	20,936,734	14.98	881
M5 10,00,000 & above	23	70,661,259	50.57	864
(*i*) 10,00,000—19,99,999	14	17,175,849	12.29	882
(*ii*) 20,00,000,—49,99,999	5	16,260,762	11.64	891
(*iii*) 50,00,000 & above	4	37,224,648	26.64	842

Note: Excludes Jammu and Kashmir where census has not been held.

The slower rate of urbanization in 1981-91 period could be explained by the failure of lowly-urbanized states to catch up with the urbanized ones on the one hand and the slowing down in the rate by the highly urbanized states even though the urbanized states have raised their level of urbanization farther during 1981-91. This has been supported by the high correlation (g = 0.939) between the levels of urbanization by states during 1971-81 and 1981-91. The rate of urbanization was consistent during 1961-71 and 1971-81 with as high as 0.752 correlation coefficient which has declined to 0.240 in 1981-91. Thanks to the success of rural development programmes in 1980's which have slowed down the tempo of rural-urban migration. The other fact that a large number of commuters who are urban in occupation but forced to stay in the rural areas because of housing shortage in the urban areas. Besides, the rapid transit system and suburban electrified train services have facilitated the commuters particularly in the immediate hinterland of the metropolitan cities. They are not warranted by the urban statistics and have escaped the urban censuses.

Urban Development Problems in India

The structurally and spatially imbalanced urbanization in India during the twentieth century specially since the Independence have concentrated the urban problems in the metropolitan cities particularly in the mega cities. The problems of housing, transportation, energy supply, sanitation, health and other civic amenities, worsening low order of urban living in slums and squatter colonies, have been most acute in them. Of course living conditions in other cities are no better. The introduction of various urban development programmes such as employment generation in the informal sector, various poverty alleviation programmes, sites and services scheme, public housing projects in the metro cities for various income groups have gone long way in improving urban living but have fallen short of our expectation, as when one problem is solved, many more crop up because, such urban improvement programme exerted pull- forces to the rural migrants. The problem solving measures such as slum improvement (sites and services scheme), water supply, sanitation etc., schemes have been piecemeal and not part of approved master plans for urban development. As a matter of fact, only a few metropolises had statutory master plans. A number of master plans prepared during 1970's and 1980's have not got statutory sanctions, nor had they been implemented, nor there were any comprehensive urbanization policy in the country. However a Task Force for planning and development of small and medium size towns was constituted in 1975.

The Task Force published its report in 1977 with the emphasis on the integrated growth and development of small and medium size towns (IDSMT) (not exceeding 100,000 population) so as to divert the rural urban migration stream towards these towns. One of the major recommendations was to formulate a national urbanization policy. Such, policy should include *inter-alia* urban land development policy for efficient utilisation, housing for the poor and low income group through mass public housing projects, locational policy of economic activities so as to create urban centres integrally linked with the regional economy and working out urban development norms and standards with the creation of statutory local authority at appropriate level. This programme (IDSMT) was vigorously launched in 1979-80 and was incorporated in the Sixth (1980-85) and Seventh (1985-90) Plans but failed to divert the migration stream away from the large cities.

The Role of IDSMT Urban Development Policy

The main emphasis of this programme was on the creation of urban infrastructure and civic amenities of life such as improvement of slum environment through drainage, sewerage and sanitation and health facilities, provision for potable water supply, conversion of open privies to sanitary ones, etc. This centrally sponsored programme was supported by central assistance by about 50 per cent for urban development subject to states' matching contribution of 50 per cent. The budgetary limit was Rs. 10 million per town in 5 years. This central assistance came as a soft loan with only 5.5 per cent interest per annum and to be repaid in 25 years including initial moratorium on loan repayment for 5 years. The loan assistance was extended to include land acquisition and services, construction of new markets, provision for industrial estates, processing and service activities, and employment generation in the unorganised sector, besides many physical development schemes. It was also envisaged that these cities and towns will be functionally and spatially linked to their regional setting and economy with the extension of services to agriculture and allied activities which in turn would find their markets in such towns. In most cases they were chosen with respect to their growth potential.

In the beginning of the Sixth Plan, 231 towns having population 100,000 or below were chosen under this scheme of urban development and by the end of the Plan period, the programme extended to 235 towns inclusive of some large towns. During the Seventh Plan, 102 more towns were brought under this IDSMT scheme with a budgetary provision of Rs. 880 million so as to complete the ongoing projects. Housing for the houseless was also incorporated in the programme including low cost sanitation, water supply and sewerage system.

National Urbanization Policy

The National Commission on Urbanization (NCU) appointed by the government of India and chaired by Charles M. Correa, submitted its interim report in January 1987 and the final report in August 1988. The main issues before the NCU were:

1. Where and how the urban population to the order of 350 mn could be accommodated and how to provide them with necessary urban infrastructure and services?,
2. The Metropolitan cities in India are already in deep crisis with overcrowding, scarcity of land, services on the verge of breaking down and defective urban planning and management. The urban agglomerations have fast been reduced to virtual slums,
3. Physical infrastructure and administrative systems have deteriorated and urban finances both in allocation of resources and raising internal revenue have collapsed. How to support urban development?
4. The urban agglomerations have become the destination of economically and socially displaced rural migrants thus bodily transferred the rural poverty to the cities and distort the rural-urban space relationship.

While deliberating on the above issues and investigating the imperative causes, the NCU had no other option except to recommend strategies to bring about healthy rural-urban relation by pre-empting development and reform measures to be carried out immediately within the rural India itself as the real causes of urban crisis are underdevelopment of rural settlements and rural people. If urbanization has to be slowed down in guiding the rural-urban migration having filtering effect, rural people have to be contained where they belong with reasonable level of living. Non-agricultural activities have to be brought to them rather than bringing the people to the jobs in urban areas. That will bring structural change in the rural settlements in themselves. The Rural Area Development should be the basis of urbanization policy of India.

The urban development programme such as Integrated Urban Development (IUDP), Integrated Development of Small and Medium Size Towns (IDSMT) was adopted in piecemeal and *ad hoc* manner in 1970's and 1980's and not as a component of comprehensive urbanization policy nor were they allowed to run their full course. Hence there is a need for a comprehensive urbanization policy for the country. The NCU has not been able to deliver a concrete urbanization policy and only highlighted certain strategies—

1. A structurally balanced urban development has to be based upon regional economic development and resource allocation thereof;
2. Decentralized urban development has to be supported by decentralized planning and dispersal of economic activities;
3. Development of the metro cities should be an integral part of national plan with the provision of self-supported urban infrastructure while initial investment in large scale is the imperative need;
4. The available infrastructure of the medium size towns and cities need to be utilized fully so as to reduce the cost of new infrastructural development and at the same time any additional cost has to be paid for by the users;
5. Besides, there should be a well thought out urban land policy, municipal finance, infrastructural need and

investment policy. Planning for balanced urban development has to be based upon sound regional development policy, rural-urban integration and decentralised urban growth. The NCU has identified 329 cities called GEMs (Generator of Economic Momentum) for integrated urban development based on their growth potential and available infrastructure.

Based on the geographic configuration of GEMs, 49 special priority urbanization regions (SPUR) have also been delineated taking into account the 15 agro-climatic regions (recently defined by the Planning Commission) and 80 natural regions used by National Sample Survey Organisation (NSSO). These SPURs will play significant role in urban decentralization provided they are backed by efficient utilisation of natural and human resources. This is the spatial planning approach to urbanization planning policy in India.

Distribution of GEMs

GEMs (329 cities and towns)

NPCs (77 cities)		*SPCs (252 cities and Towns)*	
1. State Capital Centres	3	1. Cities with potential for Generating economic momentum	103
2. Million Cities of 1981	4	2. Headquarters of District with 30% and more urban population	20
3. Million Cities Expected by 2001	27	3. Headquarters of Districts with 90% and more rural population	109
4. Economic Growth Potential Centres	9	4. Residual list (economic, social and environmental considerations)	20
5. Residual List (Socio-cultural and other considerations)	9		

The NCU has made 78-point recommendations with regard to urbanization, land policy, water and sanitation needs, energy requirement, transport and communication infrastructure, housing policy, urban finance and urban management, information system for land and environmental planning and for decision-making and above all spatial planning to supplement economic development planning by inter-sectoral co-ordination. The spatial planning (items No. 58 and 59 of NCU summary recommendation) at state and district level should concentrate on National Priority Cities (NPCs), State Priority Cities (SPCs) and Spatial Priority Urbanization Regions (SPURs) with a view to bringing about integrated development—"through multi-level planning". At the city level local government should undertake threefold urban planning *viz*. Master Directive Plan for the entire city, Execution Plan and Action Area Plans. The last one will aim at detail planning at sectoral development on employment generation, housing, transport and other infrastructure. The Execution plans should reorient the zonal plans and correspond to state and national plans in prioritisation to facilitate budgetary allocation and investments.

The Mega City problems are of international dimension. Delhi has expanded territorially to the neighbouring states and this spatial spread of urban development and the location of economic activities and housing in the vicinity of Delhi Union Territory have necessitated the constitution of National Capital Region. The spatial differentiation between the place of work and place of residences has increased the friction of space to overcome which has called for expansion of transport and communication network. The case of Bombay in a way is different because of peninsular location and concentration of central functions at the tip of peninsula where expansion has taken place vertically. Besides, the setting up of New Bombay across the Bay has farther increased the transport need.

Calcutta being the slowest growing mega city is different in many ways. The civic services, transport system and rampant poverty have reached the point of no return.

The mega city problems require a regional approach and unless their hinterland regions are developed and symbiotic rural-urban relation is established, their economies will collapse.

Historically, the mega cities or primate cities grew at the cost of the small and medium size towns in appropriating their petty surplus and pauperising the hinterland economy. All these metro cities and even the newer ones are located in the lowly urbanized and industrialized hinterland regions. The recent trend of urban growth in the resource rich backward region has failed to exert appropriate growth impulses in their regional hinterland although there are symptoms of spatial transformation in economic, social and physical development. The regional planning approach to urbanization planning is missing. The rural-urban relation is more bureaucratically structured than inter-dependent. The spatial planning related to rural development may create a favourable situation for decentralization of urban growth.

Conclusion

Our urbanization policy should aim at a comprehensive settlement policy for integrated development of the whole spectrum of rural and urban places in social, economic and physical terms.

In order to achieve spatially balanced urbanization pattern, the physical planning process has to be functionally and spatially integrated with social and economic planning at various levels of planning.

This calls for decentralized urbanization planning so that the rural-urban migrants would find place in the secondary and tertiary cities rather than gravitating towards the mega cities. The mega cities need careful planning so as to strengthen the economic base of the GEMs identified by the NCU.

The concept of multi-level planning as a system at three levels (Nation, State and Districts) of synthesis is based on the combination of bottom up and top down approach of socio-economic structuring and spatially balanced development.

The decentralized planning process related to urban industrial and rural agricultural development is to be supporterd by the philosophy of growth with equity and delegation of power to act. The participating governments, at all levels—nation, state, district and local must take decision and act upon with the participation of the beneficiaries.

References

1. Government of India (1988), "Executive Summary: India's Urbanization Policy", *Habitat International*, 12 (3), pp. 17-19.
2. Ministry of Works and Housing, Government of India (1977), *Report of the Task Force on Planning and Development of Small and Medium Size Towns and Cities*, Vols. I & II, New Delhi.
3. Nanda, A.R. (1991), *Census of India 1991*, Series-1, Paper-2 of 1991 Provisional Population Totals: Rural-Urban Distribution, New Delhi.
4. Pathak, C.R. (1989), "Spatial Planning and Development Philosophy—Priorities and Implications of SPURs, GEMs, NPCs and SPCs—a Discussion", Presented in the *AITP Workshop on* October, New Delhi.
5. *Report of the National Commission on Urbanization (1988)*, Vols. I & II, August, New Delhi.
6. Routray, J.K. (1993), "Urban and Regional Planning in Practice in India", *Habitat International*, Vol. 17, No. 4, pp. 1-20.

16

Bio-Diversity, Sustainable Development and Intellectual Property Rights

—A.C. Minocha

Bio-diversity is the sum total of all forms of life and is the simplest expression of the most complicated system on earth. It represents the notion of right of life of all living beings. It is sustainable development which takes care of bio-diversity and ensures equilibrium between its different components. Sustainable development is that process which meets the needs of present generation without compromising the ability of the future generations to meet their needs. It is essentially a question of balancing of present and future needs, though our myopic view of development prefers present to future needs. Our concern for balance between economic and ecological linkages has got operationized in the concept of sustainable development.

In any discussion on sustainable development, agriculture is often at the centre of discussions, since it is dependent mainly on natural resources, land, water and physical conditions. Sustainable development of agriculture not only involves identification and application of improved technologies but also ecological and socio-economic concerns. The objectives of sustainable development of agriculture can be, increase in productivity, measured by yield per hectare, sustainability, ensuring continuous development in the future also, equitability, measured in terms of distribution of gains of new technology across regions and size-class of holdings, stability, measured in terms of coefficient of variation of yield. A trade-off among these objectives is essential for sustainable development of agriculture.

The green revolution technology has been highly productive but at the same time marked by low sustainability since it has been resource intensive and has created problems of soil erosion, salinity, water-logging, depletion of ground water, loss of fertility due to excessive extraction from land, health hazards, loss of bio-diversity, etc. Resource intensive technologies are essentially environment degrading and, therefore, adversely affect bio-diversity and sustainable development.

The most important question relating to sustainable development of agriculture is who manages and controls natural resources like land, water, forest and other resources, who benefits from that management and who pays for current utilisation of resources. This question of resource management and resource ownership has received little attention in studies of sustainable development of Indian agriculture. The natural resources are managed through technical and institutional arrangements. The technical arrangements provide tools and knowledge, and technological improvement determines how resources are used as factors of production. The institutional arrangements determine as to who control these resources. The nature of institutional arrangements defines the extent of people's rights over resources which may assume the form of state property regime, private property regime, both individual and corporate, common property regime and open access regime. The basic requirement of any property regime is the authority system which may be the international organization, the central and state governments, the village panchayats, resource development committees, the user groups, with a view to protecting the security of right holders and ensuring sustainable development.

Intellectual property rights (IPRs) provide such an institutional arrangements for the management and control of natural resources and confer monopoly rights to the inventors of new ideas, new processes, new products, along with benefits accruing from sale and management and control. Intellectual property is the creation of human mind or intellect. Patenting is one form of protecting intellectual property. Other forms may be trade marks, designs, copy-rights. A research leading to invention can acquire the status of intellectual property. Of all these forms of IPRs, patent is the most important. It is an exclusive right to use and sell a particular invention for a specific period. The basic assumption of IPR is that people cannot innovate or generate knowledge unless they are driven by profit motive. Although IPRs are centuries old, then extension to bio-technology has increased tremendously the possibility of manipulating living organisms. Bio-technology is a general term used to describe any manipulation of living organism by altering its characteristics. It is applied not only to traditional plants and animal breeding but also to fomentation process, plant genetics, industrial tissues, dairying and animal husbandry. It has increased the potential for raising the productivity of agricultural products, by making it possible to cut out genes from one plant and transfer to another through cross-fertilization. Genes are tiny invisible particles carrying hereditary characteristics.

At the Urguay Round of negotiations, the scope of GATT was widened to include new areas, one of which was IPRs in genetically engineered varieties of seed, fertilizers and chemicals, the most critical inputs of agriculture. The inventors of these, by and large, are the multinational companies of developed countries which command tremendous resources for research and development in these areas. The authority system under the institutional arrangement is provided by WTO, the successor to GATT, and the central governments of member countries who are placed under obligation to protect their IPRs.

Intellectual property rights conflict with farmers right to bio-diversity as well as freedom of the researchers to work for the removal of hunger. Under the new regime, there will be conflict between the farmers and the seed industry, between public domain and private profit, between agriculture which produces and reproduces diversity and one which consumes diversity and produces uniformity.

Seed is a common resource of local farmers whose innovations are collective in nature and are shared. The farmers have been the original breeders, custodians and owners of seeds. The new institutional arrangements takes away this right from the farming community and gives it to such companies which can establish monopoly control. From individual and community right to international monopoly rights is a change of considerable importance. The development of thousand varieties of seeds by farmers in India and other developing countries through selection, breeding and cross-breeding have little to do with profit. The public seed breeding agencies like the agricultural universities, the Indian Council of Agricultural Research (ICAR) and other research institutes have done considerable work, motivated by public welfare.

Under the patented product regime, the farmers will have the right to use seeds and that too at a high price but no right to save and reproduce or sell them unless specifically permitted by the country where they live. It would be violation of the IPR regime, if the farmers pass on the harvested seeds or sell them to others. All this amounts to infringement of farmers rights. These rights include the right to conserve, modify and develop new varieties, the right to exchange, the right to breed for diversity and conservation of bio-diversity, the right to cultivate diverse crops, the right to get free information about the risk of chemical pollution and the right to produce diverse nutritious food for healthy consumption.

There is a fundamental conflict between the regime of IPRs and the objective of Convention on Bio-diversity held in 1992. The threefold objectives of Convention on Bio-Diversity (CBD) are conservation of bio-diversity, sustainable use of its components, the equitable use of the benefits of its use. IPRs would come into conflict with all the three objectives of CBD. Whatever may be the motive of IPRs, their extension to bio-diversity will have serious repercussions. The notion of monopolistic IPRs is an alien concept to many local and indigenous communities, since for them most knowledge and biological resources are commonly owned and are meant to be shared. In India nearly two-third of annual seed requirements of farmers are met through inter-farm exchange and the rest through agencies like the seed corporations. Informal inventions by the farmers are the main reason for stability and sustainability of agricultural system.

Article 27(2) of TRIPs recognises that the state can exclude from patentability such inventions, the prevention of whose commercial exploitation is necessary to avoid serious degeneration of environment, but the authority to examine, interpret and decide what constitutes prejudicial to environment will be that of WTO.

Under another article 27(3), the state can provide for the patenting of plant varieties either by patents of by effective *sui generis* system or combination of both. But the provision forces a country the patentability of micro-organisms and micro-biological process, leaving little scope for the countries which may not want to patent any form of life.

The existing international agreement that covers plant breeders rights is the international convention for the protection of new varieties of plants known as UPOV Convention. It may be suitable for developed countries where farmers are not a large part of population and do not have any control over breeding and seed supplies. In OECD countries, all farmers are consumers of seed supplied by the seed industry. The UPOV convention provides for a high degree of standardisation. It is inappropriate as a *sui generis* system. To be eligible for protection, the new variety must be uniform, distinct and stable. Breeders and researchers have to pay hefty royalty to the plant breeders or using patented variety for further research. A genuine *sui generis* should recognise farmers and plant breeders rights and build on CBD. The owners of IPRs of patented plant varieties are mostly the big companies. Even under plant breeders, the farmers have to pay royalty for raising and breeding seeds on their farms.

Lot of debate has taken place in respect of *sui generis* system. Does it mean non-monopolistic model of protection of plant varieties and recognise informal varieties of farming communities and provide incentives for the same? The PBR under UPOV is being put forward as a model for *sui generis*. But we have seen that PBR is another form of monopoly power to the right holders. Any *sui generis* system will be opened for review by the WTO to decide whether it is effective or not. It is doubtful whether a system of free exchange of seeds would qualify for *sui generis*. There is fundamental conflict between the coverage of IPRs and the objectives of CBD. IPRs represent a move towards the notion of "might is right." It is a global instrument that the bio-technology is using for giving monopoly control over seeds supply. IPR is a recipe for food insecurity and bio-diversity erosion. The CBD on the other hand, has been one of the responses of the world community to conserve the ideological basis of bio-diversity. It recognises the national sovereign rights of countries to their biological wealth, recognises the contribution of indigenous communities to knowledge about utilisation of bio-diversity.

The GATT agreement requires the member countries to evolve systems of protection of all the types of intellectual property rights, extending their scope to micro-organism, bio-technology and genetic resources. So far, patents were extended to chemicals and drugs.

The Indian Patent Act, 1970, which was considered to be one of the best in the world and had given a big boost to drug industry provided for only process patents. The main feature of the Indian provision was that through alternative processes, the same product could be manufactured. The WTO, on the other hand, provides for both process patents as well as product patents. Product patenting implies that the production of a patented product cannot be made by any process. The product patenting is inherently unfair. Such a system of patenting would reduce the scope of innovations in developing countries and make them dependent upon international players. India is required to amend its Patent Act of 1970 in accordance with the provisions of the WTO. Our Patent Act could not be amended by Parliament but through an ordinance of the President to enable India to become a member of WTO. A bill to replace the ordinance lapsed with the dissolution of the Lok Sabha. Pressures are now being built on the government of India to get the Act amended. The Agricultural Ministry has also adopted a new legislation entitled, "Plant Varieties Protection and Farmers Rights" Act. The proposed Act assumes the role of farmers as conservers but not as innovators.

Recently the WTO has held India guilty of violation of the 1994 TRIPs agreement about patents on pharmaceuticals and agro-chemicals. It has ordered India not only to comply with the treaty but stipulates the precise mechanism for doing so which tantamounts to interference in domestic affairs of a sovereign state.

The TRIPS Article 70.8 and 70.9 require the developing countries to take certain transitional measures during 10-year period allowed to move from process only patents to products patents. India is required to create "mail-box" to hold applications for patents to be given effect only in the year 2005. The immediate requirement for the government is to make the acceptance of product patent applications in pharmaceuticals and agro-chemicals and then begin for comprehensive legislative exercises. During the transition period, India is required to create a "mail-box" to hold applications for patents to be given effect only in the year 2005 and grant exclusive marketing rights in respect of products for which applicants have filed patents and obtained marketing clearance in another WTO member-state. India is already providing such a mail-box.

There is no unanimity among major political parties regarding the contents of comprehensive bill that India should enact to comply with the requirements of IPRs. It may be recalled that the Peoples Commission on GATT consisting of eminent jurists had examined the question of compatibility of the provisions of TRIPS agreement, with the basic provisions of our Constitution. The new government should avail of the analysis and conclusions of that Commission. The government is in the process of evolving a *sui generis* system for protection of plant varieties. This may raise important issues which include the direction of agricultural research in our country, its over-riding requirement for protecting the interests of vast number of resource poor marginal and subsistence farmers, the need to preserve the option of low cost diffusion of better varieties, due recognition of our publicly funded research institutions in envolving new varieties and by our farming community in developing large varieties. A nation-wide transparent consultation should be held with the experts and activists who have been expressing their view on these issues over the last few years. Due consideration should be given to differing perspectives so that any legislative action that we take in due course truly reflects the national consensus.

"We are signatory to the Bio-diversity Convention of 1992 also. The best way is to temper article 70.8 and 70.9 with article 7 of TRIPS which states that IPRs "should promote technological innovation and transfer and dissemination of technology in a manner conducive to social and economic welfare" and article 8 which allows measures "to protect public health and nutrition and promote public interest in sectors of vital importance and protect abuse of IPRs and practices which unreasonably restrain trade or adversely affect the international transfer of technology."

India should enact its own legislation to safeguard patent rights of traditional agricultural commodities and to India's claim for reciprocal patents with WTO countries under the TRIPS agreement. Recent decision of US government to grant patent to Rice Tee for basmati rice could have been countered, had we evolved our own legislation to protect patents of our own products in line with international standards. Such a legislation would facilitate patenting of our inventions or innovations by the country's scientific establishment, the CSIR. The US grant of patents for wound healing properties of turmeric powder 3 years ago, was challenged on the basis of application filed by CSIR on the ground that such properties were part of our traditional knowledge. The efforts of CSIR finally paid off when the US patent office rejected the patent on August 13, 1997. There is strong need for meticulous documentation of our traditional knowledge and practices by our Research and Development institutions.

References

1. Jha, A.K., "Concern for Bio-Diversity", *EPW*, March 11, 1995.
2. FAO, "Sustainable Agricultural and Rural Development in Asia and Pacific", Regional Document No. 2, FAO Conference on Agriculture and Environment, April, 1991.
3. Jodha, N.S., "Sustainable Agriculture in Fragile Resource Regions", *EPW*, March 30, 1991.
4. Reddy, Ratna, "Environment and Sustainable Development—Conflicts and Contradictions", *EPW*, March 25, 1995.
5. Chopra, Kanchan, "Forests and Other Sectors—Critical Role of Government Policy", *EPW*, January 24, 1995.
6. Thamarajshi, R. "Some Aspects of Environmental Accounting", *EPW*, November 21, 1992.
7. Mehta, R.P.S., "Public Policy and Sustainable Agricultural Development—A National Accounting Approach", *The Indian Journal of Agricultural Economics*, October-December, 1995.
8. Rao, Mohan J., "Wither Indian Environment", *EPW*, April 1, 1995.

9. Johal, S.S., "Structural Adjustment in Agriculture Sector for Growth and Productivity", Centre for Research in Rural and Industrial Development, Chandigarh, 1994.
10. Rao, CH. Hanumantha and Gulati, Ashok, "Indian Agriculture Emerging Perspectives and Major Policy Issues", *EPW*, December, 1994.
11. Minocha, A.C., "Globalisation of Indian Agriculture", *EPW*, April 15, 1995.
12. Acharya, Sarthi and Acharya, Niru, "Structural Adjustment Policies and Small Producers", *EPW*, January 7, 1995.
13. Manda, Meera, "Transnationalisation of Third World State and Undoing of Green Revolution", *EPW*, January 7, 1995.
14. Bhalla, G.S. "Globalisation and Agricultural Policy", *EPW*, January 28, 1995.
15. Nandna, Shiva, "Bio-Diversity, Totalitarianism, IPRs as Seed Monopolies", *EPW*, October 11, 1997.
16. Patel, Sujata, "Ecology and Development", *EPW*, September 20, 1997.
17. Vyas, V.S. and Ratna Reddy, "Assessment of Environmental Policies and Policy Implementation in India", *EPW*, January 10, 1998.
18. "Foreign Invasion—How the West is Trying to Steal What is Ours", *Down to Earth*, February 28, 1998.

17

Structural Adjustment in India and Its Impact on Balanced Regional Development

—G.B. Nath

Introduction

Over the last decade a lot of changes have taken place in Indian economy, due to economic reforms initiated by the then Prime Minister Rajiv Gandhi during the last 1980's. But it gather momentum only in 1991 when comprehensive structural adjustment policy was adopted by Narasimha Rao government. When they took office in July 1991 the economy was out of control, exports were declining, foreign exchange reserves had declined to no more than two weeks, import and industry was virtually crippled. Hence government had to give the highest priority to restoring macro economic stability to bring the economy back to the path of rapid growth. The subsequent government formed by the leadership of H.D. Deve Gowda and I.K. Gujral carried forward the measures initiated by their predecessors. The stabilisation and structural adjustment programme (S and SAP) otherwise known as "New Economic

Policy" (NEP) 'Reforms' etc. involves liberalisation of financial and capital market, restructuring of the industries, rationalisation of approach toward MRTP Act, privatisation of public sector undertakings, reforms in foreign trade and tax policies, globalization of the economy, opening up of the domestic economy to the world market etc.

It has been argued by the proponents of the SAP that the reform measures would promote broad base of sustainable growth process which would percolate to the poorest of the poor person and regions of the country. One of the approach of Five Year Plan in India is to reduce regional disparities. Even the Fourth Five Year Plan started paying special attention towards balanced development of regions by taking target group approaches and comprehensive area development programmes. But now after the advent of the 'NEP' in India we have given farewell to planning and shifting our loyalty towards the market-oriented economy. Now the issue before us is to analyse whether S and SAP would take care of the regional disparities or accentuate the already existing disparities between states. Whether the backward regions would able to draw the needed amount of capital for its development, or remain as supplier of raw materials to the advance states. Given the context, the present paper argues that the working of the planned economy, industrial policy and licensing policy itself has encouraged the process of economic concentration in certain regions and business houses in India. Switching over from planned economy to open economy or market economy with regulation would accentuate the existing regional disparities due to its inherent contradictions.

Disparities in Industrial Growth

Despite natural resources and huge manpower the industrial revolution had bypassed the Indian subcontinent due to the colonisation of the country. After transfer of power the Indian government wanted to decolonise the country by setting up of various industries. One of the objectives of planning was to promote regional balance in the economy through planned investment of domestic as well as foreign capital. However industrial disparities in the country persisted.

The North-Eastern states in Indian union and states like Bihar, Orissa are in the bottom of industrial development. In contrast Maharashtra, Tamil Nadu, Gujarat, Punjab, West Bengal are industrially most advanced states. Mishra and Puri's study reveals that the western region and West Bengal taken together accounted for 63.3 per cent of total persons employed, 60.41 per cent of gross in factory value of output and 63.45 per cent of value added by manufacturing (Mishra and Puri, 1988).

The government of India appointed a committee in July 1967 under the chairmanship of Subimal Dutta to enquire into the working of the licensing system. This industrial licensing policy enquiry committee or in short Dutta Committee submitted its report in July 1969. One of the objective of industrial licensing policy was the reduction in regional disparities. But Dutta Committee found that the four industrially advanced states Maharashtra, West Bengal, Gujarat and Tamil Nadu were the main beneficiaries of the industrial licensing policy for they bagged 62 percentage of the total licenses issued during the decade 1955-66. The states like Orissa, Bihar, Uttar Pradesh and Madhya Pradesh benefited the least by bagging only 15 per cent of the total licences approved. Thus instead of reducing the regional disparities the licensing policy of government of India accentuated it.

The National Development Council (NDC) in 1968 recommended the following criterion for the identification of industrially backward states and union territories

(*i*) Total per capita income together with contribution of industry and mining,
(*ii*) Number of workers in registered factory per lakh of population,
(*iii*) Per capita annual consumption of electricity,
(*iv*) Length of surface roads in relation to population and area of the state,
(*v*) Railway mileage in relation to the population and the area of the state.

The NDC in 1968 constituted two working groups to identify backward areas and recommending fiscal and financial incentives for their development—Pande Committee and Wanchoo Committee respectively. On the basis of the criteria set up by the NDC in 1968, as has been given above the Pande Committee has identified Andhra Pradesh, Madhya Pradesh, Uttar Pradesh, Bihar, Orissa, Rajasthan, Assam, Jammu & Kashmir and Nagaland as industrially backward areas. The Wanchoo Committee recommended the following fiscal incentives for industries set up in backward areas:

(*a*) grant of higher development rebate to industries located in backward areas,
(*b*) grant of exemption from period of five years,
(*c*) exemption from import duty on plant and machinery and components imported by a unit located in a backward district,
(*d*) exemption from excise duties for a period of 5 years,
(*e*) exemption from sales tax for a period of 5 years, and
(*f*) provision of transport subsidy for the despatch of finished products for five years.

Government of India constituted an 11-member Committee under the chairmanship of P.C. Nayak in August 1975 to examine the question of development of backward areas and suggest measures for balanced regional development. The Nayak Committee suggested for setting up of a central authority for backward area development at National level to assist in planning, sponsoring and promoting industrial development of the backward areas. The Committee also recommended for a system of disinventives by the central government to ensure that large metropolitan centres do not become attractive to large and medium industries. Another similar attempt was also taken in 1980 when government of India constituted a high level national committee for the development of backward areas. This Committee felt that the industrial estate programme has not helped to relocate industries away from metropolitan areas and the licensing policy could not by itself promote industrial development in backward areas.

Thus since the inception of planning in India a number of committees were set up and rule and regulations were formed to arrest industrial concentration in the metropolis and disperse them to the periphery. Only due to the persistent effort and deliberate planning and participation of the state in industrial activities certain medium and large industries have come to the backward states.

Since one and a half decade, Indian policies of central planning, state control and protection were radically altered with the ushering in of economic liberalisation and privatisation. The Nehruvian legacies of inword looking growth strategy based on self-reliance, equity and social justice, import substitution, restriction of foreign investment, nationalisation of key sectors, it is alleged, have resulted in the evolution of an inefficient economic system. Hence S and SAP was considered as a panacea for the problem Indian Economy was facing. The salient features of the industrial restructuring programme are as follows:

1. Industrial licensing has been abolished for all excepting a short list of industries related to security and strategic concerns, social reasons, hazardous chemicals and overriding environmental reasons and items of elitist consumption. The exemption from licensing will apply to all substantial expansions of existing units.
2. Foreign investment has made easy. Approval would be given for direct foreign investment upto 51 per cent foreign equity in high priority industries. For the promotion of export of Indian products in world market the government would encourage foreign trading companies to assist Indian exporters in export activities.
3. Automatic permission has been given for foreign technology agreements in high priority industries. This would inject, it is hoped, a high level of technological dynamism in Indian economy.
4. There is also public sector restructuring which continue to be poor in their performance, quality of services and returns on investments. Little has been done to improve their performance. Public sectors which are chronically sick are to be referred to the Board of Industrial and Financial Reconstruction (BIFR). This may result in closure or, privatisation of some of these public sector undertakings. As a part of restructuring of the PSUs government has resort to disinvestment. By divestiture or disinvestment public ownership is partially or fully transformed to private management through sale of equities.
5. Government has restricted the work of Monopolies and Restrictive Trade Practices Act (MRTP Act) by removing

the threshold limit of assets in respect of MRTP companies and dominant undertakings. Hence there is no need now to get prior approval of government for establishment of new undertakings expansion or merger, amalgamation of old industries etc.

All these liberalisation, globalisation and privatisation measures no doubt make Indian industries competitive within the country as well as globally, urgently address the problem of cost reduction and improvement in productivity, generate sufficient resources, invest in constant technology upgradation, modernisation and develop R and D, made quality production for the best satisfaction of the consumers etc. However, all these achievements are at a great social cost. Particularly in the context of a growing regional disparities industrial restructuring as has been envisaged in India would encourage an enclave type of development. As we know there is disproportionate concentration of industries in cities like Calcutta, Bombay, Delhi, Madras, Ahmedabad, Bangalore, Hyderabad, Bhopal, Ranchi, Kanpur, Rourkela etc. Industrial licensing policy was made the scapegoat of regional disparities. Hence decision to do away with licensing except for some specific industries is good. But the question before us is that can free market concept and de-regulation regime would ensure regional balance? What mechanism now is left over to set right the regional disparities? Hence in the absence of a regulation and control, capital again would come to these cities and mega cities. New industrial establishment and expansion of old industries would further lead towards heavy concentration of industries. In these localities creating, environmental, housing, health and transportation problems. At a time when there is a need of decentralisation of industries to achieve balanced regional industrial development there would be concentration of industries in few mega cities. There is provisions of public utility services like transport, electricity water, which attracts the industries in these cities. State participation in industrialisation in the past, has developed certain Industrial Estates for attracting industries to backward districts by providing these public utility services. But now by withdrawing state from industrialisation and doing away with licensing policies would hamper the effort of decentralisation, hence liberalisation of licensing policies and procedure in regard to the location of projects reinforces the attraction of the already developed regions and thus goes against the regional balance objective (Sandesara 1991).

Agrarian Disparities and New Economic Policy

There is considerable regional disparities between states in Indian union on agricultural front. The evolution of the post-colonial agrarian structure shows that capital penetration in agriculture to modify the pre-capitalist agrarian structure is not even throughout the country. As the process of capital penetration is weak in some parts than other the duality in agrarian structure prevailing. This has given rise to a modern capitalist sector and an isolated subsistence based pre-capitalist agrarian structure. The ruling elites in India wanted to release the productive forces arrested under colonial influence stagnating agriculture. In response to this various land reform measures which included the abolition of intermediary right in land, security of tenure, fixation of ceiling on land holding and the redistribution of ceiling surplus land were attempted. Abolition of intermediary rights which was the first stage of land reform was held as the outstanding achievement in bringing about a peaceful transition in agrarian relation. But security of tenure and fixation of ceiling inland holding and distribution of ceiling surplus land was not welcomed. Hence the landless peasants and agricultural labourers who could have the principal beneficiaries of land reform measures were neglected.

Instead of tenancy reform and distribution of ceiling surplus land state in mid-1960's adopted the Green Revolution strategy of agrarian development. Green Revolution strategy is a package: Combination of mutually dependent agricultural inputs like high yielding variety seeds, chemical fertiliser, pesticides and insecticides, along with adequate irrigation. Introduction of high yielding variety of wheat, paddy, maize, jowar and bazara depends crucially on the availability of fertiliser, adequate water supply and pesticides and insecticides. That is why these varieties could not be adopted to areas without irrigation facilities.

The technical change initiated along with the feudal structure of the economy strengthened the economic base of the rich peasants and landlords. This is because they had the political as well as the economic strength to generate a large surplus and raise credit for investment in irrigation, fertilizer, pesticide and farm machinery. They were also the major recipients of the price incentive, marketing facility and technical advice. Hence the package encouraged an enclave type of agrarian development. For it was limited to the areas which commanded necessary resources. Like, Punjab, Haryana, Maharashtra, Godavari belt in Andhra Pradesh and Western Uttar Pradesh etc. The east which was reeling under semi-feudal production relation in agriculture left out of the Green Revolution Programme. Hence this area specific programme created a lot of regional imbalance in agrarian development.

In the context of a weak structural change and uneven penentration of capital it is instructive to study the World Bank led S and SAP. In Indian economy, reforms in India has not been carried out in the agricultural sector in a big way. However the World Bank has proposed certain changes in the agricultural policy in the Country Memorandum. Some of these recommendations are:

1. Reduction in subsidies, on agricultural inputs,
2. De-regulating international trade in agricultural commodities,
3. Scaling down of the government procurement operation,
4. Reduction of the role of Food Corporation of India, and
5. Dismantling the public distribution system (PDS) etc.

It has been argued that liberalisation and globalisation in agriculture would improve terms of trade in favour of agriculture and the Indian farmer would reap much more benefit by exporting non-traditional items like horticultural, floricultural and dairy based products, poultry and marine products etc. Such diversification of agriculture would raise farm employment, income productivity and improve the socio-economic position of the weaker sections by reducing poverty and inequality (Rao and Gulati 1994, Rao 1994, V.M. Rao 1994).

Globalisation of the agriculture pre-supposes the free import and export of agricultural produce. In order to earn foreign exchange more and more exportable crops would be produced.

Hence there would be shift from low profit consumption crops to high profit cash crops like fruits and vegetables. Business houses like Tata, Godrej, Escort, IPCL, Usha-Martin, Arvind Mills have also been entering to agriculture. These industrialist-turned agriculturist and other gentlemen farmers and the rich peasants those also have been benefited from Green Revolution Programme are now demanding for the integration of the Indian agriculturalists with the world market and treatment of agriculture as industry. They are also demanding to free the lease market and scarp the ceiling on landholding. Once government conceded to these demand it would be much difficult to protect the small and marginal farmers in India, whose number is more than two-third of the farming community. Thus the Green Revolution Programme has in the past by-passed the small and marginal peasants, it has increased the gap between the rich state and not so rich states. Particularly eastern India is not a green revolution area. A number of institutional barriers inhibits agricultural growth. Similarly certain western parts and southern parts experience poor water resources. Hence agriculturally advance states like, Punjab, Haryana, Tamil Nadu, Uttar Pradesh, Andhra Pradesh would reap the full benefit out of the globalization and liberalisation of agriculture. Agriculturally poor states in North-East, and eastern India, dry areas of western India would not get much benefit due to the prevalence of subsistence farming in these states.

Besides the above factors fiscal compression in the economy has been achieved in part through cutback in agricultural infrastructure like power, irrigation, fertiliser etc. The institutional credit to rural sector has been reduced following the recommendation of the Narasimham Committee report and this has now raised cost of credit to agriculture. Similarly in order to cut back fiscal deficit government has resorted to reducing subsidies on fertilizer, power, water etc. This has resulted in loss of income and fall of production. All these factors have led to the loss of income and earnings of the working class pushing them to abysmal poverty and destitution. As Nayar and Sen (1994) have observed, the trade policy reform in Indian agriculture may change the distribution of agricultural output and income between regions, accentuating inequalities. Keeping the poor states in view, the land reform programmes, poverty alleviation schemes and subsidised food and credit has not lost its importance. Hence S and SAP should address to these issues for a balanced regional development of the vast sub-continent like India.

Growth of Basic Infrastructure and Economic Development

Development of infrastructural facilities like transport; rail road and shipping; finance; insurance and banking; energy: Coal, electricity and oil; social overheads like health and education affects the economic development to a great extent. Most of the industries in India has been localised in the area with good infrastructural facilities be it physical or human. Infrastructural building requires heavy capital, expenditure and the gestation period is quite long. Hence the private capital is quite shy in entering into these sectors. That is why since the initiation of planning in India state has been asigned with the responsibility in providing with these facilities. Heavy investment in infrastructural facilities with the state initiative has tremendously raised the quality of its service in the country. State funding of education has paid rich dividends in terms of massive expansion of education, supply of scientific and technical man-power etc. Similarly, phenomenal growth has taken place due to public investment in irrigation. It has raised farm productivity, facilitated Green Revolution etc. Public monopoly in power sector has industrialised the state by providing power at a cheaper rate. Despite these achievements the infrastructural facilities are highly unevenly distributed in the country. Taking into consideration the totality of infrastructure Punjab, Goa, Kerala, Tamil Nadu, Maharashtra are the leading states in India in providing these facilities, Rajastan, Uttar Pradesh, Orissa, Madhya Pradesh, Bihar lagging far behind. Besides, most of the infrastructural facilities are urban bias. Whether it is power or transport, banking or insurance, health or education all they have been concentrated in the urban localities.

After the initiation of the S and SAP in India, infrastructural sector is no more the public sector monopoly. World Bank's clear message is that public investment is the cause of all economic ills in India. Hence state should withdraw and that is what government of India is doing during all these years of 'reform' government want to invite private capital, both domestic and foreign to invest in infrastructural sector. Private investment has taken up in the road and port sector on the built, operate and transfer (BOT) basis. Government of India in recent years has set up Infrastructural Development Finance Company with an authorised capital of Rs. 5,000 crores. Government has also announced various measures like automatic approval for foreign equity participation upto 74 per cent in key infrastructure industries such as electricity generation, distribution, construction of roads, bridges, railways etc. in order to attract foreign investment in infrastructure.

However, despite a number of policy measures adopted by the government to attract private investment in the critical infrastructural sector, private capital domestic or foreign is not coming up. This is because private capital would like to come to the states where the markets are already in a developed stage. Since in the advance states the marketisation has already taken place, private capital would make inroad to those places. However poor social overhead capital and infrastructural facilities has obstructed the free flow of private capital to the backward areas and privatisation of infrastructural sector further would block the over all development of the backward regions.

In a federal state like India there is constitutional division of power between the state and the centre for financial matters. Articles 268, 269, 270, 272, 275, 280, 282 of Indian Constitution deals with the matter of distribution of finance between the state and centre for a cordial centre-state financial co-operation. However the centre has assigned with a greater financial resource whereas state have inadequate sources of revenue in comparison to the responsibilities and required expenditure to meet them. The resource transfer mechanism through the Finance Commission and Planning Commission over the years has put the backward states into rough weather. Their mechanism of financial devolution has widened. The already existing economic disparities in the Indian federal system. Chakraborty (1998) in a recent article has shown that the centre-state financial relation have failed to reduce the vertical imbalances (Also see Vithal 1997 and George and Gulati 1985, Sharma 1997). Frequent change at the economic criterions and the growing importance of the non-economic criterion of resource distribution has further accentuated the regional disparities. States with powerful Chief Minister and with better political connections with the centre get more funds than other states with least political clout of the Chief Ministers. Even the location of public sector units are by political manoeuvring. As has been illustrated by Das (1997) location of public sector units in backward areas has been conceived as an important instrument of removing regional imbalances the demand for second steel plant in Orissa was ignored by the centre on vested political consideration and they were handed over to Salem in Tamil Nadu, Hospet in Karnataka and Visakhapatnam in Andhra Pradesh. (For detail see Das 1997).

Given the above context it is important to note that S and SAP initiated in India in recent years with liberalisation and privatisation as the development strategy would allow the less funds to flow from the centre to the state. This would considerably reduce the social sector expenditure. Thus in a situation when the backward states depend more and more on the central funds for their expenditure in the social sector cuts in the central allotment would affect the poor more. Thus as Gupta (1995) has pointed out since 1991, Bihar, Madhya Pradesh, Rajasthan, Uttar Pradesh and Orissa has reduced per capita expenditure on medical and health in real terms. This gap is less likely to be fulfilled by way of private sector investment in health facilities. Similarly there is also considerable reduction in educational sector in various states. In a country where half of the people are illiterate state participation by investing at least 6 per cent of the GDP on education, would go a long way in educating the people as best productive resources.

Infrastructural projects are two dimensional, on the one hand, they have tremendously contributed in economic development of the country after colonial transformation, on the other hand these projects have displaced a large number of households of which a few have been effectively rehabilitated. Thus a conservative estimate of persons displaced by mines, dams, industries, sanctuaries etc. has put that 1,85,00,000 persons has been displaced through them but only 46,25,000 persons (or 25 per cent) have been rehabilitated with a backlog of 138,75,000 persons till waiting for rehabilitation. For detail (see Fernandes and Raj 1992 Table 1.4). It is most important to note that the tribals constitute a significant portion of population displaced through various projects. This is because almost all the projects, parks, wildlife sanctuaries, dams and mines are located in the tribal areas because of the location of raw materials, vast landmass, and cheap labour force etc. Fernandes and Raj (1992) has noted that among the displaced persons 78 per cent are tribals belonging to the eastern region: Chotanagpur, Bihar, Chatisgarh in Madhya Pradesh and tribal districts of Orissa. The so called infrastructural projects have destabilised the material base of the tribals, have dethroned them from their habitats and marginalised them. Capital penetration for that matter development has not integrated the marginalised section into the capitalist framework but has alienated them from it. Heavy investment in industrial sector have little effect in transforming these predominantly agricultural regions. Thus places situated a few km away from Rourkela, Durgapur, Bhilai, Ranchi bears testimony to this fact. After liberalisation of the economy and entry of multinational companies with investment portfolio of billions of rupees more and more industries; dams, power stations, coal mines are being planned in these regions. This modernisation, industrializatioin drive would pump money in an unprecedented manner which would, it is feared, further marginalised a section of tribals by alienating them from their life support system (Nath and Patel, 1998, Nath, 1995).

Despite differences in the methodology of calculating the dimension of poverty in the country trend analysis of poverty in India shows that there was slow decline of rural poverty in 1970's and a much faster decline in 1980's. The urban poverty has declined but the decline is slower than the rural poverty. But in the post-reform period a very sharp deterioration took place in rural poverty situation and marginally in urban poverty situation during the NSS survey period covering 1991-92 (Tendulkar and Jain 1995). Gupta's study based on NSSO estimate and the methodology suggested by expert group appointed by Planning Commission, has shown that the poverty ratio in rural and urban sectors dropped from 57 per cent to 37 per cent between 1970-71 and 1990-91 but moved upto 41.7 per cent in rural and 37.8 per cent in urban sector in 1992 (Gupta 1995 Tables 2 and 3). In absolute terms the number of poor between 1990-91 and 1992 has increased by nearly 19.8 million. Alok

Kumar's study (1994) shows the inter-state differences in the incidence of poverty. Region-wise the percentage of rural agricultural and non-agricultural labour below poverty line was comparatively high in all states of eastern region, Assam in the North-East, Madhya Pradesh in central region, Tamil Nadu in south, and Uttar Pradesh in north. On the other hand, in states like Andhra Pradesh, Himachal Pradesh and Punjab, poverty level was comparatively low. Globalisation of the economy, privatisation of the public sector undertaking, liberalisation of the trade sector, cutting down to subsidies in agricultural sector, dismarketing the public distribution system, withholding expenditures from the poverty alleviation programmes, reducing expenditure from health and education, etc. would neither enrich the poor states nor would reduce the gap between the rich and not so rich states. What is required for the poor states is land reform and investment in land related infrastructure, redistribution of assets. More power to village panchayat, decentralisation of the planning process, investment in health education and skill formation to bring them at par with the advance states (See for detail Nath 1995, Banerjee, 1994; Alok Kumar 1994, Gupta 1995, Raj 1997). But structural adjustment is not concerned with these issues even though time and again government of India has assured that S and SAP would be carried on with a human face by devicing various safety net measures.

Summary and Conclusion

In order to get rid of the crisis ridden economy government of India has followed an outward looking market-oriented economy. Hence measures such as devaluation of the rupee opening up the economy to external competition, globalisation of the financial market, liberalisation of the trade policy etc. have become the *sine qua non* for the S and SAP. All these policy initiatives supposed to bring about competitiveness in Indian industry, improve efficiency of the economy, accelerate the growth rate of the Indian economy. In the context of a backward country like India with considerable regional disparities in economic development here we have focused on the possible impact S and SAP on the regions which are at present lagging far behind the advance areas. The issues we have addressed whether the regional imbalance that is persisting in the planning process would take care of by S and SAP? Whether capital foreign or indigeneous would come to build up the fragile infrastructure: social or human.

As we have seen above in the agricultural sphere the Fund Bank prescription favouring liquidation of agricultural subsidies and control, curtailing public expenditure on irrigation, power, reversing the basic issue of land reforms and property distribution, reducing priority sector funding have put the backward regions in an backward position. Government is withdrawing from the economy at a time when more state intervention is necessary. Particularly the advanced states may not require the presence of government in their state for market would take care of the investment in those states. But in backward states government presence in irrigation, power, agricultural subsidies, public distribution of food grains, etc., were very much necessary. Hence for the underdevelopment of the market forces no private capital would come forward to invest in these fields.

Industrial dispersal as a major strategy to develop the backward areas was perceived from the beginning of the planning in India. In fact a number of public sector undertakings came up in the industrially backward states like Orissa, Bihar, Madhya Pradesh, Assam etc. A number of rules and regulations were framed to arrest industrial concentration. Various committees were set up from time to time to recommend for dispersal of industries from metropolis to the periphery. Despite these measures industrial concentrations took place. However certain public sector units were located in backward areas which do not have much impact in changing the pre-capitalist rural sectors in the respective states.

Given this context it is of interest to know the concessions that has given to foreign capital, MNC, Indian big bourgeoise and monopolist by privatising, liberalising and globalising Indian economy. Public sectors which were at the commanding height were subject to disinvestment. Now we are opening more areas for private investment where profitability overrides social welfare. But privatisation and disinvestment is no panacea. After liberalisation and privatisation we have eliminated the barriers to free flow of foreign capital; financial, technical and human. MNC are coming in a big way to avoid opportunity extended to them. Hence capital foreign or indigeneous flows to the regions endowed with high productivity, large buying power and good infrastructure. Backward states as they fail to attract investment is expected to remain backward.

Today development means sustainable human development and development is measured in terms of Human Development Index (HDI). Hence human capital formation is the *sine qua non* of any developmental plan. Hence health and education, safe drinking water, considered to be the primary importance. But states like Andhra Pradesh, Arunachal Pradesh, Bihar, Madhya Pradesh, Rajastan, Uttar Pradesh are far behind in providing these facilities. But privatisation of these services has put the poor people in the problem of foregoing these facilities. No private capital would come forward to backward regions to provide health care, and educational facilities. Hence there is no doubt that the role of state in providing these facilities is of supreme importance. Even the World Bank's World Development Report 1997 has recognised the importance of state in the changing world. Even the so called success stories of East Asia and South-East Asia is a consequence of the state intervention in providing the basic infrastructural facilities. State presence in these countries is quite visible in basic health, universal education, roads and communication, power etc. In contrast public spending in these areas is very low in India (see Ghosh 1997, Dasgupta 1997).

It is not surprising to note that territorial economic resources are unevenly distributed and capitalist growth process has a tendency to exploit the raw materials for private gain. Hence capitalist growth process is an uneven growth process. Internationally also the gap between the rich and not so rich countries has widened (see Kuzerts 1969, Boldwin 1967, Rosentein Rodan 1972). Even in United States all the 50 states have not developed uniformly. Similarly in UK the northern part of the country considered backward in comparison to the southern regions. The economic disparities between states in a country over the years have provided space for different form of conflicts: caste, communal and ethnic. A number of separatist movement in India: like people of Dakshina Kannada have been demanding for Tululand, a separate state for Coorg in Karnataka, the tribal belt of Bihar, Orissa and Madhya Pradesh agitate for Jharkhand; for Vidarbha and Konkan in Maharashtra, for a Bodoland in Assam, for a Gorkhaland in West Bengal, for a Uttarakhand in Uttar Pradesh; for a Kosal in Western Orissa are some of the illustrations. Internationally, the IMF sponsored reforms have led to the outbreak of ethnic strife, religious fundamentalism and civil war in Yugoslavia, Somalia and Rwanda (Chossudousky 1997). After globalisation, modernisation, liberalization and privatisation of the economy in India these backward regions would face similar situation of conflict, caste, communal and ethnic. The entire tribal belt of Orissa, Bihar, Madhya Pradesh, the North-East etc. are rich in natural resources but there is little economic development. Now the type of development process we are adopting would provide only enclave type of development due to the cheapness of labour and natural resources. But there may not be any genuine self sustained growth of these regions.

Very often state attempts of resolving the development contradictions by setting up of regional development boards with insignificant power to deal with the basic issues of regional imbalances. The Kalahandi-Bolangir-Koraput (KBK) plan in Orissa; the development boards in Vidarbha Maharashtra and Konkan in Maharashtra; Gorkha Hills Development Council in West Bengal; Jharkand Development Council in Bihar are some of the cases in point. However in the scenario of economic reforms these boards and council would not cut much ice. Hence there is a need of corrective measures which can be provided by the visible hand of the state, but not by the invisible hand of the market. Visualising development as a social process our recommendation would call for developing regional planning as a tool of development planning, devicing a meaningful federalism for the correction of regional imbalances. However working out a detail of regional planning is beyond the scope of this paper.

References

Baldwin, R.E. (1972), *Economic Development and Growth*, John Wiley and Sons Inc., New York.

Banerjee, Amalesh (1994), "Rural Labour and Anti Poverty Programme", *Indian Journal of Labour Economics (IJLE)*, Vol. 37, No. 4, October-December, pp. 653-58.

Chakraborty, Pinaki (1998), "Growing Imbalance in Federal Fiscal Relationship", *Economic and Political Weekly (EPW)*, February 14s, pp. 350-54.

Chossudousky, Michel (1997), "Economic Reforms and Social Unrest in Developing Countries", *EPW*, No. 29, July 19-25, pp. 1786-88.

Das, Keshabananda (1997), "Politics of Industrial Location: Indian Federation and Development Decisions", *EPW*, No. 51, December 25-26, pp. 3268-74.

Dasgupta, Biplab (1997), "SAP: Issues and Conditionalities: A Global Review", *EPW*, Nos. 20-21, May 17-23/24-30, pp. 1091-1104.

Fernandes, Walter and S. Anthony, Raj (1992), *Development, Displacement and Rehabilitation in the Tribal Areas of Orissa*, Indian Social Institute, New Delhi.

George, K.K. and I.S. Gulati (1985), "State Resource Transfers 1951-84: An Appraisal", *EPW*, No. 7, February.

Ghosh, Jayati (1997), "India's Structural Adjustment: An Assessment in Comparative Asian Context", *EPW*, Nos. 20-21, May 17-23/24-30, pp. 1113-31.

Gupta, S.P. (1995), "Economic Reforms and Its Impact on Poor", *EPW*, June 3.

Kumar, Alok (1994), "Determinants of the Incidence of Poverty Among Rural Labour: A Cross-sectional Study", *IJLE*, Vol. 37, No. 4, October-December, pp. 639-52.

Kuznets, S. (1969), *Economic Growth and Structure: Selected Essays*, Oxford and IBH Publishing Co., pp. -142-75.

Mishra, S.K. and Puri, V.K. (1985), *Development and Planning*, Himalaya Publishing House, New Delhi.

Nath, G.B. and J. Patel (1998), "Structural Adjustment and Its Impact on Tribal Areas and People in India", in S.N. Tripathy edited *Tribals in India: The Changing Scenario*, Discovery Publishing House, New Delhi.

Nath, G.B. (1995), "Human Dimension of Structural Adjustment in India: Problems and Possibilities", *IJLE*, Vol. 38, No. 4, October-December, pp. 617-22.

Nayyar and Sen (1994), "International Trade and Agricultural Sector in India", *EPW*, No. 20, May 14.

Rao, C.H.H. and Ashok Gulati (1994), "Indian Agriculture: Emerging Perspective and Policy Issues", *EPW*, No. 53, December 31.

Rao, C.H.H. (1994), "Reforming Agriculture in the New Context", *EPW*, Nos. 16-17, April, 16-23.

Rao, V.M. (1994), "Agriculture and Liberalisation: Some Implications for Development Policies", *EPW*, Nos. 16 and 17, April 16-23.

Ray, Sumit (1997), "Globalisation, Structural Change and Poverty: Some Conceptual and Policy Issues", *EPW*, Nos. 33 and 34, August 16-22/23-29, pp. 2117-35.

Rosentein-Rodan, P.N. (1992), *The Have's and Have-nots Around the Year in Economic and World Order*, (ed.) Jagadish N. Bhagwati, Orient Longman Ltd., Bombay.

Sandesara, J.C. (1991), "New Industrial Policy: Question of Efficient Growth and Social Objectives", *EPW*, Nos. 31 and 32, pp 1869-72.

Sarma, J.V.M. (1997), "Federal Fiscal Relation in India Issue of Horizontal Transfers", *EPW*, No. 28, July 12-18, pp. 1719-23.

Tendulkar, S.W. and L.K. Jain (1995), "Economic Reform and Poverty', *EPW*, No. 23, July 10.

Vithal, B.P.R. (1997), "Role of Articles 275 and 282 in Federal Fiscal Transfers", *EPW*, No. 28, July 12-18, pp. 1689-91.

PART IV

AGRICULTURAL PLANNING AND SUSTAINABLE DEVELOPMENT

18

Sustainable Development: Concept and Issues with Special Reference to Agriculture

—*M.V. Nadkarni*

Concept

The widespread, almost universal, acceptance by economists of the need for sustainable development during the 1980s is an evidence of their attempt at internalisation of the ecologists' concern for conservation into economics. The basic idea of conservation is the preservation of the stock of nature's capital both in quantity and quality in such a way that the access of future generations to this stock is not in any way reduced below what the present generation enjoys. Conservation does not preclude the use of natural resources by the present generation. It expects, however, that such a use is not at the cost of future generations. It followed logically that economic development at present should not be at the cost of future

This paper was earlier published in *Indian Journal of Agricultural Economics*. It is published with kind permission of the editor and author. (Vol. 48, No. 3)

generations. The Brundtland Report defined Sustainable Development as "development that meets the needs of the present generation without compromising the ability of the future generations to meet their own needs" (World Commission on Environment and Development, 1987, p. 8). Through this concept, economists tried to reconcile the need for conservation with the need for development almost at one stroke.

This reconciliation is, however, more apparent than real. At best, it could be said to be accomplished in part. Both at conceptual and policy level, there remain several unresolved issues about which there is need for a debate. There are still areas of conflict between considerations of ecology and economic growth which we cannot push under the carpet of 'Sustainable Development'. This paper is a modest attempt to raise some of these issues rather than to give definitive solutions, though the author's own policy preferences also may be projected in the process.

The first issue is about the definition and content of 'Development'. Even before the term Sustainable Development became popular, this issue had emerged when there was an attempt to distinguish between Growth and Development, making the latter a more comprehensive concept. It was realised that there was need for a broader concept which would do justice to the requirements of developing countries to improve the quality of life of their masses, and to remove poverty and hunger. Though 'Development' became an imprecise term in the process, it became more sensible and relevant to developing countries. It is noteworthy, however, that 'Development' was not interpreted to preclude growth of Gross National Product (GNP). Other criteria or indicators were added, but GNP did not lose its place of eminence.

When, however, environmental concern was to be incorporated into Development, the eminence of GNP came under sharp attack. In this context, it is possible to see two distinct ideological positions; one which rejected GNP altogether, and another which continued to accept it though with due qualifications and adjustments. The former would minimise material acquisitions that tax natural resources and frowns upon the economists' conventional objective of maximising production and consumption. Development, however, would still be possible in terms of information, knowledge, skills, technological improvements that improve the efficiency of resource use, culture, equitable distribution of given income and wealth, and freedom. In his proposal for a Steady-State Economy, Daly (1980) clarifies that development in these terms can very well be promoted, though two things need to be held constant, namely, the stock of human bodies and the stock of inventory of artifacts. He also adds that the levels at which the two populations are held constant in a Steady-State Economy are sufficient for a good life and sustainable for a long time. However, "the rate of throughput of matter-energy by which the stocks are maintained is reduced to the lowest feasible level. For a population this means that the birth rates are equal to death rates at low levels so that life expectancy is high. For artifacts, it means that production equals depreciation at low levels so that artifacts are long lasting, and depletion and pollution are kept low" (Daly 1980, p. 325).

This school regards the present rates of economic growth and consumption of natural resources unsustainable. There are definite limits to growth of material consumption imposed by the Entropy Law. If the human welfare has to be sustained in the long-run, the only way to ensure it is by taking care to see that there is no depletion of natural resource base. Boulding (1966) characterised the Earth as a spaceship with finite resources on board. Such a perspective calls for minimisation of throughput and hence of GNP, and not its maximisation.

Most of the advocates of sustainable development would not however go thus far. They would readily take into account other measures of the state of human welfare or progress like the Physical Quality of Life Index. They would even come round to accept that estimates of GNP need corrections to reflect the depletion of environmental capital of the country or region concerned, but they would not be willing to totally give up GNP or sectoral rates of growth of production. They share a more optimistic perspective of growth prospects, pointing out at continuous technological advance and substitution possibilities made by it. New sources of energy and new metals developed have not allowed real prices of raw materials to rise in the long-run, which have in fact tended to decline. A policy of not touching exhaustible resources—that is what the maintenance of the physical stock of nature's capital would require in their case—would deny growth opportunities to the present generation. They do not regard the problem of pollution so grave as to totally give up growth as they believe that pollution could be countered to a great extent, if not fully, by the adoption of clean technologies.

It is noteworthy that even this optimistic school would not any longer advocate blind pursuit of growth irrespective of environmental costs. If growth and development have to be sustainable what conditions have to be met? Is it enough to maintain the total capital stock constant including man-made capital? Man-made capital can substitute for natural capital only to a very small and limited extent. Some forests can be replanted and redeveloped by man, but bio-diversity lost with forests cannot be replenished. The assimilative capacity of nature as a waste sink is also very limited, and there are definite limits to recycling and pollution abatement. There are important irreversibilities like ozone depletion, extinction of species, and loss of natural forests rich in bio-diversity, which cannot be made good by man-made capital. Even renewable resources can become exhaustible if their rate of exploitation exceeds the rate of regeneration and there is a risk of irreversible loss even in the case of renewable resources. In view of these irreversibilities and the grave impact they may have on human welfare in future, we have to play safe. This would require that economic activity has to be such that it does not in any way result in the depletion of natural wealth over time, and improve upon it where possible. Economic growth and development have to be subject to this important constraint, only in which case they can be termed as sustainable.

A Few Tricky Problems

The interpretation of the requirement of non-depleting natural capital stock raises problems in the case of exhaustible resources. Any exploitation of these resources would lead to their depletion. A way out of this problem could be to rely on the real price of the concerned resource as an indicator. If it rises over time, it means that depletion of the resource is not offset by the availability of substitutes and that net depletion is occurring.

When resources were abundant, their prices may have indicated extraction and transport costs alone but not their *in situ* scarcity. When, however, scarcity begins to be felt, markets also begin to reflect it. Prices of gold and silver since long and of petroleum since the mid-seventies could be said to have been reflecting not merely production costs but also *in situ* scarcity. Monopoly element may be a factor behind price levels, but a monopoly cannot emerge where a resource is abundant. A difficulty in relying on prices as indicator is that irrespective of whether we refer to renewable or exhaustible resources, if their present rate of extraction is imprudent, there could be an over-supply in the present and prices may be down. Only when the impact of the resource depletion begins to be felt affecting the current rates of exploitation, the prices would begin to reflect the *in situ* scarcity. It may then be too late to reverse the depletion even in the case of renewable resources.

In any case, market prices do not reflect environmental costs. They do not cover negative externalities imposed on present and future generations. Nor do they indicate the option value of resources which are forgone by their present use. They do not reflect the existence value of resources like forests, wild animals, and of historical monuments, which are independent of any use value derived by human beings. A consensus appears to be emerging in favour of artificially deriving prices which reflect these environmental costs at least as an aid for decision-making. There is now a growing literature on non-market valuation of environmental costs (for a review, see Markandya, 1992; Smith, 1993). However, the problems in this area remain unresolved.

An important problem is that in the absence of guidance from the market, we have no proper criteria to judge the reliability of a valuation. There can be implausible extremes that serve no useful purpose. For example, using surrogate market techniques to evaluate environmental benefits provided by a single medium sized tree over a period of 50 years of its life span, T.M. Das calculated its environmental value as Rs. 15.7 lakhs (at 1980-81 prices). This includes the valuation of environmental services like production of oxygen, conversion to animal protein, soil conservation, control of humidity, sheltering of birds, etc. and control of air pollution (quoted by Lal, 1992, p. 46). Would it be right to value the production of oxygen by a tree at the same rate as the cost of oxygen cylinders produced by man, or to value the shelter provided by a tree to birds and insects at the same rate as the cost of artificial shelter provided by man. There is a basic confusion between the value at the margin and value at the average in such calculations. As an environmental good or service becomes scarce, its value can be expected to increase at an increasing rate, so that the value at the margin can be significantly higher than the average value. When man operates to produce or relocate an environmental good or service in specific or isolated circumstances, he operates at the extreme margin. Using these values for valuation of the total stock of environment in a region can produce such extraordinarily high estimates that there can be no question of any growth and development. We will have to go back to the stone age!

A more plausible approach is the assessment of impact caused to the economy by the damage to the environment. For example, the impact of pollution by a factory could be measured in terms of decline in crop output, increased expenditure on the treatment of illness of animals and human beings, man-days of employment and hence output lost as a result, decline in fish harvested, increased time and expenditure on getting potable water, etc. But such estimates can err on the lower side because some of the damage goes beyond the proximate area and is not captured by market or proxy signals adequately. Secondly, they are too anthropocentric to care for the existence value of environment. Forests, wild life and other components of natural environment have rights and a value independent of their use to human beings.

Ascertaining the maximum one is willing to pay for preserving an environmental resource or the minimum amount of compensation one is willing to accept for its loss is being increasingly proposed for non-market valuation. It can be used to include the existence value even of things like whales at the global level. The method can appear more plausible for proximate situations. Even here, there are other problems. Supposing an irrigation project submerges an uninhabited forest, whose willingness to pay should be considered here? Farmers and others benefiting from the project would not be willing to pay for its preservation. However, those whose environmental awareness is high may express high levels of willingness to pay. Ultimately more than the arithmetic of sample surveys, a qualitative judgement about how valuable the forest is, about the uniqueness of its bio-diversity, about its replicability in another area through compensatory forest, etc., may guide the decision-making. In spite of these difficulties, a proper social cost-benefit analysis is a very helpful guide in decision-making which includes the valuation of all environmental costs. Where environmental costs cannot be quantified but are to be prevented nevertheless, the cost of so preventing environmental damage and that of paying proper compensation for damage if it occurs have to be incorporated into social cost-benefit analysis and project proposals.

Valuation is not the only issue here. It is pertinent to mention that some projects create difficulties not because proper compensation and rehabilitation package for displaced people cannot be theoretically provided, but because in practice this package may not reach the people. There could be significant leakages of funds provided for the purpose or simple inefficiency in execution, so that ultimately the project may produce more illfare than welfare.

There is also the further question of whether the use of the valuation of environmental costs should be restricted to merely decision-making, or also for actual pricing of the goods and services produced in the course of the concerned development project. Take for example, the environmental value of a tree. If none is expected to pay this price for cutting a tree, how would you ensure its preservation? The 'Polluter-to-Pay' principle has been accepted as a requisite for sustainable development, so that the externalities are internalised and the tendency to over-produce or over-consume a good involving negative externality is corrected. In agriculture, it has been particularly hard to follow this principle. The subsidies are so huge that even the direct production costs are not covered by the pricing of inputs. Let alone reflecting environmental costs, let alone reflecting depreciation and interest on fixed capital, water charges do not even cover the current costs of maintaining and running an irrigation project. Not to speak of environmental costs, fertiliser prices do not even cover production costs.

Even if goods are priced reflecting environmental costs, there are problems arising from concentration of purchasing power in the hands of a few which may defeat the purpose of so pricing. The hike in petroleum prices has not reduced the demand for private transport and petroleum, though it may have stimulated the emergence of more fuel-efficient cars. High prices may merely price out the poor, while the rich are hardly affected. In such a case, the shadow prices can be used for deciding the level of production, and then the supply of the good may have to be rationed. For example, even if irrigation charge does not cover full costs, water availability can be properly regulated and rationed so that the farmers maximise output per unit of water and not waste it.

Indicators

Ecologists like Gordon Conway have developed operational or observable indicators of sustainable development, which are helpful to the economists in assessing the development performance from the point of sustainability. They are particularly relevant for assessing agricultural systems. They appear more as economic than ecological indicators. This would show that what is ecologically unsustainable would also be economically unsustainable. The indicators are:

"1. Productivity (measured in terms of yield or net income),
2. Stability of yield or net income,
3. Sustainability of yield or net income, and
4. Equitability in terms of income distribution" (as quoted in Tisdell, 1988, p. 375).

It should be clarified that productivity in gross terms cannot be an indicator of sustainable development. Productivity achieved at high cost per unit of output cannot be sustainable. Ecological sustainability requires economic efficiency too. Productivity or net income as an indicator of sustainable development also needs a time perspective. Obviously, it should refer to the long run. Productivity or net real income should be high and non-declining, that is, constant or preferably increasing, subject also to stability and sustainability. Productivity and net income both per hectare and per capita in Indian agriculture are quite low relatively to world averages and also compared with some developing countries like China though they have been increasing. But we seem to fail the test of even other indicators of sustainable development. Whatever increase we have achieved in productivity seems to have involved some price in terms of increased instability and vulnerability. There is now considerable literature on instability in Indian agriculture, and the consensus seems to be to indicate that instability has increased after the mid-sixties during the Green Revolution period (Rao *et. al.*, 1988). This has required more attention to maintenance of soil health and the natural resource base of agriculture, instead of focusing merely on chemical inputs. Insofar as increased instability in output is due to the extension of Green Revolution to regions with less assured water supply, developing drought resistant yet more productive varieties of crops and a more holistic approach to farming may have to be on the agenda of the country. This would mean attending to long-term productivity of farms as a whole and not of single crops alone.

Though the problem of instability has received some attention, agricultural economists have tended to ignore the problem of vulnerability. Combining different crops and animal husbandry to reduce risk and vulnerability of the farm as a whole has received attention, but not vulnerability of the agricultural system as such. Among Conway's indicators of sustainable development, 'sustainability ' refers to "the propensity of a system to withstand collapse under stress. It has to do with robustness or continuing viability of a system" (see Tisdell, 1988, p. 375) or low vulnerability. Tisdell points to the ecologists' worry that some agricultural systems may be highly productive but subject to substantial risk as far as their sustainability is concerned. This is particularly so regarding advanced agriculture which depends on a narrow genetic base. Harlan observes here (as quoted by Tisdell, 1988, p. 375): "The trend for more and more people to be nourished by fewer and fewer plant and animal food sources has reached the point today where most of the world's population is dependent on a handful of species. This . . . was not characteristic of the traditional subsistence agriculture. . . . As the trend intensifies, man becomes even more vulnerable. His food supply now depends on the success of a small number of species, and the failure of one of them may mean starvation for millions of people."

It would be foolhardy to recommend that modern agriculture should, therefore, revert entirely to traditional agriculture. But we have to be concerned as much with vulnerability of agricultural systems as with their productivity, and about the need for maintenance of bio-diversity and conservation of crop genetic material. Such material can be conserved *ex situ* in artificial gene banks only to a limited extent. Hence we have to ponder over how to treat the remaining part of agriculture that is still relying on traditional practices and local varieties. Can we afford to push traditional agriculture to extinction and depend only on high-yielding varieties (HYVs) and chemical farming? Do we treat farmers practising traditional agriculture as backward to be merely converted to modern ways, or do we regard them as a source of conserving diverse crop varieties *in situ*, encourage them and learn from them? What incentives and institutional arrangements are necessary to preserve bio-diversity and richness of traditional varieties? Is it not possible to advance productivity even within traditional agriculture through methods such as those adopted by Fukuoka (1984) so that it is economically worthwhile to preserve it at least in some areas?[1] These questions may have to be on our agenda of research to help sustainable development of agriculture.[2]

It is equally important that agriculture does not make human life in general and other productive systems vulnerable. There is enough cause for worry on this account. Not only are the factories producing pesticides and chemical fertilisers a source of pollution hazard in themselves, their output spreads pollution wider (*cf.* Myers, 1985, p. 123; WCED, 1987, p. 127). Their use is hazardous for the farmers themselves, particularly in the case of pesticides, unless they handle them with all safeguards. In the course of zealous extension of these inputs, the farmers are not properly made familiar with risks associated and precautions to be taken. The chemical inputs damage other life supporting systems and destroy natural enemies of pests. They get into water bodies including groundwater and affect their potability and fish raising capacity. There is a tendency to underplay the severity of the problem in India by comparing per capita consumption of these inputs with other countries. Such comparisons hide excessive use in some regions. Their use, however, cannot be discontinued totally at the present juncture when we have to meet the needs of a growing population, until at least alternative and safer technologies are developed. In any such situation, a proper weighing of environmental costs involved against the advantages is necessary to arrive at correct dosage. But this judgement is often vitiated by two factors—subsidies by which prices do not even cover production costs let alone environmental costs, and the tendency of several enterprises to supply substandard inputs which reduce the advantages even while costs including environmental costs are incurred. The farmers often believe so much in the efficacy of these inputs that they do not use some of the practices of natural farming like the adequate use of organic manure and tank silt to condition the soils, and planting crops of different species between rows of given crops so that the spread of diseases is checked. This excessive faith in the efficacy of chemical inputs, to the neglect of the other practices and precautions and protective measures necessary, has made the farmers generally vulnerable both to ecological and economic risks. The vulnerability to economic risks arises under modern agriculture because the modern inputs are purchased from the market, unlike in the traditional agriculture and natural farming where most of the inputs are produced in the farm itself. The question is how far we can encourage the farmers to become vulnerable in the name of higher productivity. In the absence of effective crop insurance measures, other safeguards have to be developed which the farmers themselves can adopt easily and economically.

Poverty and Sustainable Development

The last, but by no means the least important of the indicators of sustainable-development listed above is equitable distribution of income and wealth and reduction in poverty levels. Though the economists' concern with equity and poverty reduction has a long history, the ecological significance of these is not often appreciated. A particular resource may be scarce from the point of view of the society as a whole and has, therefore, to be used frugally and carefully to last long. If, however, the purchasing power is concentrated in the hands of a few, the resource may not be perceived to be scarce by such people and may be used wastefully. Land, for example, is scarce for the society, but not to the landlord who owns hundreds of hectares. Care of land needs more labour, which the landlords find as scarce. So instead of economising on a scarce resource and using it sustainably, a relatively abundant resource is economised and under-employed. In this perspective, equity in the distribution of income and wealth is a requirement or a condition of sustainable development, and not merely an indicator.

Since sustainable development is expected to produce a favourable impact in terms of reducing inequity and poverty, it would be proper to treat it also as an indicator of sustainable development. Most of the worlds' poor depend directly on natural resources for livelihood. Insofar as sustainable development improves this capital base — soil health, water, forests, fisheries, etc.—it should help in reducing their vulnerability and poverty. The natural resources are used often as common property resources (CPRs), and help those with inadequate private property to increase its productivity and also compensate for it. For example, poor peasants can meet their requirement of fuelwood, green manure, small wood for implements and fodder and thus increase the productivity of their small holdings. Even landless labour can afford to keep some animals if CPRs are available as a source of fodder. Regeneration of CPRs thus would help both ecology and poverty alleviation.

A grave problem arises in the regeneration and sustainable management of village forests and grazing lands. It is the possibility of a general perception that while a sacrifice may be imposed on the local people in the form of restricted grazing, the gains would go to the Forest Department or the Panchayat and not to themselves as individuals. In spite of this, there are several examples of success in carrying out eco-development projects, particularly in reversing land degradation and rehabilitating the grazing lands in India. This requires, however, three conditions. One is that there is a well defined area—usually a village—which is identified as the exclusive beneficiary of the project, so that a free-rider problem is avoided and community rights over the land taken up for development are established. Secondly, the development of the land is done with close involvement of the people. Examples of modest success merely involve people's co-operation, while examples of more significant success involve people's active participation in planning, executing and managing the project. The third condition is that the gains from the project should be equitably distributed, not on the basis of land or animals owned by households, but on per household basis irrespective of their other assets. We may call the last condition as the 'Principle of Incremental Equity' in contrast with total equity. The latter involves redistribution of land on equitable basis, which has been politically difficult. We cannot wait for rehabilitation of wastelands until total equity is attained. 'Incremental Equity' is not applied to all produce or all assets, but only to additional benefits that accrue from an eco-development project. It requires that all usufruct and timber, etc., obtained from common lands be distributed on an equal basis to all households as a matter of right. A prominent example is that of Pani Panchayat in Maharashtra where water is considered as a community asset and every household has equal right to it. They can trade it if they like, but they must have the right.

To satisfy these three conditions, particularly the last one, there has to be a socio-political environment in villages where villagers can meet, talk and settle matters of management of community assets on an equal footing. It has been found from experience that class or caste homogeneity is not an indispensable condition for success, though it can be very helpful. The community, however, has to be small enough to make interactions between individual members possible, and large enough to make it a viable unit. Often voluntary agencies or the Forest Department have acted as catalytic agents to form Village Forest Committees or simply Village Committees, but it is important that they work on their own in due course so that peoplel's co-operation and participation is on a sustained basis.

Land Reforms and Sustainable Development

Though we have emphasised Incremental Equity more than total or revolutionary equity, ceilings on the ownership of agricultural holdings and redistribution of surplus continue to have relevance in the context of sustainable development. A stricter implementation of ceilings will make the distribution of land reflect the scarcity of land more realistically and could lead to a more efficient land use. The proper care of land needs a higher endowment of labour which small and medium holdings have more than the large holders. Moreover, co-operative as well as collective participation of individual holders is necessary for implementation of soil and moisture conservation measures in watershed development projects and for efficient and equitable management of canal and tank irrigation. The possibility of securing such a co-operation and group participation is enhanced when there is a greater economic homogeneity among individual holders.

It is not quite clear whether tenancy is favourable to sustainable development or not. It would be reasonable to argue that a tenant-at-will without security of tenure is not interested in the sustainable use of land. But it is not necessary that tenants with security of tenure will behave so. Moreover, if the landowner is responsible for long-term improvements in land and for ensuring that healthy agricultural practices are adopted, and if he/she gets the returns for his/her investment under the tenancy arrangements, sustainable development may still be possible. This would require a formal contract between the tenant and landowner. A legal ban on tenancy, pushing tenancy underground with no possibility of legal security of tenure to tenants, appears to be hardly favourable for sustainable agriculture. In general, owner cultivation seems to be the best system, but there could be problems where the owner is unable to cultivate himself/herself and yet would not like to lose the land. If leasing out involves the risk of losing land altogether, the landowner may prefer to keep it idle rather than lease it out. Institutional conditions of agriculture have obviously an impact on sustainable land use, but this is an area where more research is required.

Land degradation due to deforestation, erosion and waterlogging are the gravest problems of Indian agriculture. Land degradation of all forms, principally soil erosion, affects almost 174 million hectares of the country's 329 million hectares of territory (Government of India, 1989, p. 15). Watershed development programmes have now been undertaken in many areas which promise to reverse this degradation. Yet, lands taken up so far for conservation measures are a small fraction of the total land that needs treatment. Thus only 31 million hectares out of 174 million hectares were reported as treated till 1986-87 (Government of India, 1989, p. 19). Much of the problem is caused by faulty land use and preventive measures are as necessary as curative. People displaced by irrigation and hydro-electric projects used to be often settled in catchment areas by clearing forests. This led to problems of siltation of reservoirs sooner than expected. A major reason for land degradation is continuous extension of cultivation to marginal lands which ought to be under tree and grass cover. This extension at the expense of common lands has been permitted officially under political pressures, through periodical granting of ownership rights on encroached lands. The encroachers are not always poor people, since field studies have shown that the major part of such land is encroached by the non-poor (*Nadkarni et al.*, 1989, pp. 127-130; Pasha, 1992, p. 2500). A bold political decision as well as its strict implementation is necessary about whether extension of cultivation into common lands and forests can be permitted any more. To facilitate this decision and implementation, the productivity of these lands has to be increased and the local communities should be made to feel that they have a stake in their preservation and development—a theme already discussed above. At present, however, there is no system of legally recognised community tenure by which local communities can enforce their rights. This gap needs to be filled.

New Economic Policy and Sustainable Development

Macro economic policies can considerably affect the sustainability of development in agriculture. The new economic policy of liberalising the economy, making it more market led and open, has mixed implications, but leaning more on the adverse side. The emphasis on reducing subsidies and making prices reflect the economic costs should promote resource use efficiency. The policy has been followed in a half-hearted and piece-meal manner, and, therefore, may not have the expected salutary impact. Subsides to agriculture are a world-wide phenomenon, and unless they are cut in the developed countries first, the necessary political environment cannot be created in favour of reducing subsidies in developing countries. Opening up of the economy to new, clean and efficient technologies and stimulating their adoption will also have a positive impact.

There are some adverse implications which the country should try to overcome. First, the new economic policy seems to be more encouraging to capital intensive technology and save on labour. Insofar as capital goods are artifacts that consume more energy and other natural resources, this could be a negative development. If, however, the new artifacts are more fuel and resource efficient, we can expect some environmental gain.

The new economic policy also intends to make the economy more export-oriented. This includes agriculture. Export orientation of agriculture should never be at the cost of self-sufficiency in food grains, so that we are not made more vulnerable in the process. Inducing the economy to produce more for exports can mean more environmental costs which should be weighed against any temporary gains in foreign exchange. It is sometimes contended that export crops like rubber, tea, coffee and pepper are more environment-friendly than food crops. It is argued that the former mean more greening and do not involve soil erosion. But usually plantation crops are raised at the cost of rich natural forests, in which case it is no environmental gain. Besides, they usually involve more use of pesticides and fertilisers which seep into water bodies. The initial stages of plantations such as for tea also involve significant amount of soil erosion since the ground has to be cleared of all other plants including grass. Thus a lot of safeguards to keep the environmental costs down to the minimum tolerable level are necessary.

Agriculture and forests can suffer in other ways in reckless export promotion of mineral ores and granite. Miners do not often take the necessary step to correct the damage caused by mining in the form of increased soil erosion and siltation. If the mines happen to be in hilly forest areas, the environmental implications are all the more grave.

The decline of the state and its regulatory power in the course of economic liberalisation can also have adverse environmental implications, if it leads to tax monitoring and implementation of environment laws. There is already a call to exempt small scale industrial units from environmental regulations and at the same time to promote more of them.[3] This kind of economic development is extremely short-sighted and suicidal.

Conclusion

There is much in the concept and strategy of Sustainable Development that is vague and not palpable. Further debate should clarify some of the issues involved. We cannot, however, adopt the strategy of environmentally costly growth merely because some of these costs cannot at present be precisely quantified. As a wag put it, it is better to be imprecisely correct than be precisely wrong.

Notes

1. It is heartening to find an Indian periodical, *Honey Bee,* devoted to compiling and publishing traditional practices which promote sustainable agriculture.
2. Vulnerability due to instability in output prices also seems to have increased during the Green Revolution period. This is because of increased commercialisation of output and increased market dependence for inputs. Food grains have a relatively stable demand, thanks to the stabilising role of the procurement system. Other crops are more vulnerable on the price front. We have not discussed this problem as our main focus here is on problems related to natural resource environment. However, this problem is also no less important.
3. According to a PTI Report, the Minister of State for Small Scale Industry, government of India, M. Arunachalam, said during the Small Scale Industries (SSI) Ministers Conference at New Delhi that: "SSIs should be left out of the purview of the proposed notification under the Environment Protection Act 1986. He felt that extensive environment controls should be applied only to projects above a certain size as long as SSIs did not underatke Hazardous processes", (*Deccan Herald,* June 8, 1993).

References

1. Boulding, K. (1966), "The Economics of the Coming Spaceship Earth", in II. Jarrett (Ed.) (1966), *Environmental Quality in a Growing Economy,* The Johns Hopkins University Press, Baltimore; Reproduced in Daly, Herman (Ed.) (1980), *op. cit.,* pp. 253-63.
2. Daly, Herman (1980), "The Steady-State Economy: Toward a Political Economy of Biophysical Equilibrium and Moral Growth",

in Herman Daly (Ed.) (1980), *Economics, Ecology, Ethics: Essays Toward a Steady-State Economy*, Freeman and Co., New York.

3. Fukuoka, Masanobu (1984), *One Straw Revolution—An Introduction to Natural Farming*, Indian Edition (Original Edition 1978), Frends Rural Centre, Rasulia, Hoshangabad.
4. Government of India (1989), *Indian Agriculture in Brief*, 22nd Edition, Directorate of Economics and Statistics, Ministry of Agriculture, New Delhi.
5. Lal, J.B. (1992), "Economic Value of India's Forest Stock", in Anil Agarwal (Ed.) (1992), *The Price of Forests*, Centre for Science and Environment, New Delhi.
6. Markandya, Anil (1992), "The Value of the Environment: A State of the Art Survey", in Anil Markandya and Julie Richardson (Eds.) (1992), *Environmental Economics*, Earthscan Publications Ltd., London, pp. 142-65.
7. Myers, Norman (Ed.) (1985), *The Gaia Atlas of Planet Management*, Pan Books, London and Sydney.
8. Nadkarni, M.V., Syed Ajmal Pasha and L.S. Prabhakar (1989), *The Political Economy of Forest Use and Management*,Sage Publications India Pvt. Ltd., New Delhi.
9. Pasha, Syed Ajmal (1992), "CPRs and the Rural Poor: A Micro Level Analysis", *Economic and Political Weekly*, Vol. 27, No. 46, November 14.
10. Rao, C.H. Hanumantha; S.K. Ray and K. Subbarao (1988), *Unstable Agriculture and Droughts*, Vikas Publishing House Pvt. Ltd., New Delhi.
11. Smith, V. Kerry (1993), "Non-Market Valuation of Environmental Resources: An Interpretative Appraisal"; *Land Economics*, Vol. 69, No. 1, February, pp. 1-26.
12. Tisdell, C. (1988), "Sustainable Development: Different Perspectives of Ecologists and Economists, and Relevance to LDCs", *World Development*, Vol. 16, No. 3, March, pp. 373-84.
13. World Commission on Environment and Development (WCED) (1987), *Our Common Future*, Oxford University Press, London.

19

Agricultural Sustainability Status of the Agro-Climatic Sub-Zones of India: Empirical Illustration of an Indexing Approach

—R. Maria Saleth

Introduction

Since the critical dimensions of sustainable development in general and sustainable development of agriculture (SDA) in particular are ecology, economics, and intra- and inter-generational equity (Barbier, 1989; Daly, 1990; Swaminathan, 1991), any approach for developing an indicator for SDA should necessarily reflect all these three dimensions. Unfortunately, the applicability and practical utility of the currently available approaches for evaluating SDA like the agro-ecosystem analysis (Conway, 1985), mathematical programming-based simulation (*e.g.*, Parikh, 1988), dynamic programming (Saleth, 1991), and 'carrying capacity' evaluation

This paper was earlier published in *Indian Journal of Agricultural Economics*. It is published with kind permission of the editor and author. (Vol. 48, No. 3)

[Food and Agriculture Organization (FAO), 1984] are severely limited by their methodological inability to capture all the critical concerns of SDA, excessive data demand and limited transparency.

While the current information is not a match for the data requirements of sophisticated approaches, the easy availability of simple information on the ecological, economic and equity aspects of agriculture points to the need for an operational approach and an unifying framework for integrating such diverse set of data to develop an indicator for SDA which is simple, transparent and information-efficient, *i.e.*, the ability to generate policy relevant information within the currently binding information constraint. This paper aims to

(*i*) expose the concept and methodology of the Sustainable Livelihood Security Index (SLSI) proposed by Swaminathan (1991) and operationalised by Saleth and Swaminathan (1992, 1993), and

(*ii*) empirically illustrate the practical utility and policy relevance of SLSI as a litmus for evaluating the relative agricultural sustainability status of 80 agro-climatic sub-zones of India using easily available data.

I
CONCEPTUAL BASIS AND ANALYTICAL FRAMEWORK FOR SUSTAINABLE LIVELIHOOD SECURITY INDEX (SLSI)

The major goal of SDA in developing countries like India is to create and maintain livelihood security options (Chambers, 1986; Swaminathan, 1991; Chambers and Conway, 1992). The concept of Sustainable Livelihood Security (SLS) is defined by Swaminathan (1991) as livelihood options which are ecologically secure, economically efficient and socially equitable. The intimate conceptual and casual linkages between the SLS and other welfare goals like poverty alleviation, meeting basic needs, human development and quality of life (see Saleth and Swaminathan, 1993) justify SLSI as a legitimate indicator for SDA.

The analytical framework essential for operationalising SLS in the form of SLSI is identified by the following propositions about SDA; (*i*) given the three-dimensional conception of SDA, the necessary conditions for sustainability are ecological security, economic efficiency and social equity—both in intra- and inter-generational contexts—and (*ii*) given the dynamic and contextual nature of SDA, sustainability needs to be relative rather than absolute both in time and space.

In an operational context, the multi-dimensional conception of SDA requires the SLSI to be a composite of three indices, *i.e.*, Ecological Security Index (ESI), Economic Efficient Index (EEI) and Social Equity Index (SEI), so that it can take stock of both the conflict and synergy between ecological, economic and equity aspects of SDA. The relative nature of SDA requires the SLSI to be also relative, *i.e.*, the sustainability potential of any region should be contrasted with that of other regions or against some established norms or conventions (*e.g.*, the poverty line or minimum dietary requirement to obtain a relative picture. Since the contextual nature of SDA implies that the relative significance of the three components of SLSI varies by regions, there is a need for identifying suitable weighting scheme to assign component and regional-specific weights.

II
SLSI METHODOLOGY

The SLSI methodology is actually a generalisation of the relative approach underlying the Human Development Index developed by the United Nations Development Programme (UNDP) (1990). While the SLSI methodology is explained in detail elsewhere (see Saleth and Swaminathan, 1992, 1993), here, a brief outline is given. Let X_{ijk} and $SLSI_{ijk}$ denote respectively the value and index of the i-th variable representing *j*-th component of the SLSI of *k*-th region. Then,

$$SLSI_{ijk} = \begin{cases} \dfrac{X_{ijk} - \min\limits_{j} X_{ijk}}{\max\limits_{j} X_{ijk} - \min\limits_{j} X_{ijk}} & \quad \ldots (1) \\[2em] \dfrac{\max\limits_{j} X_{ijk} - X_{ijk}}{\max\limits_{j} X_{ijk} - \min\limits_{j} X_{ijk}} & \quad \ldots (2) \end{cases} \qquad \begin{array}{l} (i = 1, 2, \ldots, I) \\ (j = 1, 2, \ldots, J) \\ (k = 1, 2, \ldots, K) \end{array}$$

The numerators in equation (1) measure the extent by which the *k*-th region did between the *i*-th variable representing *j*-th component of its SLSI as compared to the region of showing the worst performance. The denominator is actually the range, *i.e.*, the difference between the maximum and minimum values of a given variable across regions, which is simple statistical measure of total variation present in that variable. The denominator, fact, serves as a scale or measuring rod by which the performance of each region is evaluating in a given variable. We note that such a scale can also be identified exogeneously utilising scientific standards, social norms and policy targets.

Having calculated the $SLSI_{ijk}$ for all the variables, the indices for the various components of SLSI are calculated as a simple mean of the indices of their respective representative variables. That is,

$$SLSI_{jk} = \frac{\sum_{i=1}^{I} SLSI_{ijk}}{I} \qquad (j = 1, 2, ..., J) \quad (k = 1, 2, ..., K) \quad ...(2)$$

Then, the composite indicator for each region is calculated as a weighted mean of the component indices obtained from equation (2). That is,

$$SLSI_{k} = \frac{\sum_{j=1}^{J} W_{jk}\ SLSI_{jk}}{J} \qquad (k = 1, 2, ..., K) \ ... \ (3)$$

The W_{jk} in equation (3) denotes the weight assigned to the *i*-th component of the SLSI of *k*-th region and has the property that: W_{jk} +... + W_{jk} = 1. If the weights are identical and sum to unity, then SLIS is calculated as a simple mean. But when the weights are different across all *j* and *k*, SLSI is calculated as a weighted mean. For distinction, the former is denoted simply as SLSI and the latter as SLSI*. Obviously, all the indices and hence, both the SLSI and SLSI*, will be bounded by 0 and 1.

III
EMPIRICAL PROCEDURE AND DATA

To empirically construct SLSI, we follow a simple approach involving the selection of a set of variables having the ability to say something more relevant and substantial about the ecological, economic and equity aspects of SDA. Although more variables can be selected, here, we have selected just three variables each to represent three dimensions of SDA. Ecological security is reflected by the three variables: the proportion of geographical area under forest, per capita utilisable groundwater potential and population density per square kilometre. Since forest occurrence and growth are governed by regional-specific geo-physical conditions, the critical minimum forest cover essential for ensuring ecological security does vary by regions. For instance, the respective critical minimum forest cover norms suggested for the plains, plateau and hills and mountainous regions are 20 per cent, 33.3 per cent and 66.6 per cent respectively (Government of India, 1952). The per capita utilisable groundwater potential indicates the degree of pressure on groundwater resources especially when it is contrasted with the 'water barrier' norm. According to Falkenmark (1984), the water barrier is approached whenever per capita water availability is less than 500 cubic metre. The variable population density was chosen in view of its capacity to reflect the extent of human pressure on the overall environment/resources.

Economic efficiency is represented by the three variables: land productivity in rupees/hectare (Rs./ha), labour productivity in Rs./ha and cereal output per capita. Although expressing productivity in monetary units does help to capture not only physical productivity as influenced by soil fertility, climate, irrigation, technologies, etc., but also the performance of marketing and other rural institutions affecting farm prices, it has, however, the potential to bias the evaluation in favour of regions specialised in high-valued cash crops. It is to counter such a bias, we have included the variable per capita cereal output that also has the potential to say something about the food security status especially when it is contrasted with the critical minimum per capita grain availability, *i.e.*, 180 kilograms/capita/year, suggested by Brown (1991, p. 11).

Social equity is reflected by the three variables: people below the poverty line, female literacy and current groundwater use as percentage of its ultimate potential. While rural poverty captures the effects of employment, income, asset ownership and food consumption, female literacy capturing social equity indicates the potential not only for women's social and economic participation but also for population stabilisation. The intra-generational equity as indicated by poverty and literacy is supplemented by inter-generational equity indicated by current groundwater use.

Despite their limitations, the selected variables do have a good capacity to reflect the overall ecological, economic and equity aspects of a region's agricultural system. Two observations are due in this regard. First, the variables actually selected to represent a given dimension reflect also the concerns in the other dimensions of agricultural sustainability. For instance, the variables representing the ecological dimension could also indicate indirectly the inter-generational equity potential in view of the direct relationship between ecological security and inter-generational equity. Similarly, groundwater utilisation rate and the two productivity variables reflect also the effects of technology. And, second, most of the variables display both positive and negative correlation among them which, rather than being a problem, actually enhances the capacity of SLSI to capture both the inherent conflicts as also the intrinsic synergy among various aspects of agricultural sustainability.

The data for the nine candidate variables pertaining to the triennium ending 1984-85 for some 80 agro-climatic sub-zones were obtained from Government of India (1991). The sample covered three zones each in Haryana, Kerala and Punjab, four in Karnataka, five each in Bihar, Orissa and Rajasthan, six each in Andhra Pradesh, Maharashtra and West Bengal, seven each in Gujarat and Tamil Nadu, eight in Uttar Pradesh and 12 in Madhya Pradesh. The remaining sub-zones were excluded in view of the absence of comparable data.

Although the SLSI and SLSI* of each sample region were calculated by a straightforward application of equations (1), (2) and (3), a few additional points related to the calculation procedure quality attention. When developing the individual indices, equation (1a) was applied for four variables (*i.e.*, forest cover, land and labour productivities and female literacy) having a positive effect on SDA and equation (1b) was applied for all the remaining variables having an inverse effect on SDA. The identified norms were used as follows. Whenever the value of the variables exceeded their respective norms, then the indices for these variables will be assigned a value of 1. Else, their indices will be based on equation (1).

Even though a number of approaches can be considered for developing weights (see Saleth and Swaminathan, 1992), here, we follow a simple approach. Under this approach, first, the inverse of the proportional contribution of ESI, EEI and SEI to the SLSI was obtained. And then, the weight to be assigned to each component will be the ratio of its inverse contribution to the sum of all the three inverse proportions. Despite its heuristic nature, it has the following appeals:

(*i*) since the relative significance of the components of SLSI varies by regions, it assigns differential weights not only across components but also across regions, and

(*ii*) the weights assigned are also inverse to the relative significance of the three components are reflected by their values. This is due to the fact that as one has more (less) of something(s) he will value it less (more).

IV
AGRICULTURAL SUSTAINABILITY STATUS OF THE AGRO-CLIMATIC SUB-ZONES

The relative agricultural sustainability status of the sample agro-climatic sub-zones as indicated by the values and ranks of their SLSI and SLSI* as well as ESI, EEI and SEI is shown in Table 14.1. The values of ESI, EEI and SEI range respectively from 0.992 to 0.147 from 0.885 to 0.068 and from 0.844 to 0.253. This indicates that the agricultural systems of the sample regions display wider variation in their ecological and economic aspects that in equity aspects. While the SLSI shows a range of 0.645 to 0.214, the SLSI* displays a range of 0.623 to 0.147. Consequently, the SLSI ranking of regions differs significantly

Table 14.1

The Relative Agricultural Sustainability Status of the Agro-Climatic Sub-zones, India, 1984-85

Sr. No.	States/ Agro-climatic sub-zones	Ecological security		Economic efficiency		Social equity		Sustainable livelihood security			
		ESI	Ranks	EEI	Ranks	SEI	Ranks	SLSI	Ranks	SLSI*	Ranks
(1)	(2)	(3)	(4)	(5)	(6)	(7)	(8)	(9)	(10)	(11)	(12)
	Andhra Pradesh										
1.	North Coastal Andhra	0.915	6	0.190	57	0.542	23	0.549	15	0.366	43
2.	South Coastal Andhra	0.675	24	0.607	10	0.592	14	0.625	3	0.623	1
3.	Nellore	0.717	14	0.521	18	0.535	27	0.591	8	0.579	3
4.	Rayalaseema	0.663	27	0.189	58	0.413	58	0.422	47	0.326	52
5.	South Telangana	0.351	51	0.129	70	0.470	41	0.317	70	0.235	69
6.	North Telangana	0.954	4	0.465	25	0.464	44	0.628	2	0.560	5
	Bihar										
7.	North Bihar Plains	0.147	79	0.159	66	0.336	73	0.214	80	0.187	78
8.	North-Eastern Plains	0.225	72	0.121	72	0.390	67	0.245	78	0.197	76
9.	South Bihar Plains	0.272	66	0.135	69	0.392	65	0.266	76	0.220	72
10.	Chhota Nagpur Hills	0.382	45	0.105	76	0.442	50	0.310	73	0.208	74
11.	Chhota Nagpur Plateau	0.460	36	0.093	77	0.454	47	0.336	66	0.198	75
	Gujarat										
12.	Southern Hills	0.802	9	0.297	41	0.621	13	0.574	10	0.482	17
13.	South Gujarat	0.690	20	0.301	39	0.649	9	0.547	16	0.475	21
14.	Middle Gujarat	0.334	55	0.195	54	0.590	15	0.373	61	0.306	54

15.	North Gujarat	0.315	59	0.184	60	0.526	29	0.342	64	0.286	59
16.	North-West Arid Area	0.430	38	0.159	65	0.537	25	0.376	60	0.286	57
17.	North Saurashtra	0.353	50	0.224	50	0.578	17	0.385	58	0.332	48
18.	South Saurashtra	0.397	41	0.327	37	0.579	16	0.434	44	0.411	33
	Haryana										
19.	Shivalik Foothills	0.291	65	0.750	4	0.538	24	0.526	24	0.453	23
20.	Plains	0.237	70	0.682	6	0.371	69	0.430	45	0.358	45
21.	Arid Area	0.313	61	0.539	17	0.555	19	0.469	36	0.438	29
	Karnataka										
22.	Northern Dry Region	0.348	52	0.189	59	0.452	48	0.330	68	0.289	56
23.	Central Dry Region	0.292	64	0.167	63	0.451	49	0.303	74	0.258	65
24.	Southern Region	0.373	47	0.639	7	0.486	37	0.500	28	0.476	19
25.	Hills/Coastal Region	0.850	7	0.276	44	0.692	8	0.606	5	0.480	18
	Kerala										
26.	Coastal Midlands	0.200	77	0.191	56	0.830	4	0.407	51	0.262	64
27.	Midlands	0.244	63	0.297	42	0.844	1	0.478	34	0.377	38
28.	Hills	0.688	22	0.338	36	0.832	3	0.620	4	0.535	7
	Madhya Pradesh										
29.	Chhattisgarh Plains	0.699	17	0.441	28	0.467	43	0.536	22	0.514	11
30.	Northern Hills	0.795	10	0.122	71	0.414	57	0.444	43	0.253	67
31.	Bastar Plateau	0.992	1	0.430	31	0.394	64	0.605	6	0.511	12
32.	Bundelkhand	0.677	23	0.447	27	0.436	52	0.520	25	0.500	14
33.	Chhattisgarh Hills	0.691	19	0.112	75	0.397	62	0.400	54	0.233	70
34.	Satpura Hills	0.727	12	0.088	78	0.396	63	0.403	53	0.196	77
35.	Vindhya Plateau	0.706	16	0.437	29	0.489	36	0.544	17	0.522	10
36.	Satpura Plateau	0.742	11	0.456	26	0.428	55	0.542	19	0.510	13

(Contd.)

(1)	(2)	(3)	(4)	(5)	(6)	(7)	(8)	(9)	(10)	(11)	(12)
37.	Central Narmada Valley	0.711	15	0.433	30	0.506	33	0.550	14	0.527	8
38.	Gird Region	0.722	13	0.474	23	0.501	34	0.565	12	0.546	6
39.	Jhabua Hills	0.406	40	0.085	79	0.441	51	0.311	72	0.181	79
40.	Malwa/Nimar Plateau	0.370	48	0.426	32	0.357	70	0.384	59	0.382	37
	Maharashtra										
41.	Eastern Vidarbha	0.608	32	0.408	34	0.519	30	0.512	27	0.498	15
42.	Western Hills/Plains	0.384	43	0.247	47	0.716	7	0.449	41	0.373	41
43.	Scarcity Region	0.692	18	0.213	51	0.546	22	0.484	30	0.377	39
44.	Central Plateau	0.377	46	0.118	74	0.473	39	0.323	69	0.226	71
45.	Central Vidarbha	0.688	21	0.119	73	0.535	26	0.447	42	0.256	66
46.	Konkan	0.270	68	0.160	64	0.801	5	0.410	50	0.268	63
	Orissa										
47.	Inland	0.958	3	0.506	20	0.472	40	0.645	1	0.584	2
48.	Northern Plateau	0.959	2	0.137	68	0.461	45	0.519	26	0.286	58
49.	South-Western Hills	0.929	5	0.466	24	0.399	61	0.598	7	0.524	9
50.	Coastal Region	0.648	29	0.202	53	0.640	10	0.497	29	0.373	42
51.	Ganjam	0.647	30	0.247	48	0.547	21	0.480	32	0.404	34
	Punjab										
52.	Northern Punjab	0.313	60	0.741	5	0.568	18	0.541	21	0.476	20
53.	Central Punjab	0.228	71	0.885	1	0.629	12	0.581	9	0.422	31
54.	Southern Punjab	0.303	62	0.825	3	0.458	46	0.529	23	0.448	24
	Rajasthan										
55.	Northern Arid Region	0.317	58	0.594	11	0.373	68	0.428	46	0.399	35
56.	Southern Plains	0.392	42	0.546	14	0.273	79	0.404	52	0.373	40
57.	Eastern Plains	0.369	49	0.634	9	0.392	66	0.465	37	0.439	27

58.	Southern Plateau	0.433	37	0.411	33	0.337	72	0.393	57	0.389	36
59.	Western Arid Region	0.343	53	0.068	80	0.353	71	0.254	77	0.147	80
	Tamil Nadu										
60.	Northern Region	0.383	44	0.246	49	0.253	80	0.294	75	0.282	61
61.	Central Region	0.337	54	0.267	45	0.424	56	0.343	63	0.331	49
62.	North-Eastern Coast	0.270	67	0.299	40	0.428	54	0.332	67	0.320	53
63.	Delta	0.209	76	0.639	8	0.500	35	0.449	40	0.359	44
64.	South-Eastern Coast	0.330	57	0.170	62	0.516	32	0.339	65	0.277	62
65.	Southern Region	0.237	69	0.583	12	0.838	2	0.552	13	0.421	32
66.	Hills Region	0.554	34	0.309	38	0.761	6	0.541	20	0.472	22
	Uttar Pradesh										
67.	Western Hills	0.669	26	0.291	43	0.476	38	0.478	33	0.426	30
68.	North-Eastern Plains	0.544	35	0.512	19	0.332	74	0.463	38	0.441	26
69.	Eastern Plains	0.167	78	0.204	52	0.289	78	0.220	79	0.209	73
70.	Vindhya Hills	0.819	8	0.400	35	0.408	59	0.543	18	0.486	16
71.	Central Plains	0.557	33	0.543	15	0.322	75	0.474	35	0.445	25
72.	North-Western Plains	0.213	74	8.875	2	0.298	77	0.462	39	0.327	51
73.	South-Western Plains	0.224	73	0.559	13	0.402	60	0.395	55	0.343	46
74.	Bundelkhand	0.651	28	0.485	22	0.308	76	0.481	31	0.438	28
	West Bengal										
75.	Barind Region	0.212	75	0.504	21	0.468	42	0.395	56	0.340	47
76.	Alluvial Region	0.147	80	0.259	46	0.528	28	0.311	71	0.239	68
77.	Coastal Region	0.333	56	0.178	61	0.517	31	0.343	62	0.284	60
78.	Rarh & Eastern Plains	0.609	31	0.540	16	0.549	20	0.566	11	0.565	4
79.	Terai Region	0.669	25	0.157	67	0.433	53	0.420	48	0.295	55
80.	Hills Region	0.417	39	0.195	55	0.638	11	0.417	49	0.330	50

from their ranking based on SLSI*. The downward movement of the SLSI* range is due to the effect of the weighting procedure that deflates the better performance slightly but inflates the poor performance substantially. Such an equalising effect is favourable for regions with poor performance as inter-regional priority for investment allocation will be inverse to their ranking. The relatively narrower range of SLSI and SLSI* as compared to their component indices indicates that the performance of regions is not consistent across the three aspects of SDA.

While the mountainous regions in Madhya Pradesh, Karnataka, Kerala and Uttar Pradesh dominated in ecological security, the agriculturally advanced regions in Punjab, Haryana, Uttar Pradesh and Tamil Nadu topped in economic efficiency. The regions that performed better in social equity are mostly in western coastal regions of Kerala, Tamil Nadu, Karnataka, Maharashtra and Gujarat. Regarding the overall performance of the sample regions in terms of their SLSI*, only about a third of the 80 sample regions located mostly in Madhya Pradesh, Andhra Pradesh, Kerala, Orissa and West Bengal have an SLSI* of above 0.5 and another third of them located mostly in the arid and hilly tracts of Bihar, Rajasthan, Madhya Pradesh, Uttar Pradesh, Gujarat and Tamil Nadu have an SLSI* lower than 0.3. Contrary to expectation, the regions having greater potential for SDA are not in Punjab, Haryana or western Uttar Pradesh but in Andhra Pradesh, Orissa, West Bengal and Madhya Pradesh as the latter group showed relatively consistent performance across all the components of SLSI as well as the variables representing them.

V
POLICY RELEVANCE OF THE SLSI APPROACH

The policy relevance of the SLSI* approach emerges from the fact that it helps not only to establish inter-regional priority for the allocation of agricultural investment but also to prioritise programmes/projects relevant to each region. While all the regions need attention, under conditions of capital constraints, it is the regions with the poor conditions for SDA, *i.e.*, those with an SLSI* of less than 0.3, that should receive the top priority in agricultural investment. Given the inter-regional investment allocation, the SLSI* approach could also provide further policy guidance as to the specific programmes and projects through which such investment should be channelled to improve the overall agricultural sustainability of each region. Such a regional-specific prioritisation over programmes and projects can be identified by the relative values of the ESI, EEI and SEI. For instance, if the ESI of a given region is having a lower value as compared to the other two indices, then, projects focused on afforestation and water conservation should receive higher priority over the economic and social oriented programmes.

In terms of the results presented in Table 14.1, the ten regions requiring the most immediate policy attention at the western arid region of Rajasthan, Jhabua hills and Keymore plateau regions of Madhya Pradesh, all the five sub-zones of Bihar, the central plateau of Maharashtra and finally, the eastern plains of Uttar Pradesh. While in the case of the two Madhya Pradesh regions, the programmes for SDA should focus more on economic and equity aspects, in the case of the remaining eight regions, the programmes should focus more on ecological and economic aspects.

VI
CONCLUDING COMMENTS

The major limitation of the SLSI approach is its assumption of the agricultural system of a given region as a closed system independent of that of other regions. The weighting scheme, though intuitive, is heuristic rather than scientific. While the cross-sectional basis of the SLSI approach enables it to be generalised for ranking various households, projects and programmes and even nations in a global context, it is not of much help for evaluating sustainability in an inter-temporal context. Thus SLSI functions only as a mere litmus test or screening device for ranking different entities but fails to provide any accurate quantitative information on agricultural sustainability. Despite these and other drawbacks of the SLSI approach, its simplicity, information-efficiency and generalisability make it a readily available and easily understandable tool for evaluating the relative potential for agricultural sustainability within the currently binding information constraint.

References

1. Barbier, E.B. (1987), "The Concept of Sustainable Economic Development", *Environmental Conservation*, Vol. 14, No. 2, pp. 101-10.
2. Brown, L.R. (1991), *State of the World*, W.W. Norton, New York.
3. Chambers, Robert (1986), *Sustainable Livelihoods: An Opportunity for the World Commission on Environment and Development*, Institute of Development Studies, University of Sussex, Brighton, England.
4. Chambers, Robert and Gordon R. Conway (1992), *Sustainable Rural Livelihood: Practical Concepts for the 21st Century*, Discussion Paper 296, Institute of Development Studies, University of Sussex, Brighton, England.
5. Conway, G. (1985), "Agro-Ecosystem Analysis", *Agricultural Administration*, Vol. 20, No. 1, pp. 31-35.
6. Daly, Herman, E. (1992), "Allocation, Distribution and Scale: Towards an Economics That is Efficient, Just and Sustainable", *Ecological Economics*, Vol. 6, No. 2, pp. 185-93.
7. Falkenmark, M. (1984), "New Ecological Approach to Water Cycle: Ticket to the Future", *Ambio*, Vol. 13, No. 2, pp. 152-60.
8. FAO (1984), *Potential Population Supporting Capacities of Land in the Developing Countries*, Rome.
9. Government of India (1952), *National Forest Policy 1952*, New Delhi.
10. Government of India (1991), *Agro-Climatic Regional Planning at State Level*, ARPU Working Paper No. 5, Planning Commission, Agro-Climatic Regional Planning Unit, Ahmedabad.
11. Parikh, J.K. (Ed.) (1988), *Sustainable Development in Agriculture*, Martinus Nijhoff, Amsterdam.
12. Saleth, R.M. (1991), "Measuring Sustainability in a Regional and Resource-Specific Context: The Case of a Groundwater Aquifer System", Discussion Paper No. 46, Indira Gandhi Institute of Development Research, Bombay.
13. Saleth, R.M. and M.S. Swaminathan (1992), "Sustainable Livelihood Security Index: A Litmus Test for Sustainable Development", Discussion Paper, M.S. Swaminathan Research Foundation, Madras.

14. Saleth, R.M. and M.S. Swaminathan (1993), "Sustainable Livelihood Security Index: Towards a Welfare Concept and Robust Indicator for Sustainability", in Anton Moser, C. Krotschek and M. Narodoslansky (Eds.) (1993), *Ecological Sustainability and Biotechnology,* Inter-Science Wiley, London (Forthcoming).
15. Swaminathan, M.S. (1991), *From Stockholm to Rio de Janeiro: The Road to Sustainable Agriculture,* Monograph No. 4, M.S. Swaminathan Research Foundation, Madras.
16. UNDP (1990), *Human Development Report 1990,* Oxford University Press, New York.

20

Agro-Climatic Regional Planning: An Approach Towards Sustainable Development

—V.V. Jugale & Mrs. Y.V. Jugale

Agriculture sector in India has undergone into number of changes since independence. We couldn't determine our long-term agriculture plan strategy before independence due to the colonial rule. But after independence lot of changes in the mixed economic system have been introduced for the welfare of the overall population. There is a general shift of one position to another particularly in the agricultural scenario of some states like Punjab, Haryana. It is because of the Agricultural Universities and research institution, lot of organisational and farm level practices have been brought up. But still our agriculture sector has to go up through number of challenges. Present paper deals with the coming challenges and alternatives to it have been discussed thoroughly.

Dimensions of Agricultural Growth

Agriculture is a culture that has been exercised with the use of material inputs and human work force. Its earliest thrust was subsistence to the living beings in the universe. Now-a-days it has been practiced as a agri-business. Man has identified its potentialities of growth for the benefit of human beings. Population growth and agricultural growth in fact play the game of light and shadow. Consequently the development takes place with an innovation in the technology use.

Overall agricultural development in India can be classified into five phases. These phases are the outcome of the strategy of extension and development.

The first phase of agricultural development had begun from 1947 to 1961. During the period the efforts were made to eliminate the traditional farming technique in agriculture sector. Number of institutional and infrastructural policy measures were introduced during the period. The ultimate aim of these policies was to solve the problems of starvation and food supply. Agricultural production was the ultimate end of the development.

Intensive agricultural development programmes started from 1961 and were under implementation till at the primary phase of the Green Revolution. In this strategy the intensive package programmes like, use of improved seeds, implements, land and water management in selected districts were introduced. This led the foundation for the Green Revolution. The period between 1966 to 1978 was actually belonged to the primary phase of the Green Revolution during which new land management techniques were introduced for specific crops like paddy and wheat.

Self-sufficiency in food grains production was created during the period from 1978 to 1985. This period was well-known for speedy development of agriculture sector. The food grains production rose to 150.44 million tonnes in 1985-86. The compound growth rate of Punjab state was 6.5 per cent during that period.

As a result of use of irrigation water and chemical fertilisers, food grains production increased phenomenally. A sense of self-sufficiency was emerged during the period since 1985. Indian agriculture took a differential dimension of stagnance. There is a minor addition in the food grains production during the end of the eighties.

The structural and quantitative changes that took place in the agricultural development process since independence was because of the following reasons:

1. According to Dr. M.S. Swaminathan the Green Revolution was successful more than expected because of successful quantitative dynamism in the policy accompanied with infrastructure development, incentives and intensive research in the agriculture sector.
2. An experimental attitude has raised due to improved seeds and implements.
3. More emphasis was given to the irrigation, consequently raising to the crop intensity.
4. Infrastructural development programmes including agriculture, extension, transport, education, credit and market helped for raising the agricultural production.
5. Multivariate bio-technology and mechanical technology intensified the agricultural development resulting to the increasing land productivity.
6. Agricultural credit input played a significant role in channelising the agricultural growth process.
7. Fair prices, employment and income generation tends to change the phase of traditional agriculture.

Distortions in Agricultural Growth

Varieties of distortions in the growth performance of agriculture sector have been observed in the process of agricultural growth. To-do-away such distortions, there actually arised a need of second Green Revolution which will bring structural as well as attitudinal changes in the farm and farm community, respectively. Before we proceed towards a new ethos of sustained growth in agricultural sector, we must try to diagnose the distortions in the agricultural sector.

Inter-state disparity is a grave problem of balanced agricultural growth. Though there is a wide range of diversity in the resource availability, the dispersion of agricultural development was not balanced. Punjab and Haryana have got ample opportunities of agricultural growth whereas the other states like North-Eastern states, Karnataka, Maharashtra, Rajasthan, Madhya Pradesh have to face slow growth rate.

The share of agricultural income in national income has declined from 56-45 per cent in 1950-51 to 33.88 per cent in 1990s. However the dependancy on agriculture has not yet come down. The forward and backward linkages of agricultural sector cannot be discarded in the overall economic system. Till today our agriculture is gambling with monsoon. A mere increase in the buffer-stock may not be considered as the self-sufficiency in food grains front. The future projections led by Planning Commission emphasises the need to increase the per capita availability of food grains by raising the agricultural productivity. By the end of 2007, our population will reach to 110.20 crores, which requires the food grains to the tune of 276 million tonnes. This is rather a challenge to the Indian agriculture because since last fifty years, every alternative season, there are updowns in agricultural production particularly after 1986-87. The annual growth rate has come down to 0.6 per cent (1987-88).

The Green Revolution no doubt has rewarded the Indian agriculture by increasing its productivity. But the per capita availability of food grains has come down with minor changes in it. During 1976 to 1980 the import of food grains come down but it do not reached to zero. Out of the total food grains production, 87.5 per cent is used for human consumption and rest of the food supply is used for animals. The per capita availability of pulses is a serious constraint of the human nutritions. Same is the case of oil seeds production. As a result of government programmes the cultivation of oil seeds is increasing now-a-days.

Agricultural poverty is a major concern to the human standard of living. A dichotomy is being observed in the process of development and the poverty level. This intensified the problem of distributive justice in the framework of the human welfare. Like the industrial sector, risk and uncertainties in agricultural sector are the regular phenomenon. Still the potentialities have to be identified hidden in human and natural factors.

I.J. Singh (*IJAE,* Volume 44, No. 1, 1984) had tried to measure the level of poverty in agricultural sector. In 1970-71 below poverty level income was Rs. 1,728 which has raised to Rs. 11,000 in 1990s. The below poverty level of the holding size in Maharashtra was 3.20 hectares. In Madhya Pradesh and Rajasthan, the below poverty level holding size was 2.96 hectares and 2.86 hectares, respectively. Whereas the states like West Bengal, Punjab and Assam the above ratios were 0.73 hectare, 0.86 hectare and 0.91 hectare respectively. Because of the high productivity of wheat and paddy in Punjab, the below poverty level holding size in Punjab is less. During the Seventh Five Year Plan, the below poverty level holding size in Maharashtra has come down to 1.62 hectares and 2.16 hectares. (Categorised into two groups of families having the income level of Rs. 4,800 and Rs. 6,400). This has come down to 0.46 hectare, 0.56 hectare, 0.67 hectare, in West Bengal, Punjab and Assam respectively. During 1970-71 to 1985-86 the number of below poverty level families has increased by 9.3 million whereas in Punjab the number of below poverty level families has come down to 0.24 million.

The size of holding is continuously declining causing a heavy burden of increased population on agriculture sector. Besides subdivision and fragmentation are also the serious concerns to it. In 1960-61 the average size of holding was 2.69 hectares. This had come down to 2.30 hectares in 1970-71, 1.84 hectares in 1980-81, 1.68 hectares in 1985-86. An average size of holding of middle farmers has come down very fastly. On the contrary the size of holding of small farmers has slightly diminished. Similarly the number of size holding has gone up from 48.88 million in 1960-61 to 97.73 million in 1985-86.

Immediately after independence the private and public expenditure in agricultural sector had gone up comprising 424 crores in 1960-61 to Rs. 9,120 crores in 1980-81. The share of public investment in it had gone up from Rs. 126 crores to Rs. 3,219 crores and private investment from Rs. 298 crores to Rs. 5,001 crores during the same period. The figures have inflated because of the high rate of inflation. But since 1980s both types of investment in agriculture sectors are declining. This is rather a more serious concern to the policy makers. Since 1990s the government investment has purposively been increased in our almost all budgets. The private investment in 1988-89 was 7.51 per cent only.

The use of agricultural workforce is still a major concern

to the theorists. The total workforce is increasing with an increase in population but no employment opportunities are increasing with that. On an average we have two per cent employment growth rate during last 20 years. Unless we increase it by four per cent by 2000 A.D., we will not be in a position to give employment opportunities to all unemployed. In India, an average employment per hectare-per crop is 103 mandays. In North-East Asian countries this average is around 200 to 300 mandays. Whereas in Japan, Korea, Taiwan this rate is around 400 mandays. There is a wide range of inter-state and inter-crop disparities in average employment opportunities. The range of hired workers for paddy cultivation in Tamil Nadu is 182.12 mandays per hectare, in Madhya Pradesh it is 82.53 mandays. As compared to paddy, wheat requires less hired workers. Even after the use of bio-technology and mechanical technology, the use of animal workforce has not yet minimised. On the contrary it has raised after the use of these technologies. However this depends upon number of factors like geo-climatic conditions, cost and benefits of crop cultivation, size holdings, crop intensity, wages, rent etc. With the existing technological conditions agriculture has no opportunities of employment. Unless we bring major changes in the structural and institutional aspects of the agricultural sector, we couldn't generate an employment opportunities. This can be made possible only through the expansion of non-farm sector in rural areas. It has been confessed that the non-farm economic activities in rural areas are increasing tremendously since 1991 census.

The terms of trade to agriculture sector goes always adverse. Besides there is a wide range of differences in input prices and output prices. Between 1960 to 1975, the terms of trade were little favourable (104.73 per cent) to agriculture. Similarly in 1990-91 the price index of manufacturing commodities was 182.8 per cent and that of agricultural price index was 198.3 per cent. Agricultural prices, no doubt should remain remunerative to the agriculturists and simultaneously to the consumers also. Thus terms of trade between agriculture and industry has become more complicated and controversial issue.

Weak rationalisation of agriculturists has created the ecological and environmental problems. Of late sustainable agricultural development has necessitated to have an efficient use of resources. However an attitude of agri-business has created the mind of our agriculturists towards rationalisation. To attain this stage of development, we should march towards the second Green Revolution, focusing on human resource development in agricultural sector.

The problem of optimum use of water potentials and increasing water table in the undergrounds is rather a challenge to the existing technologies. Besides there is no distributional justice sought in the distribution of irrigation water among the people, among the crops and among the regions. Out of the total river water, we are able to store it only upto 19.68 per cent. Rest of water goes waste flowing towards the oceans. This is a more concerned challenge to our technicians and the policy makers.

The foregoing analysis exhibits varieties of distortions in agricultural growth since last 50 years. Farm entrepreneurship should be developed to eliminate such distortions and this can be made possible through agro-climatic regional planning.

Agro-Climatic Regional Planning

In a vast country with a diversified agro-climatic conditions like India, needs to follow agro-climatic regional planning. The Planning Commission has initiated this project in 1988. The strategy of agro-climatic planning aims at a more scientific utilisation of available resources both natural and man-made. Within this planning strategy India has been divided into fifteen regions delineated on the basis of commonality of agro-climatic factors, like soil type, rainfall, temperature, water resources, etc. They are as follows:

(*a*) Western Himalayan Region
(*b*) Eastern Himalayan Region
(*c*) Lower Gangetic Plains Region
(*d*) Middle Gangetic Plains Region
(*e*) Upper Gangetic Plains Region
(*f*) Trans-Gangetic Plains Region
(*g*) Eastern Plateau and Hills Region

(*h*) Central Plateau and Hills Region
(*i*) Western Plateau and Hills Region
(*j*) Southern Plateau and Hills Region
(*k*) East Coast Plains and Hills Region
(*l*) West Coast Plains and Ghats Region
(*m*) Gujarat Plains and Hills Region
(*n*) Western Dry Region
(*o*) The Islands Region

The Macro *objectives* of the agroclimatic regional planning exercises are as follows:

(*a*) Attempt a broad demand-supply balance of major commodities at the national level but based on a careful analysis of potentials and prospects of various Zones;
(*b*) Maximise net income of producers;
(*c*) Generate additional employment for the benefit particularly of landless labourers;
(*d*) Provide the framework for the scientific and sustainable use of our natural resources, particularly land water and forests, in the long-run.

Each region is again divided into zones and sub-zones. Two to three districts come under one sub-zone. Zonal profiles with feasible cropping pattern has been prepared by the Planning Commission under the chairmanship of Y.K. Alagh (see Table 15.1).

Simultaneously the Planning Commission has given zone wise crops specialisation which is rather a guiding principles given to the Indian farmers. Table 15.2 illustrates the cropping specialisation in the Zones. Crops specialisation is more in crops like sugarcane, cotton, jowar and wheat. Whereas in case of rice, pulses, fruits and vegetables, distribution appears to be more widespread, large variations in the yield level of major crops are observed among zones.

While arriving to the agro-climatic regional planning strategy, livestock, mineral resources, marine resources, allied activities are also taken note of. Zone-wise irrigation and soil conservation strategy has also been highlighted.

Table 15.1
Selected Agro-Climatic Features of Sub-Regions

Sr. No. (1)	*Sub-zone* (2)	*Rainfall (mm)* (3)	*Climate* (4)	*Soils* (5)	*Crops* (6)
I.	**Western Himalayas**				
1.	High Altitude Temperature	165	Humid to cold arid	Hill soils, mountain meadow skeletal, tarai	Wheat, Maize, Rice, Jowar
2.	Hill Temperate	2000	Humid	Brown hill	Rice, Maize, Rapeseed, Wheat
3.	Valley Temperate	400	Sub-humid	Sub-mountain, mountain, meadow, skeletal	Wheat, Maize, Rice, Sugarcane
4.	Sub-tropical	1030	Semi-arid to humid	Alluvial (recent) brown hills	Wheat, Barley, Potato
II.	**Eastern Himalayas**				
1.	Himalayan Hills	2641	Per humid to humid	Brown hills	Rice, Maize, Ragi, Tomato
2.	NE Hills	3528	Per humid to humid	Red sandy, laterite	Rice, Rapeseed, Maize
3.	Southern Hills	2052	Per humid to humid	Acidic soils	Rice, Maize, Sesamum, Sugarcane
4.	Lower Brahmaputra	1840	Per humid to humid	Alluvial, red loamy tarai soils	Rice, Rapeseed, Wheat, Jute, Potato

5.	Upper Brahmaputra	2809	Humid to per humid	Alluvial, red loamy	Rice, Jute, Rapeseed, Wheat
III.	**Lower Gangetic Plains**				
1.	Barind Plains	1587	Moist sub-humid to dry sub-humid	Red and yellow alluvial (recent)	Rice, Jute, Wheat, Rapeseed
2.	Central Alluvial Plains	1449	Moist sub-humid to dry sub-humid	Red and yellow, deltaic, alluvium, red loamy	Rice, Jute, Wheat, Rapeseed, Potato
3.	Alluvial Coastal Saline Plains	1607	Dry sub-humid to moist sub-humid	Red and yellow deltaic, alluvial	Rice, Jute, Rapeseed
4.	Rarh Plains	1302	Moist sub-humid to dry sub-humid	Red and yellow red loamy	Rice, Wheat, Maize, Sesamum
IV.	**Middle Gangetic Plains**				
1.	North-West Alluvial	1211	Moist sub-humid to dry sub-humid	Alluvial (recent), calcareous	Rice, Wheat, Maize, Sugarcane
2.	North-East Alluvial	1470	Dry sub-humid to moist sub-humid	Alluvial, tarai	Rice, Wheat, Maize, Jute, Gram
V.	**Upper Gangetic Plains**				
1.	Central Plains	979	Dry sub-humid to semi-arid	Alluvial	Wheat, Rice, Tur

(Contd.)

(1)	(2)	(3)	(4)	(5)	(6)
2.	North-Western Plains	907	Dry sub-humid to semi-arid	Alluvial tarai	Wheat, Sugarcane, Rice, Maize
3.	South-Eastern Plains	701	Semi-arid	Alluvial	Wheat, Bajra, Rice, Maize, Tur, Potato
VI.	**Trans-Gangetic Plains**				
1.	Foothills of Shivalik and Himalayas	890	Semi-arid to Dry sub-humid	Alluvial (recent) calcareous	Wheat, Rice, Maize, Sugarcane
2.	Plains	561	Semi-arid to Dry sub-humid	Alluvial (recent) calcareous	Wheat, Rice, Bajra, Maize, Sugarcane
3.	Scare Rainfall Arid Zone	360	Arid and extreme arid	Calcareous, sierozemic alluvial (recent) desert	Wheat, Cotton, Gram, Bajra, Rice
VII.	**Eastern Plateau and Hills**				
1.	Eastern Plain	1271	Dry sub-humid	Medium to deep black red and yellow	Rice, Linseed, Jowar, Wheat, Gram, Groundnut
2.	Eastern Highland	1436	Moist sub-humid to dry sub-humid	Red sandy, red and yellow	Rice, Maize, Nigerseed, Wheat
3.	North-Central Plateau	1296	Moist sub-humid to dry sub-humid	Red sandy, red and yellow	Rice, Maize, Wheat, Ragi
4.	Eastern Plateau	1369	Moist sub-humid to dry sub-humid	Red and yellow, red loamy	Rice. Maize, Ragi, Wheat
5.	Tribal	1338	Moist sub-humid to dry sub-humid	Red sandy, red and yellow, red loamy laterite	Rice, Ragi, Nigerseed, Maize

VIII.	**Central Plateau and Hills**				
1.	Bundelkhand (UP)	780	Dry sub-humid to dry arid	Mixed red and black	Wheat, Gram, Jowar, Rice
2.	Bundelkhand (MP)	700	Dry sub-humid to semi-arid	Mixed red and black	Wheat, Gram, Jowar, Rice
3.	North Hills	1570	Moist sub-humid to dry sub-humid	Red and yellow	Rice, Wheat, Nigerseed Maize
4.	Kymore Plateau and Satpura Hills	1100	Dry sub-humid	Red and yellow medium black.	Wheat, Rice, Gram, Linseed
5.	Vindhya Plateau	1130	Dry sub-humid	Medium black	Wheat, Gram, Jowar, Rice
6.	Satpura Plateau	1220	Dry sub-humid	Shallow black, mixed red and black	Jowar, Wheat, Tur, Rice
7.	Central Narmada Valley	1300	Dry sub-humid	Deep black, skeletal	Wheat, Gram, Soyabean, Jowar
8.	Gird	670	Semi-arid (half drier and wetter)	Medium black, alluvial	Wheat, Gram, Jowar, Rapeseed, Bajra
9.	South-Eastern Plains	760	Semi-arid (half drier and wetter half)	Medium black	Wheat, Jowar, Gram, Maize
10.	Southern Plains	760	Semi-arid (wetter half)	Medium red and black, grey, brown	Maize, Rice, Wheat, Gram

(Contd.)

(1)	(2)	(3)	(4)	(5)	(6)
11.	Transitional Plain	490	Semi-arid to arid	Desert soil, grey brown	Bajra, Wheat, Sesamum Rapeseed, Jowar
12.	Semi-arid Eastern Plains	500	Semi-arid (wetter half)	Red and yellow, grey brown	Maize, Wheat, Gram, Jowar
13.	Semi-arid Western Plains	500	Semi-arid (drier half)	Alluvial	Wheat, Bajra, Jowar, Gram
14.	Flood-prone Eastern Plain	500	Semi-arid (drier half)	Alluvial (recent)	Bajra, Wheat, Rapeseed, Gram, Jowar
IX.	**Western Plateau and Hills**				
1.	Hills Zone	988	Semi-arid	Medium to deep black shallow red, red loamy	Jowar, Bajra, Rice, Groundnut
2.	Scarcity Zone	602	Semi-arid	Medium black, deep black	Jowar, Cotton, Wheat, Gram
3.	Plateau Zone North	874	Semi-arid (wetter half)	Medium black, deep black, mixed red and black, shallow red	Jowar Cotton, Wheat, Gram
4.	Plateau Zone South	1040	Semi-arid to dry sub-humid	Medium black, shallow black	Cotton, Jowar, Tur, Wheat
X.	**Southern Plateau and Hills**				
1.	Sub-zone 1	769	Semi-arid and arid	Medium black, laterite, deep black, red loamy	Jowar, Cotton, Groundnut, Bajra
2.	Sub-zone 2	677	Semi-arid	Red loamy, medium black, red sandy, coastal alluvium, laterite	Groundnut, Ragi, Jowar Rice
3.	Sub-zone 3	725	Semi-arid and arid	Red sandy, medium to deep black	Jowar, Rice, Castor-seed, Groundnut

4.	Sub-zone 4	1001	Semi-arid (wetter half)	Deep black, medium black	Rice, Jowar, Maize, Cotton, Groundnut
5.	Sub-zone 5	865	Semi-arid	Red loamy, red sandy	Ragi, Jowar, Groundnut, Rice
6.	Sub-zone 6	841	Semi-arid to dry sub-humid	Mixed red and black red loamy, deltaic alluvium	Rice, Jowar, Groundnut, Bajra
XI.	**East Coast Plains and Hills**				
1.	North Orissa Coast	1287	Moist sub-humid	Deltaic alluvial, coastal alluvial laterite, red loamy	Rice, Groundnut, Jute, Sesamum, Ragi
2.	North Coastal Andhra	1128	Dry sub-humid	Red loamy, laterite, medium black red sandy, coastal alluvial	Rice, Ragi, Groundnut, Bajra, Sesamum
3.	South Coastal Andhra	996	Semi-arid	Deltaic alluvium, deep black, red, sandy, red and black	Rice, Cotton, Jowar, Tobacco, Groundnut
4.	North Coastal Tamil Nadu	1036	Semi-arid	Red loamy, red sandy, coastal alluvium	Rice, Groundnut, Bajra, Jowar
5.	Tanjavur	1113	Semi-arid to dry sub-humid	Deltaic alluvium, red loamy	Rice, Groundnut, Sesamum, Sugarcane
6.	South Coastal Tamil Nadu	780	Semi-arid (drier half)	Mixed red and black coastal alluvium	Rice, Cotton, Bajra, Groundnut
XII.	**West Coast Plains and Ghats**				
1.	Coastal Hilly	3127	Per humid and humid	Laterite, red loamy, coastal alluvium	Rice, Ragi, Sesamum, Nigerseed

(Contd.)

(1)	(2)	(3)	(4)	(5)	(6)
2.	Coastal Midland	3127	Dry sub-humid and per humid	Red loamy, coastal alluvium, laterite	Rice, Tapioca, Ragi, Banana
3.	Midland	2727	Per humid	Laterite, red loamy, coastal alluvium	Rice, Tapioca, Groundnut, Banana
4.	Hilly	2626	Per humid	Red loamy, mixed red and black	Rice, Ragi, Jowar, Groundnut
XIII.	**Gujarat Plains and Hills**				
1.	South Gujarat 'A'	1793	Semi-arid to dry sub-humid	Deep black, coastal alluvium	Rice, Ragi, Sugarcane, Jowar
2.	South Gujarat	974	Semi-arid to sub-humid	Deep black, coastal alluvium	Jowar, Tur, Cotton, Wheat
3.	Middle Gujarat	904	Semi-arid	Medium black	Rice, Cotton, Maize, Bajra
4.	North Gujarat	735	Arid to semi-arid	Grey brown, deltaic alluvium	Bajra, Cotton, Jowar, Wheat
5.	North-west Arid	340	Arid to semi-arid	Grey brown, deltaic alluvium	Bajra, Groundnut, Jowar, Cotton
6.	North Saurashtra	537	Dry sub-humid	Medium black	Groundnut, Cotton, Bajra, Jowar
7.	South Saurashtra	844	Dry sub-humid	Coastal alluvium, medium black	Groundnut, Wheat, Bajra, Cotton
XIV.	**Western Dry**				
1.	Western Dry	395	Arid to extremely arid	Desert soil, grey brown	Bajra, Gram, Wheat, Rapeseed

Table 15.2
Cropping Specialisation in the Zones

Sl. No.	*Crop/Crop Group*	*Zones of Concentration*				*Percentage to Total Area*	*Percentage to Total Production*
1.	Rice	3	4	7	11	62.0	55.3
2.	Wheat	4	5	6	8	80.0	86.2
3.	Jowar	8	9	10		86.3	87.0
4.	Pulses	6	8	9		66.6	65.5
5.	Oilseeds	8	9	10	13	70.0	70.3
6.	Cotton	6	9	10	13	92.0	85.3
7.	Sugarcane	4	5	9	10	74.3	72.6
8.	Fruits and Vegetables	3	4	5	12	56.4	60.8

To achieve the aim of such strategy, we should have institutional multi sectoral linkages with an organisational framework. Since independence we have created lot of institutional framework but not an effective linkages with such institutions. Institutions have rather become more bureaucratic than competitive. In the second phase of our Green Revolution programmes we must stress on more competitiveness among the organisational framework.

Agriculture sector has more concentrated and related to supply side economics whereas industrial activities rely upon demand side economics. Agro-based industries are the resource based industries. Agro-produces can be manufactured and processed which again have the forward and backward linkages with agro-input and agro-service activities. The non-farm economic activities are being well established in rural areas. As a result they are held responsible in generating employment opportunities. Besides the market-oriented pre-harvest and post-harvest technologies in farm activities have better future to deal with particularly rural women have better opportunities of employment in such activities.

Conclusions

Thus agro-climatic regional planning has better future, in fact that is the only alternative way to deal with the development activities in India. However the strategy should properly be followed with an institutiional linkages in the economy. The distortions in agricultural growth can be co-related through human resource development activities. The strategy can better be deep rooted through farmers training and be created confidence among the farmers for competitive economic conditions. We should march towards this direction to eliminate the distortions and to bring the sustained development of agricultural sector in the economy that is to march towards the second Green Revolution is though essential.

References

Alagh, Yoginder K. (1996), "Ninth Plan in Perspective: Role of Agricultural Research", *Agricultural Situation in India*, Vol. LIII, August, No. 5.

Alagh, Yoginder K. (1988), *Agro-Climatic Regional Planning in India*, Planning Commission, GOI.

Bhalla, G.S., and Singh, Gurmail (1997), "Recent Developments in Indian Agriculture: A State Level Analysis", *EPW*, March 29.

Swaminathan, M.S. (1996), "Sustainable Agriculture and Hunger Free India", *Agricultural Situation in India*, Vol. LIII, August, No. 5.

Singh, I.J. (1989), "Agricultural Instability and Farm Poverty in India", *IJAE*, Vol. 44, No. 1.

Index